Run for your supper
gr 1 #6                              166

# Physical Education
# for the
# Classroom Teacher

BRING
SNEAKERS !!!

1- 4
① Exercises                          5 Relay
② Steal the Bacon   176
③ Nodge Ball
④ Crows ~ Cranes    180

5 & 6
Exercises
Nodge Ball - Prison    194

# Physical Education for the Classroom Teacher

## A Physical Education Curriculum for Elementary School Children

### Helen Fabricius

*formerly Coordinator of Elementary School
Health and Physical Education*

*Corvallis Public Schools
Corvallis, Oregon*

Second Edition

WM. C. BROWN COMPANY PUBLISHERS
Dubuque, Iowa

**PHYSICAL EDUCATION**

Consulting Editor
*Aileene Lockhart*
*University of Southern California*

**HEALTH**

Consulting Editor
*Robert Kaplan*
*The Ohio State University*

**PARKS AND RECREATION**

Consulting Editor
*David Gray*
*California State College, Long Beach*

# Preface

This book was originally written to provide the elementary school classroom teacher with a planned, progressive curriculum in physical education, grades one through six. Its purpose has not changed with the second edition. While the physical education specialist is becoming more common in the elementary school, nationwide the classroom teacher continues to teach most of the physical education that is taught. As stated by Margie R. Hanson, Elementary Education Consultant, American Association for Health, Physical Education and Recreation, in the 1969 edition of "Promising Practices in Elementary School Physical Education, ". . . we must not neglect the preparation of the classroom teacher because we can never do the job alone. Enlightened classroom teachers and principals will make possible even better programs." In those school systems fortunate enough to have elementary physical education specialists, this curriculum may serve as a guide from which to expand, explore and add variations.

This book can be used as a college text for prospective elementary teachers as well as for the physical education major in training or already in service. The major student will find the book useful in acquiring an over-all view of methods and curriculum at the elementary school level. Likewise, elementary principals and supervisors, in training or in the field, can quickly and easily recognize the basics of an adequate physical education curriculum for an elementary school.

The physical education curriculum contained in this book is based on the following beliefs held by the author:

1. Physical education activities are important—and perhaps essential—for the development and health of the elementary age child. "Development" and "health" are assumed to include physical, social and emotional development and health.

2. While in general it may be considered desirable for both the elementary teacher and the children to have physical education taught by a specialist, the classroom teacher *can* plan and teach a physical education curriculum that will contribute to the growth and development of boys and girls.
3. The opportunity to develop physical, social and emotional fitness is the right and privilege of every child in our country.
4. The development of the total fitness of every child up to his potential is a basic necessity for the present and future vitality of our nation.

The physical education curriculum for elementary age children herein proposed is to be considered *a* program for elementary schools and not necessarily the only acceptable program. Curriculum, methods and teaching suggestions are the results of the author's own experience in teaching elementary youngsters and in helping classroom teachers teach physical education.

The curricular activities described in this book are classified by type of activity, i.e., self-testing activities, games and sports, rhythms and relays. They are further classified by grade level so that a progression will be guaranteed from grade to grade. Progression, from the simple to the more complex, is as important in physical education as in any other subject in the curriculum if maximum results are to be achieved.

In this edition some activities and teaching suggestions for the elementary grades have been added as well as an introduction to movement education and perceptual motor training. Included also is an expanded, updated and annotated bibliography.

The section on Junior high school physical education contains a curriculum which has been successfully used with seventh, eighth and ninth grade girls. It is a continuation of the elementary curriculum heretofore mentioned, and meets most of the needs of the junior high age group. The material proposed is not designed as a complete program, nor the only acceptable program, for junior high girls. It should, however, help the junior high teacher who might have had little preparation in this field.

Acknowledgement, with sincere thanks, is due Phyllis A. Glaser, Special Education and Physical Education Resource Teacher, Minneapolis, Minnesota Public Schools, for the material on movement education and perceptual motor training. Appreciation is due Lucille Lewis, Corvallis, Oregon for some of the sketches, Mallory Zahn, Supervisor of Elementary Physical Education, and Maurice Nichols, Assistant Superintendent of the Alexandria, Virginia Public Schools for their cooperation in taking pictures on the Alexandria playgrounds.

"It is of great importance that we take immediate steps to ensure that every American child be given the opportunity to make and keep himself physically fit — fit to learn, fit to understand, to grow in grace and stature, to fully live."

John F. Kennedy
AAHPER publication, "Your Child's Health and Fitness." *NEA Journal,* Feb. 1962

To R., C. and M.

in Appreciation

# Contents

## The Curriculum: Rhythms

## The Curriculum: Relays

## PART THREE

### Other Considerations

## PART FOUR

### Physical Education for Junior High School Girls

**Part**

# Basic Considerations

# A Point of View

## INTRODUCTION

The purpose of this book is to help the elementary classroom teacher — the nonexpert in physical education — plan and teach a physical education curriculum that will benefit the children in her class. The average — and sometimes the superior — elementary teacher, by training and by experience, is not an expert in all fields. Usually she is skilled in the teaching of the so-called academic subjects of language, social studies, arithmetic and science. Usually she is not as well skilled in the teaching of art, music and physical education. Many school systems provide special teachers to teach these subjects, or to guide and assist the elementary classroom teacher in these areas. Many more school systems provide no such assistance. The teacher is then left on her own, to try to do her best in an area of education where she feels inadequate and where she knows little except what her own experience as a pupil has taught her. Many elementary teachers feel that they should include a physical education class in their daily schedules but, beset by many other responsibilities and duties, omit this part of the curriculum and just "let the kids go out and play."

It is acknowledged that the elementary classroom teacher is not usually an expert in the teaching of physical education. It is the purpose of this book to present an elementary physical education curriculum that will be of benefit to children and that can be planned, directed and taught by the elementary teacher with no special training in physical education.

The elementary teacher often recognizes that there are values for children in a well planned and taught physical education program. This fact can be proven by statistics which show that boys and girls who have participated in a good elementary school physical education program score higher on fitness tests than those who have not had this opportunity. It is known that boys and girls having the advantage of a good physical education program have better skills in sports and rhythmic activities. They have a better understanding of the need of exercise as a requisite of good health. They have better standards of sportsmanship, of fair play, of teamwork, of cooperation and respect for the abilities of their colleagues. They have greater interest in sports as leisure time and after school activities. They should have learned how to release tensions and to relax. In addition, and not the least important, are the joy and satisfaction that children receive from participating in physical activities, of developing skills in sports and contributing to team or group success, thereby gaining status with their classmates.

What then is the nonexpert elementary teacher to do about the physical education curriculum? She consciously or subconsciously realizes that this is a part of the school program to which the pupils are entitled, that this is an area of learning which they all need and which can make tremendous contributions to the physical and emotional development of boys and girls.

This book suggests a physical education program that can be planned and taught by the elementary teacher with little or no training in physical education. This suggested curriculum is not an ideal curriculum. It does not require large amounts of expensive equipment or luxurious facilities. It does not require the teacher to dress in gymnasium clothes. It does not demand that the teacher actively lead the class and participate with the children. It does not require the teacher to demonstrate activities or handle or lift children. It does not involve the teaching of difficult or complicated skills. Technical and detailed physical skills can be taught only by the physical education expert who has a background in anatomy and kinesiology and who has had years of experience in the teaching or coaching of these skills. In fact, it is highly probable that even the expert in physical education, in a school situation, cannot teach every child in a class correct skills, attitudes and knowledges about physical education. This is possible only on an individual basis — one teacher to one child — and this situation, as we know, does not exist in American public schools. As in any other subject in the curriculum, however, the needs of all children can be met to varying degrees depending upon their maturity, ability and motivation.

The program suggested here does require.that:

1. The primary grade teacher include in each day's program a minimum of 20 minutes for physical education; and that the fourth, fifth or sixth grade teacher allow a minimum of 30 minutes per day for physical education.
2. The teacher plan and follow a progressive curriculum, such as presented in this book, depending on the skill and maturity of her class.
3. The school system provide a place for physical education, preferably an outdoor and an indoor area.
4. The school system provide a minimum amount of physical education supplies such as balls, ropes, mats and rhythm records.
5. The teacher's immediate superior, her principal, allow and preferably encourage her in her endeavor to provide a good physical education program for her class.

These are minimum requirements without which the conscientious teacher will find it difficult, if not impossible, to conduct even a minimum, but effective physical education program.

The curriculum here presented is consistent with the foregoing requirements. It is a curriculum that has been used successfully in elementary schools with good results in achieving the objectives of physical education.

## WHAT ARE THE TRAITS, QUALITIES AND PURPOSES OF THE ELEMENTARY AGE CHILD WHICH DETERMINE THE CURRICULUM IN PHYSICAL EDUCATION?

To help the classroom teacher plan, teach and understand a physical education curriculum, consideration must be given to the physical and emotional characteristics of boys and girls of elementary age.

Everyone, teacher or layman, recognizes the great diversity in human beings. It is true, beyond doubt, that each human is a unique individual — there being no other in the world exactly like him. Yet, and fortunately, we have our similarities too, and for the purposes of discussion and planning, it is necessary to group or classify. For educational planning, the most common classification is by age, though we recognize the weaknesses of this method. Every teacher, and every observing layman, knows that all six year olds are not alike, nor are all six year old boys — or girls — alike. However, certain general traits or characteristics are observable in *most* six year olds, or ten year olds or fourteen year olds. While we treasure the uniqueness of each individual, the fact that most children of a given age are somewhat like in physical, social, emotional and mental development is most helpful to teachers and other persons working with groups of people. With this in mind, consider the following general characteristics of the healthy elementary school age child — particularly those characteristics which apply to the construction of a physical education curriculum.

## PHYSICAL TRAITS OF THE HEALTHY CHILD

1. He has an instinctive and intensive need and desire for activity. He has need to *move* for growth, for development, for release from tension. He loves to run, to climb, to throw, to roll and 'wrestle' with other children.
2. He possesses a tremendous amount of energy. A healthy child is a hardy, resiliant organism. The healthy child has more endurance than adults think he has. A healthy heart cannot be damaged by exercise.
3. While it is true that children fatigue more easily than adults, they also recover from fatigue more quickly.
4. Children are much more flexible than adults. The skeleton is partly cartilage until the late teens. The spine grows increasingly less flexible as the child grows and develops. Lack of flexibility is a symptom of ageing.
5. There is great variation at all ages between six and twelve years in structure, weight, height and strength, and between boys and girls. Test results show that in general boys are stronger than girls even at an early age. Girls are more flexible than boys. Girls are usually heavier and taller than boys until the early teens when boys catch up and pass girls in height and weight. Great variation in physical maturity is present. It is not uncommon for third and fourth grade boys and girls in the United States to be physically mature. In unskilled, lower economic groups, children are smaller in all measurements than those children who come from professional groups.

6. Variation in physical ability and coordination is as great as variation in intelligence. Some of this variation is dependent upon previous practice, interest and experience.
7. Variation in posture is often due to the state of muscular development, especially in the shoulder and trunk areas.
8. The physical skills of walking, running and climbing are generally well developed by the time the child enters school. Object handling, such as throwing, catching, batting, etc. are less developed and many times, are completely absent.
9. The elementary age child likes physical contact. This is especially true of boys.

## SOCIAL AND EMOTIONAL TRAITS OF THE HEALTHY CHILD

1. The child has a pronounced desire for status with his group. His need to be considered as an individual, to receive attention, to be liked by his peers and to a lesser extent by his superiors, seems instinctive. The 'show-off', the clown, the so-called naughty or problem child is usually a child seeking attention and status.
2. Partly because of No. 1 above, the elementary age child is intensely competitive. He wants to be first, he wants to succeed. At five or six years, he is primarily an individual concerned more with his own desires than that of the group. He wants to be 'IT'. As, and if, the child develops normally, by the time he is nine, ten or eleven, he will want to be a member of a group, or a team, rather than an individual. He does not want to be 'left out'. He will then readily conform to group plans and aims.
3. He recognizes the need for rules, limitations and supervision, if these are fairly and impartially imposed.
4. He is often impatient with his colleagues of lesser ability, who 'spoil the game' or weaken the team. He is, indeed, often intolerant in this respect.
5. The child receives great satisfaction from successful accomplishment in learning a new skill or in winning a game or in being first in a race.
6. The child needs and wants to learn self-control in play or game situations.
7. He enjoys rhythmic and repetitive activities done individually or in groups.
8. He is creative, explorative and curious. In many instances, this aspect of his nature is restrained because of the desire for security, so he prefers doing the things with which he is familiar.

9. The child is eager for fun and participates in physical activities with enthusiasm and vigor.

## OBJECTIVES OF PHYSICAL EDUCATION

Most college students and teachers, reading a book on some aspect of education, hope to pass quickly over the sometimes uninteresting section on 'objectives.' This word, objective, has been a part of the educational vocabulary for so long that we tend to consider it superficial and unimportant. "Let's get through this, and proceed to the part that tells us what to *do*." However, in reality, this is the most important part of any educational plan or curriculum. Once objectives or aims or goals have been established and are understood, the plan or curriculum falls into place. Without a clear understanding of objectives or goals, we aimlessly flounder on a course that can have no good results except those that are accidentally or inadvertently accomplished.

The American College Dictionary defines objective as: "An end toward which efforts are directed; something aimed at." Any act has a conscious or subconscious objective. To avoid inefficiency, to avoid waste of a teacher's time and energy, to avoid waste of the pupil's time and energy, to avoid injury or actual retardation in the growth and development of children, all educational programs must be based on worthy objectives. To have no objectives, or to ignore them is unethical, unprofessional and perhaps even dishonorable in that the public and parents are misled as to what the school is doing for their children.

Let us therefore assume and admit that objectives are necessary and basic to any successful school program or curriculum. The establishment of objectives is a requisite for any physical education curriculum that is worthy of a place in the total school program. The teacher who is not an expert in physical education will find many questions answered and many problems solved by thinking through and, from time to time, referring back to, the objectives of the program.

Children will play and grow to maturity without the help of an organized, physical education curriculum. However, they will have a better opportunity for developing physical health, desirable social traits, good sportsmanship and profitable use of leisure time if they have the opportunity to participate in a good, planned and organized program of physical education.

Sometimes the child's purpose in a subject or a class differs from the objective or purpose of the teacher. In a well planned and well taught curriculum which considers the needs and characteristics of children, these purposes and aims should be nearly the same or even identical.

The school is a service agency for the improvement of living. The school's major concern is the "development of each child to his greatest capacity — physically, socially, emotionally, mentally, morally and spiritually — so that each child may become a contributing member in the democratic society to which he belongs."[1] "True educational effort is basically aimed at self education . . . self direction.[2]

Physical education, as part of the total school program, makes its greatest contribution to the growth of boys and girls in the areas of physical, social and emotional development, and should always consider the freedoms permitted and the responsibilities imposed by the democratic society in which we live. Physical education is "the subject in elementary school curriculum in which learning of neuro-muscular skills and understandings, intellectual skills and understandings, social skills and understandings, and value systems are taught through the medium of movement. It is the only subject in the curriculum which is solely responsible for the child's physical development."[3]

Considering the characteristics of children of elementary school age, the main objectives of physical education fall into these major areas:

I. Physical Development

This is the unique contribution of physical education to the school program. No other subject in the curriculum is primarily concerned with the development of physical endurance, strength, and coordination.

---

[1]Physical Education in Oregon Secondary Schools, Oregon State Department of Education, Salem, Oregon, 1958. p. 1.

[2]Journal of Health, Physical Education and Recreation, April, 1970, p. 47, American Association for Health, Physical Education and Recreation, 1201 Sixteenth Street, N. W., Washington, D. C. 20036.

[3]Evelyn L. Schurr. "Movement Experiences for Children." Meredith Company, New York, 1967. p. 17.

A. To develop strength of muscle groups — primarily those of the shoulder area, trunk, legs and feet.
B. To develop endurance — ability to perform physical activity for increasingly longer periods of time without undue strain or fatigue.
C. Through strength and endurance, to increasingly learn control of the body so that it will function to meet the needs of the individual and his safety.
D. To understand the value of exercise to health, and to develop pride in one's physical accomplishments and the development of the body.

II. Physical Skills

Basic skills and recreational skills

A. To learn the basic skills correctly — walking, running, bending, lifting, climbing, dodging, falling, relaxation; for efficient, fatigue-less, creative and safe use of the body.
B. To learn sport and rhythmic — or dance — skills — for ability to participate in such activities with confidence and security.
C. To explore one's physical capacity — and limitations — in relation to the environment, including one's own body.

III. Individual Emotional Development

A. To gradually, but consistently, improve in self-control, self-discipline and self-direction. To do what is right and/or acceptable without threats or help from others. To control self in 'stress' situations.
B. To play according to the rules, whether observed or not. To be honest.
C. To grow in self-confidence, courage, initiative and poise, willing to try new things.
D. To recognize one's strengths and limitations, and to accept them as part of 'knowing thyself.'

IV. Social Development — Human Relations Skills

A. To learn to be a contributing group member; to listen to and follow directions; to cooperate with the group for the welfare of all; to carry responsibilities as a team member or a leader. The playground is a laboratory for learning 'how to get along with others.'

    B. To begin to learn that life is governed and made more pleasant and fruitful for all by adherence to certain unwritten social customs, rules and traditions.

    C. To try to be a good sport; to win without gloating or razzing the loser; to lose without griping, arguing or making alibis.

    D. To be courteous to, and thoughtful of, one's playmates and peers.

    E. To learn 'to take it' gracefully.

V. Fun

    A. To participate in physical activities with joy and enthusiasm.

    B. To achieve release of physical and mental tension through activity.

    C. By successful and enjoyable participation in activity, to use physical activities as after-school and leisure time activities.

    D. To become aware of the role of sports in American life, and to enjoy participating as a player and/or as a spectator.

The teacher will readily recognize that these objectives will not, and cannot be achieved in a month or even a year. It is sad but true that some people never satisfactorily achieve these goals. Learning — particularly habits of action, attitude and behavior — is a slow, gradual process. The responsible and conscientious teacher, knowing the weaknesses and strengths of her pupils, will guide them along the path to the realization and achievement of these goals.

In this period of history with the strong influence of television, and the great spectator sports, physical education must be made interesting and fun, and should motivate boys and girls toward the goal of developing their bodies and having pride in their physical skill and accomplishment. This pride of body and of good health should be correlated with the teaching of good nutrition, of adequate rest and sleep and freedom from drugs, tobacco and alcohol. "Parents cannot just assume that their children will learn to play and enjoy sports on their own. Good instruction, in an atmosphere where good sportsmanship and real concern for the child's welfare are the rule, is important. Children who are properly taught derive more good and more enjoyment from sports, and they are more likely to become active and healthy adults."[1]

---

[1]Statement by Stan Musial from "Teaching Lifetime Sports Skills." President's Council on Physical Fitness, Washington, D. C., 1968.

If we believe that the function of the school is to aid each child to develop to his maximum capacity "physically, socially, emotionally, mentally, morally, and spiritually," then physical education is justifiably a part of the school program. To keep its place as a part of the school curriculum and to retain the respect of administrators, teachers and the lay public, physical education teachers must conscientiously and consistently strive for the achievement of the objectives herein stated.

# Fitness

During the past decade a great deal has been written and said about fitness. There have been attempts to define fitness as well as how to achieve and measure it. This emphasis on fitness — for all ages, but particularly children — began when the results of a physical fitness test, comparing European and American children, was brought to the attention of President Eisenhower in 1956. Commonly known as the Kraus-Weber test, it showed that the 4,000 American children tested were far less physically fit than the 3,000 European children who were tested. The Kraus-Weber test, measuring certain muscular strengths and body flexibility, is a test of minimum achievement. The children either passed the test or failed. Nearly 58 per cent of the American children failed the test whereas only approximately 8 1/2 per cent of the European children did not pass.[1]

President Eisenhower, concerned with this situation, in September, 1956, appointed a "President's Committee on the Fitness of American Youth" and named Shane McCarthy as executive director. The responsibility of the committee was to encourage and help plan programs of physical education and recreation that would increase the fitness of American boys and girls, to stimulate participation, by all ages, in activities that would tend toward increasing physical fitness.

Since 1960, concerned about the increasing evidence of the lack of fitness of the American people and the need of exercise for all ages,

---

[1]Hans Kraus and Ruth P. Hirschland. "Minimum Muscular Fitness Tests in School Children." *Research Quarterly*, 25:178-188 May, 1954.

the late President Kennedy continued and enlarged the presidential effort toward improving fitness.

He established the President's Council on Youth Fitness and appointed a special presidential consultant on youth fitness, Charles (Bud) Wilkinson of the University of Oklahoma. The Youth Council has, with the cooperation of national and state organizations for physical education and leading medical authorities, initiated pilot programs, devised fitness tests and standards, and distributed free to the schools of the country a great deal of material to aid the teacher in planning and teaching activities to develop physical fitness. This interest in and attention to fitness, emanating from the highest office in the land, has aroused interest in this topic throughout the country.

Concurrent with the interest shown by Presidents Eisenhower, Kennedy and Johnson was considerable research by physical educators and members of the medical profession; all of the results pointed to the fact that most Americans are below par physically, and that exercise is a requisite for optimum health at all ages. Dr. Paul Dudley White, a nationally known specialist in heart and circulatory ailments has periodically and consistently advocated more exercise for all ages as a means of achieving and preserving a state of mental and physical health. Much research, done in the past 20 years by individuals and universities, indicates that American youth are less fit than their forefathers[2] and less fit than their contemporaries in England,[3] Denmark[4] and Japan.[5]

> There seems little doubt that, as summarized by the late President Kennedy, "the harsh fact of the matter is that there is an increasingly large number of young Americans who are neglecting their bodies — whose physical fitness is not what it should be — who are getting soft. Any such softness on the part of individual citizens can help to strip and destroy the vitality of the nation.[6]"

---

[2]Bryant Jack Cratty. "A Comparison of Fathers and Sons in Physical Ability." *Research Quarterly*, March, 1960, p. 12-15.

[3]Louis Means. "British Youth Take Fitness Test." *Journal of Health, Physical Education and Recreation.* January, 1961, p. 75.

[4]Howard Knuttgen, "Comparison of Fitness of Danish and American School Children." *Research Quarterly*, May, 1962, p. 190-196.

[5]Louis Means. "Are Japanese Youth More Fit than American Youth?" *Journal of Health, Physical Education and Recreation*, Feb. 1960, p. 61.

[6]John F. Kennedy. "The Soft American." *Sports Illustrated*, December 26, 1960.

## WHAT IS FITNESS?

At least in a vague sort of way, everyone understands what is meant by the word fitness. To be completely or totally fit means to be in a state of optimum health — physically and emotionally — to be able to function, to be well adapted, qualified, competent, prepared, ready to meet and achieve any goal that may be set or deemed desirable. Immediately one is aware of the limitations that are inherent in the individual — his heredity and the environment in which he lives. Thus, fitness is largely an individual matter. "Fitness is . . . . . a matter of achieving an optimum state of well-being that enables us to live and to enjoy living to the maximum extent that our mental development and environment offer us."[7]

> "Fitness is that state which characterizes the degree to which the person is able to function . . . Fitness is an individual matter. It implies the ability of each person to live most effectively within his potentialities. Ability to function depends upon the physical, mental, emotional, social and spiritual components of fitness, all of which are related to each other and are mutually interdependent."[8]

Physical fitness is that part of total fitness that applies to the physical aspect of the human being. To achieve physical fitness, good habits of nutrition, rest and exercise must be practiced and the individual must be free from disease and remedial defects.

> "Physical fitness is not merely muscular development or the ability to pass one of the fitness tests which are being used more and more in our schools. Instead it is a happy mixture of the best possible bodily health plus the physical condition to perform everyday tasks more effectively and to meet emergencies as they arise. This combination in a child or an adult means having the zest and vitality for a full and productive life."[9]

Although physical fitness involves all the ingredients that make for good health, it can be narrowed still further for the purposes of the teacher of physical education. To make its greatest contribution to the fitness of boys and girls, the physical education curriculum

---

[7]Frank Neu. "We May be Sitting Ourselves to Death." *American Dairy Association,* 20 North Wacker Drive, Chicago 6, Illinois. November, 1961.
[8]"Fitness for Youth." *American Association for Health, Physical Education and Recreation.* Chart. 1960.
[9]Fred V. Hein. "What is Physical Fitness?" *National Education Association Journal,* February, 1962. p. 34.

should concern itself mainly with the development of strength and the improvement of circulatory-respiratory endurance. Along with the development of these two components of fitness will come improvement in flexibility and other aspects of physical fitness and almost simultaneously, better mental health, increased self-esteem, confidence, courage and poise — and a zest for living and achievement that will permeate all of the individual's activities.

> "Physical fitness is the ability to carry out daily tasks with vigor and alertness, without undue fatigue, and with ample energy to enjoy leisure time pursuits and to meet unforeseen emergencies. Thus, physical fitness is the ability to last, to bear up, to withstand stress, and to persevere under difficult circumstances where an unfit person would give up."[10]

## WHAT IS THE CAUSE OF LACK OF FITNESS?

Although most people in the United States today have better medical care, better nutrition, and more health knowledge than ever before in our history, our mode of life actually discourages us from exercising our bodies either in our work or in our leisure time or recreational activities. This is true for both children and adults. One must make a conscious effort to exercise regularly. One must fight to avoid a totally sedentary life. This not easy to do with the result that most people do not get exercise sufficient to achieve or maintain an optimum state of fitness and health.

Man's genius in inventing the automobile, television and labor saving devices in the home and in the factory, has made us a nation of sitters instead of doers. Lack of the need to walk and to do physical work and fewer places to play are all part of the situation that makes us less likely to get physical exercise.

Experts say that children need three to four hours of physical activity every day for proper growth and development. This is very difficult, if not impossible, to obtain. Television has made a great impact on all of our lives. Wilbur Schramm in the June, 1961, issue of the *Phi Delta Kappan* says: "The average child spends on the television in his first 16 years of life as much time as he spends in school." "The human body . . . may suffer when it is subjected

---

[10]H. Harrison Clarke and Franklin Haar. "Health and Physical Education for the Elementary School Classroom Teacher." Prentice-Hall, Inc., Englewood Cliffs, N. J., 1964. p. 7.

either to under or over stress. It is becoming more and more evident that the state of physical under-stress, represented by sedentary occupations, is responsible for early aging and degenerative changes in the body so that, for most people in such positions, a vegetative existence is not only conducive to poor job efficiency but leads to premature degeneration."[11] To compound the problem is the fact that, to keep physically fit, one must have some kind of physical activity often and consistently. To exercise once a week is not sufficient, though it is better than no exercise at all.

## WHY BE FIT?

It is difficult to condense, for the narrow confines of this book, the evidence that we now have concerning the value of exercise. This evidence is growing all of the time. The following is, at best, only a summary of what we now know. The goal in the pursuance of fitness is a body that is efficient, skilled, attractive and less susceptible to fatigue. Concomitant with physical fitness, and an "extra dividend," is improved mental health with alertness, poise, self-confidence and self-control. Following are some of the values of physical exercise:

1. a. A lower resting pulse rate.
   b. A lower oxygen consumption for the same work output.
   c. A lower stroke volume of the heart (more blood ejected per contraction).
   d. A faster return to normal of blood pressure and heart rate after exercise.
   e. An ability to perform greater amounts of work.[12]
      Highly trained athletes have a pulse rate as low as 45 to 50 beats per minute whereas the normal pulse rate is from 68 to 72 times per minute. The lower pulse rate indicates a more efficient heart and blood circulation.
2. Exercise keeps the muscles of the body strong and prevents stiffness, thus helping to eliminate or ameliorate pain in the back, legs, feet and joints while helping to maintain good posture.

---

[11]Thrift G. Hanks, M. D. "Health Values and Their Part in Business and Industry." *Management Information,* Boeing Co., Seattle, Wash. Vol. 10 #38, October 6, 1959. P. 2.
[12]Paul Hunsicker. "Physical Fitness." *American Education Research Association,* National Education Association. February 1963, p. 6.

3. Boys and girls, men and women "look better" when they are physically fit.
4. Exercise is an important factor in weight control. Overweight is a definite health hazard imposing extra strain on muscles, joints, the heart and other organs.

"The stronger one's muscles the more he can experience with less fatigue. The weaker one's muscles the more quickly does fatigue discourage activity, whether physical or mental. Fatigue affects the quality as well as the quantity of what one does. It reduces the service one may render. The individual who builds up greater resistance to fatigue comes to the end of the day and the end of the week much less exhausted. He can enjoy life more and his disposition is better."[13]

"All sorts of evidence points to the need for vigorous activity in childhood and youth and we are coming to recognize the necessity for maintaining appropriate exercise through the middle years. This points up the importance of inculcating in boys and girls an appreciation and desire for physical activity that will persist throughout life." So said Dr. Dwight H. Murray, a past president of the American Medical Association.[14] To this Dr. Paul Dudley White, the heart specialist from Boston adds, "Physical fitness should be uppermost in the minds of everyone in the middle-age bracket. . . . Disciplined eating and vigorous exercise, throughout life, are keys to positive buoyant health."[14] The words of another Boston physician, Howard B. Sprague, advise us that "The best insurance against coronary disease is exercise . . . lots of it. A combination of diet and exercise may reverse the present trend of coronary disease."[14]

"Muscles that aren't used become flabby, sluggish. They are, so to speak, not in tune, not ready to respond quickly and efficiently . . . . Muscles are the motors of the human body. Their efficiency and the ease and grace with which they perform depends on their tonus. That is one of the reasons why physicians now try to get patients up and on their feet as soon as possible after surgery or childbirth or any number of illnesses." "A little physical activity can work wonders when you go home at the end of the day feeling all done-in." "A sensible program of regular exercise will contribute more to our future health, physical and emotional, than all of the

---

[13]Arthur Esslinger. "If I were Superintendent." A paper delivered to the Oregon Association of School Administrators, October 12, 1961. p. 5.
[14]Clem W. Thompson. "A Source of Strength." *Journal of Health, Physical Education and Recreation*, January, 1962. p. 32.

new medicines or new operations in the world." "Sudden death from a heart attack isn't actually sudden," according to Dr. Paul Dudley White, "the sedentary life and the wrong diet are the two most important causes for this kind of heart trouble." "Age itself should be no deterrent to exercise." "Exercise isn't just a matter of muscular activity. It steps up all the body's functions, improves posture, helps you get rid of pent-up anxieties and frustrations."[15]

"Extensive research at the University of California has demonstrated that taking regular physical exercise markedly increases a person's sense of well-being and definitely boosts his capacity for taking nervous strains, disappointments and frustrations in his stride. The study employed two control groups — one of which engaged in daily supervised exercise and one which did not. The exercise group's morale and ability to adjust to nervous stress was found to be far superior to the nonexercise group. Conclusions of the investigators: exercise (swimming and walking were the most highly recommended) provides one of the most effective means for the release of moral-sapping nervous tensions."[16] "It appears that exercise is the master conditioner for the healthy and the major therapy for the ill."[17]

"Exercise gained in the sports and games . . . stimulates growth. The heart and the rest of the circulatory system develop with use and their efficiency increases markedly with vigorous exercise. All the muscles of the body are strengthened through activity. Recent research tells us that desirable changes in the bones and tissues of the body result directly from exercise. Furthermore, all of these effects are reversible; deterioration occurs when exercise is discontinued."[18]

". . . . . I am reasonably certain that there are several things sport does for you. It is good fun, and that is not to be sneezed at. It is healthful, in the main, and that is not to be sneezed at. It is the one way to get some absolute experience. Even though it is an artificial and manufactured environment, you are constantly being exposed to critical situations which require performance under pressure and you have to respond."[19]

15John J. Lentz. "To Exercise or Not to Exercise." *Today's Health*, March, 1963. Vol. 41, # 3, page 28.
16John E. Gibson. "What Makes you Happy?" *Today's Health*, June 1960, p. 14.
17Edward L. Bortz, M. D. Lankenou Hospital, Philadelphia, Pa. *Family Weekly Magazine*, September 17, 1961, p. 2.
8Anna S. Espenshade. "Why Be Physically Fit?" *National Education Association al*, February, 1962, p. 35.
19Byron R. (Whizzer). White from interview with Seattle Times Sports Editor. *Sports Illustrated*, April 13, 1962.

The foregoing statements and quotations from experts in the medical and education fields should be sufficient to answer the question, "Why be Fit?"

## WHAT KINDS OF EXERCISE WILL PRODUCE FITNESS?

To answer this qustion one must first consider the age and physical condition of the individual or individuals concerned. Assuming that the child or adult is basically healthy and free from disease or organic defects, and this should be determined by a physical and medical examination, all kinds of physical activity contribute toward the goal of fitness. The kinds of fitness activities one should use will depend largely upon health status, amount of time available, and a place in which to perform the activities.

The child who has the opportunity to participate in a planned physical education program in school will receive fitness benefits therefrom. If he is permitted and encouraged to participate in physical play activities during his out-of-school hours; if he does physical work around his home such as shoveling snow, cutting lawns, scrubbing floors and washing cars; and if he walks, climbs, runs, swims or skis or any of the myriad types of physical and sports activities, we can be pretty well assured that he will be physically fit or grow toward that goal. We may venture to say, however, that if any of these factors are missing or omitted, the child's achievement of physical fitness will be less than it could be. We should aim toward the goal of three to four hours of physical activity every day for every child. Parents can encourage the development of fitness in their children by buying toys that promote physical instead of sedentary activity and by equipping the backyard and/or the basement with objects that invite physical exercise. In addition doing exercises together is fun for the whole family.

For adolescents and adults whose time for activity in all probability is more limited than that of the child, fitness can be maintained by a series of calisthenics or conditioning exercises performed daily. To this should be added regular periods of more sustained activity such as swimming, walking, running, folk dancing, bicycling, bowling, golf or other sports.

Walking is one of the best exercises for all ages. As one's fitness improves, walking can be interspersed with jogging or running. Swimming, like walking, exercises all of the muscles of the body and aids cardiorespiratory endurance.

There are numerous series of calisthenics or exercises that can be done by children and/or adults. On the radio and television, in newspapers and magazines, in doctors' and teachers' professional periodicals are found series of calisthenics which, if performed correctly and regularly, will greatly increase fitness especially in the areas of strength development and flexibility. These can be done in one's own home, in the school gym or classroom, or on the playground, and need no special equipment. Before starting on a program of fitness development by means of calisthenics it would be advisable to have the doctor and the physical education specialist in your school system check the proposed list of exercises to be sure that no harmful activities are included.

The series of calisthenics suggested here was designed to exercise all parts of the body, to promote strength, flexibility, good posture, and to a lesser extent, cardiorespiratory endurance. Reference to other systems or series of calisthenics will be found at the end of this chapter.

Mention should be made also of isometric exercises which produce muscle strength and muscle endurance by means of a sustained contraction of muscle groups instead of by means of repeated contractions. There is evidence that this method of increasing strength is very effective and may be of value when used with other types of activities, or for a specific purpose, such as the strengthening of certain muscles or groups of muscles. Isometric exercise alone is not enough, however; continuous, prolonged effort is necessary to produce endurance.

### Suggested Series of Calisthenics to Exercise all Parts of the Body

For best results, exercises should be done in this order:
1. Run slowly or jog for two minutes, or about three laps around a gym. Increase to five or more laps over a period of a month. (General warm-up)

2. Airplane Exercise. Ten times, increase to 20 times over a period of a month. (Flexibility and strength of trunk muscles; posture)

3. Jumping Jack Exercise. Twenty times, increase to 40 times over a period of a month. (Warm-up, legs and feet, upper arms and shoulders)

4. Arm Circling Exercise. Twenty-five times, increase to 50 times over a period of a month. (Shouders and arms; posture)

5. Burpee Exercise. (squat kick). Eight times, increase to 15 times over a period of a month. (Legs, arms, trunk)

6. Push-ups. Ten times, increase to 25 times over a period of a month. (Shouders, arms, trunk)

7. Sit-ups. Ten times, increase to 25 times over a period of a month. (Abdominal area, thighs.)

8. Squat Bend Exercise. Eight times, increase to 15 times over a period of a month. (Legs, feet, trunk flexibility, posture)

9. Heel-toe Exercise. Ten times, increase to 20 times over a period of a month.

Total time necessary for this series of exercises is about five minutes. Exercises should be done in a pleasing rhythm, one after the other. Increase gradually to maximum number of times. Generally speaking, by midyear the pupils should be able to do the exercises the maximum number of times. Some, however, may be unable to do the maximum push-ups.

AIRPLANE EXERCISE

Count 1—Touch left foot.
Count 2—Starting position.
Count 3—Touch right foot.
Count 4—Starting position.

Count 1

Starting Position

Check—
1. Knees straight, but easy.
2. Arms straight and at shoulder level.
3. Good posture in upright position.

# JUMPING JACK EXERCISE

Count 1 — Jump to stride position.

Count 2 — Assume starting position.

Do 20 times, increase to 40 times over a period of a month.

Check —

1. Arms straight and alongside ears on Count 1. May clap hands above head.
2. Land on toes on 'Jump' rather than flat footed.

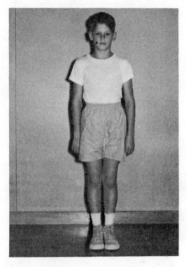

Starting Position

Count 1

## ARM CIRCLING OR 'SHOULDER ROLLER'

Count 1 for each small circle described by hands.

Do 25 times, increase to 50 times over a period of a month.

Check —

1. Palms of hands facing up.
2. Elbows straight.
3. Good posture in trunk area.

Circling or Shoulder Roller

Count 1

Count 3

Count 4

SQUAT KICK or
'BURPEE' exercise

Count 1—(see illustrations).
    Assume squat position,
    hands on floor, head up.
Count 2—Kick legs backward,
    trunk straight, head up.
Count 3—Squat position.
Count 4—Stand.

Do 10 times, increase to 15 times
over a period of a month.
Check—
    1. Head up on all counts.
    2. Body straight on count 2.

## GIRLS' PUSH-UPS

Count 1 — Lower body by bending elbows till chin
touches floor, or nearly
touches.

Count 2 — Assume starting position.

Do 10 times, increase to 25 times
over a period of a month.

Check —

1. Head in line with body
   on both counts.
2. Trunk straight.
3. Feet off floor.

Starting Position  Count 1

## BOYS' PUSH-UPS

Count 1 — Lower body by bending elbows till chin
(or chest) touches
floor.

Count 2 — Assume starting position.

Do 10 times, increase to 25 times
over a period of a month.

Check —

1. Toes turned under.
2. Head in line with body.
3. Trunk straight.
4. Hands on floor beneath
   shoulders, and shoulder
   width apart.

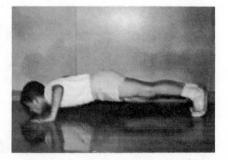

Starting Position  Count 1

## BOYS' SIT-UPS

Count 1 — Sit up and touch right elbow to left knee.
Count 2 — Starting position.
Count 3 — Sit up and touch left elbow to right knee.
Count 4 — Starting position.

Do 10 times, increase to 25 times over a period of a month.

Check —

1. Hands clasped behind base of head or neck. Elbows out straight.
2. Knees may bend slightly when pupil sits up.
3. Lower back curve *should not* increase when pupil sits up.

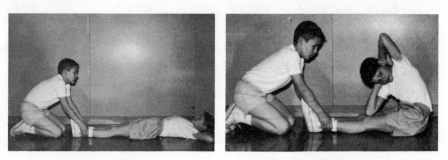

Starting Position          Count 1

## GIRLS' SIT-UPS

Count 1 — Sit up and touch toes, or as near to toes as possible.
Count 2 — Assume starting position.

Do 10 times, increase to 25 times over a period of a month.
May be done with partner holding ankles as in boys' sit-ups.

Check —

1. Knees may bend slightly as pupil sits up.
2. Lower back curve *should not* increase as pupil sits up.
3. Pupils may do this exercise, *or* curl-ups.

Starting Position          Count 1

26

# GIRLS' CURL-UPS

May be done in place of, or on alternate days with girls' sit-ups.

Count 1 — Sit up.

Count 2 — Assume starting position.

Do 10 times, increase to 25 times over a period of a month.

Check —

1. Feet flat on floor.
2. Knees bent in comfortable position.
3. Arms folded and resting on chest throughout exercise.

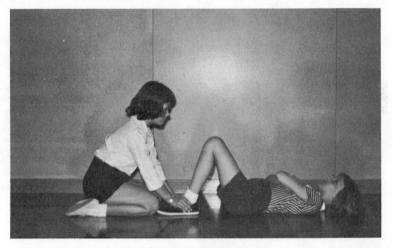

Starting Position

Count 1

Count 1

Count 2

Count 4

Count 3

## SQUAT BEND EXERCISE

(sometimes called Rocking Chair)
Start in standing position.

Count 1 — Squat with arms outstretched in front,
shoulder height.

Count 2 — Straighten knees and
touch toes, or floor,
with fingers.

Count 3 — Repeat Count 1.

Count 4 — Assume starting position, hands on hips.

Do 8 times, increase to 15 times
over a period of a month.

Check —

1. Trunk straight on
Counts 1 and 3.

2. Knees straight on Count
2.

## HEEL — TOE EXERCISE

Count 1 — Raise on toes.
Count 2 — Starting position.
Count 3 — Roll back on heels, lifting toes off the floor.
Count 4 — Starting position.
Do 10 times, increase to 20 times over a period of a month.

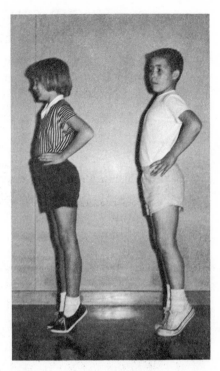

Count 1

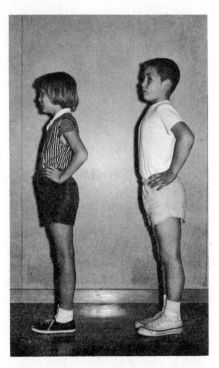

Starting Position

Check —

1. Get maximum movement on counts 1 and 3.
2. Good posture throughout.

# SELECTED CONDITIONING EXERCISES
## A More Comprehensive List

(If conditions prohibit pupils lying or sitting on the floor or ground, note that certain exercises may be done in the standing position. It should be understood, however, that better results will be achieved if pupils can sit or lie on the floor.)

**A. Endurance and Warm-Up** (Do one exercise)

1. Running in place or around gymnasium floor or playground. *Do not* run fast. Run at "trot" speed. Start at 30 seconds and increase to three minutes.
2. Treadmill. Body supported on arms and feet, body straight. Bring alternate knees up to chest, and return to straight leg position. Not too fast. Do exercise 20 times, increase to 60.
3. Jumping Jack. Stand, arms at side, feet together. Jump to stride position and fling arms above head. Repeat. Do exercise 20 times, increase to 50. (This may be done in three counts for variety, adding an extra jump when feet are together.)

**B. Upper Back, Shoulder and Arm Strength** (Do two exercises)

1. Standing, arms at shoulder level, elbows bent and wrists straight, push elbows back eight counts, relax. Do exercise 4 times.
2. Same as (1) except sit on floor.
3. Arm circling. Standing, arms out to side, elbows straight, shoulder level. Make small circles with arms, increasing to large circles in eight counts. Do exercise 4 times.
4. Same as (3) except sit on floor with legs crossed.
5. Alternate front and back clap. Standing, arms at side. Clap hands, alternately, in front and back of body. At "clap," hands should be as near shoulder level as possible. Do exercise 12 times.
6. Push-ups. Prone lying (on face) hands on floor next to chest. Keeping body straight, raise body off floor until elbows are straight. Body will be supported on hands and feet. Lower body till chin touches floor and repeat.

   *Note:* Pupils unable to do push-ups should try them with knees on floor or, if unable to do this, practice against a wall. Girls may do push-ups with knees on floor, but should be encouraged to try regular push-ups. Do exercise as many times as possible up to 20 times.

7. Pull-ups. Use horizontal ladder, horizontal bar on playground or chinning bar in gym. Grip bar with palms away from body. Pull body up till chin is over the bar. Lower body till elbows are straight. Repeat. Do exercise 3 times, increase to 10.

   *Note:* Pupils unable to do pull-ups may have slight support from standing on chair or stool until they can support their own weight.

8. Elbow Fling. Standing, arms at shoulder level, elbows bent and palms down. Pull elbows back three counts, fling arms back on count 4. Do exercise 8 times.

9. Same as (8) except sit on floor with legs crossed.

## C. Abdominal Strength (Do two exercises)

1. Standing, feet slightly apart, arms at side. Raise alternate knees and squeeze to abdomen. Keep trunk erect. Do exercise 4 times with each leg.

2. Steam Engine. Standing, hands behind neck. Touch left elbow to right knee. Raise to erect position. Touch right elbow to left knee. Be sure to raise to standing position each time. Do exercise 6 times with each leg.

3. Standing, arms at side. Contract lower abdominal muscles and attempt to flatten lower back. Action should be confined to pelvic area; shoulders and chest should not change position. Hold contraction for three seconds, increase to six seconds. Do 10 times, increase to 20 times.

4. Long sitting (legs out straight) hands clasped behind neck. Draw knees up toward chest as far as possible, keeping chest high and back flat. Do exercise 5 times, increase to 20.
   *Note:* Feet may be slid along the floor at first; later, feet and legs should be lifted off floor.

5. Prone lying, arms extended overhead on floor, legs together. Raise arms, head, chest and legs off floor slowly. Lower to floor, slowly. Do exercise 4 times, increase to 10.

6. Lie on back, hands under head. Raise alternate legs off the floor with knees straight — 12 to 15 inches off floor. Do 8 times each leg, then 4 times both legs. Do slowly. Do not hold breath. Do exercise 1 time, increase to 4.

7. Curl-ups. Lie on floor, knees bent. Raise to sitting position and curl arms around legs. Do 4 times, increase to 20. Exhale while coming up, inhale while going down. Partner may hold feet until pupil can do it alone.

8. Sit-ups. Same as (6) except that knees are straight. Hands go over to touch toes when in sitting position. Exhale while coming up, inhale while going down. Partner may hold feet until pupil can go alone. Do 4 times, increase to 20.

D. **Flexibility Exercises** (Do two exercises)

1. Trunk Bobbing. Stand, feet slightly apart, arms at side. Bend forward in 3 counts (3 "bobs") or bounces, arms relaxed, knees straight, touching floor on third count. Roll up to standing position on count four. Do 8 times increase to 12.

2. Side bobbing. Same as (1) except bend to the side, letting hand on that side slide down leg as far as possible. Do 4 times each side, increase to 8.

3. Airplane. Standing, stride position, arms out to side, shoulder height. Keeping arms and knees straight, touch right hand to left foot, return to erect position. Touch left hand to right foot. Do 4 times increase to 12.

4. Trunk Twister. Standing, stride position, arms stretched up and out at a 45 degree angle from shoulder. Twist trunk to the side as far as possible. Do 8 times each side, increase to 12.

## HOW TO GET THE BEST RESULTS FROM EXERCISE

The following suggestions apply mainly to a calisthenics program, but should also be applied to other forms of exercise.

1. Exercise must be done consistently and regularly. Having a certain time of day and a certain place for exercising aid in forming the habit of regular exercise. A daily period produces the best development, but two periods per week can result in some improvement in strength.

2. "Fitness is maintained at a high level only if motivation is continuously present."[20] Teachers and parents need to motivate children — not to play — but to perform the activities necessary

---

[20]Fitness for Youth — A chart. American Association for Health, Physical Education and Recreation, 1201 16th Street, N.W., Washington, D. C.

for all-round fitness development. Creating a desire in the individual to succeed, or to exceed his classmates' or his former score, will greatly enhance the possibility of improvement in fitness. Doing exercises with music may make them more fun. The wise teacher will find ways to avoid monotony.

3. Exercise must be vigorous and strenuous. Sloppy performance of calisthenics is an utter waste of time. In order to develop strength, endurance and other factors in fitness, the individual must exercise to the point where he is out of breath, "puffing," and experiencing at least temporary fatigue. Most children and adults don't realize their physical capacity. They can do much more than they think they can.

4. An exercise period should start with a warm-up exercise to loosen and stretch the muscles and prepare them for more strenuous activities. When the body is "cold", do not force movements. This can result in muscle strain.

5. To improve fitness, more and more strenuous activities are needed. This can be accomplished by increasing the number of times an exercise is done, by the manner in which an exercise is performed (as in push-ups or sit-ups) or by adding more difficult and more strenuous exercises.

    For most effective results, it is necessary

    a—"to execute the exercise in good form, i.e., exactly as described, and with energy in each movement.
    b—to increase the number of times each exercise is performed as the capacities of the individual pupil develop.
    c—to strive for sustained effort without rest or pause between exercises."[21]

6. The exercise period should leave one with a feeling of satisfaction and well-being, even if somewhat fatigued. One should feel relaxed, freer from tension and ready to proceed with the next item on the day's agenda.

## SUGGESTED PLAN FOR USING STUDENTS TO LEAD EXERCISES

1. As a class project, choose eight or ten exercises which the children like and which have effect on all parts of the body.

---

[21]*Youth Physical Fitness*, President's Council on Physical Fitness, Revised 1967, Superintendent of Documents, Washington, D. C. 20402. p. 56.

2. Have a student leader each day. Use any method to pick the leader. This could be done alphabetically or using everyone in Squad 1 first, then Squad 2, etc. In this manner, children can know a day or two ahead of time that they will be leaders on a certain day and will have an opportunity to prepare.

3. A good leader keeps these things in mind — He

   a. Announces the name of the exercise so the entire class can hear it.
   b. Gets into position to begin and then looks over the class to see if they are ready.
   c. Gives starting signal — "Ready, begin."
   d. Counts loud enough and clear enough so the entire class can follow easily.
   e. Does the exercise in good form so the class follows his example.
   f. Plans ahead on how to stop the class correctly, i.e. 1, 2 — 1, 2 — 1, stop. OR 1, 2, 3, 4 — 1, 2, 3, 4 — 1, 2, 3, Stop.

## FITNESS TESTS

There are a number of reasons why a fitness test should be included in the physical education curriculum. It is helpful to administrators and teachers to know whether or not the physical education curriculum is producing the desired goals in fitness development. Parents also have the right to know the status of their child's physical fitness. As for the pupil himself, testing, as in other subject areas, is a motivating factor that will encourage him to exert himself and do his best. Fitness testing should be done in all grades, but especially from the fourth grade up.

It should be recognized by all concerned, but especially by administrators and teachers, that fitness testing is a time-consuming affair. The testing of a class of 25 or 30 boys and girls will take the better part of a week of physical education classes if the teacher has no outside help — and most do not. In order to make the test worthwhile, scores must be tabulated and ranked, and each pupil and his parents should be informed of his results.

Assuming that the decision has been made to include a fitness test in the physical education curriculum, the question arises as to what kind of a test should be used and how often it should be given during the school year.

The two major types of fitness tests are
1. A test of minimum achievement
2. A test of maximum achievement

The first type of test is a screening test. It usually includes three or four test items and sets up standards which any boy or girl of that particular age or grade should be able to pass. The chief purpose is to determine which pupils cannot pass the test and are thereby below standard, or are not, according to the test, physically fit. The task of the teacher then is to help those who are not physically fit so that the next time the test is given, these pupils will pass or show improvement. Examples of this type of test are the Kraus-Weber test[22] and the test suggested by the President's Council on Youth Fitness.[23] Advantages of this kind of test — a screening test — are that it is less time-consuming, more easily administered and the tabulating and reporting are simpler.

The second type of test is, as its name implies, a test of maximum achievement, i.e., the pupil does as many or as much as he can, rather than merely enough to pass or to reach a set standard. If they have accompanying scores and ratings, and most do, tests of this type serve also as a screening test, but in addition show the pupil's maximum achievement. The main advantage of the maximum achievement test is that of motivation. The pupil strives to get into the "good" or "superior" group, to excel, to be as good or better than his classmates. In many cases, it is the pupil's only opportunity to go "all out." The disadvantages of this type of test are that it takes more time to give and to tabulate results. If the teacher is willing to spend extra time on testing, the achievement test should be used rather than the screening test. Examples of the maximum achievement test are the Oregon Motor Fitness Test for grades four through twelve[24] and the Youth Fitness test of the American Association for Health, Physical

[22]Hans Kraus, M. D. and Ruth P. Hirschland. "Minimum Muscular Fitness Tests in School Children." *Research Quarterly* of American Association for Health, Physical Education and Recreation, May, 1954. 25:178-188.

[23]*Youth Physical Fitness.* Revised 1967. Superintendent of Documents, Washington, D. C. 20402. pages 19-24. 40 cents.

[24]*Oregon Motor Fitness Test,* Grades Four through Twelve. Oregon State Department of Education, Salem, Oregon. 1960.

Education and Recreation.[25] These tests are available at little if any cost. The booklet published by the President's Council on Physical Fitness[26] also contains, in addition to the previously mentioned screening test, the AAHPER (American Association for Health, Physical Education and Recreation) test of maximum achievement.

There are numerous fitness tests other than those mentioned. Many of the larger school systems and nearly all state departments of education are able to provide the teacher with a test. Most physical education departments at colleges and universities are willing and eager to help the teacher select a test. Tests are also available from organizations such as the Four-H Clubs and other youth groups.

In selecting a test to be used by the teacher who is not an expert in physical education, consideration should be given to simplicity in administering the test and in tabulating the results. For the teacher testing fitness for the first time, it is advisable to use a screening test, and this author recommends the one provided by the President's Council on Youth Fitness. It is available to everyone, inexpensive and the only equipment required is a chinning bar and a watch to measure seconds. If a test of maximum achievement is to be used, the Oregon Motor Fitness Test is one of the best for elementary age youngsters.

For the most effective use, tests should be given in the fall and again in the spring. Some school systems advocate a midyear test in addition to the fall and spring test. This can be valuable in showing teachers and pupils what progress is being made.

For the convenience of the teacher, the tests included in the screening test recommended by the President's Council on Physical Fitness are described here. The teacher who wishes to use this test should secure a copy of the booklet. This booklet contains all necessary information about the test and also suggestions for teaching activities which will improve fitness.

---

[25]*Youth Fitness Test Manual*, American Association for Health, Physical Education and Recreation, 1201 16th Street, N.W., Washington, D. C. 20036. The AAHPER test serves as the basis for the Presidential Physical Fitness Award. Scores which pupils must match or excel to qualify are indicated in the charts accompanying the test descriptions and illustrations. Teachers may obtain official application forms and complete information on the Presidential Awards program by writing to the Council, or to Presidential Physical Fitness Awards, 1201 Sixteenth Street, N. W., Washington, D. C. 20036.

[26]*Ibid.*

Also included herein is the Oregon Motor Fitness Test for Grades Four, Five and Six with instructions for giving the test, scoring and rating tables.

## SCREENING TEST

Recommended by the President's Council on Physical Fitness

1. **Pull-ups** (Boys)

    Equipment: A bar of sufficient height, comfortable to grip. Adjustable, if possible.

    *Starting position*:

    Grasp the bar with palms facing forward; hang with arms and legs fully extended. Feet must be free of the floor. The partner (or teacher) stands slightly to one side of the pupil being tested and counts each successful pull-up.

    (Boys may jump to reach the bar, or step off of a stool or chair)

    *Action*:

    1. Pull body up with arms until the chin is placed over the bar. Chin must not rest on the bar.
    2. Lower the body until elbows are fully extended.
    3. Repeat the exercise the required number of times.

    *Rules*:

    1. The pull must not be a snap movement.
    2. The knees must not be raised.
    3. Kicking of the legs is not permitted.
    4. The body must not swing. If pupil starts to swing, his partner (or teacher) stops the motion by holding an extended arm across the front of the pupil's thighs.
    5. One complete pull-up is counted each time the pupil places his chin over the bar.

    *To Pass*:

    Boys, ages 10-13 — 1 pull-up.
    Boys, ages 14-15 — 2 pull-ups.

Pull-ups (Boys)

## 2. Modified Pull-ups (Girls)

*Equipment:*

A bar adjustable in height and comfortable to grip. A piece of pipe, placed between two stepladders and held securely, can be used.

*Starting Position:*

Adjust height of the bar to chest level. Grasp bar with palms facing out or forward. Extend the legs under the bar, keeping the body and knees straight. The heels are on the floor. Fully extend the arms so that they form an angle of 90 degrees with the body line. The partner (or teacher) braces the pupil's heels to prevent slipping.

*Action:*

1. Pull body up with the arms until the chest touches the bar.
2. Lower body until elbows are fully extended.
3. Repeat the exercise the required number of times.

*Rules:*

1. The body must be kept straight.
2. The chest must touch the bar and the arms must then be fully extended.
3. No resting is permitted.
4. One pull-up is counted each time the chest touches the bar.

*To Pass:*

Girls, ages 10-17, 8 modified pull-ups.

**Modified Pull-ups (Girls)**

3. **Sit-ups** (Boys and Girls)

*Equipment*:

None required, but lying on mat rather than floor is more comfortable.

*Starting Position*:

Pupil lies on his back with legs extended, feet about 1 foot apart. The hands, with fingers interlaced, are grasped behind the neck. Another pupil holds his partner's ankles and keeps his heels in contact with the floor while counting each successful sit-up. Teacher can do counting.

*Action*:

1. Sit up and turn the trunk to the left. Touch the right elbow to the left knee.
2. Return to starting position.
3. Sit up and turn the trunk to the right. Touch the left elbow to the right knee.
4. Return to starting position.
5. Repeat the required number of times.
6. One complete sit-up is counted each time the pupil returns to the starting position.

*To Pass*:

Boys, ages 10-17 — 14 sit-ups.
Girls, ages 10-17 — 10 sit-ups.

Sit-ups

**4. Squat thrust** (Boys and Girls)

*Equipment*:

A stop watch, or a watch with a second hand.

*Starting Position*:

Pupil stands at attention.

*Action*:

1. Bend knees and place hands on the floor in front of the feet. Arms may be between, outside or in front of the bent knees.
2. Thrust legs back far enough so that the body is perfectly straight from shouders to feet (the push-up position).
3. Return to squat position.
4. Return to erect position.

*Scoring*:

The teacher carefully instructs the pupil how to do correct squat thrusts. The teacher tells the pupil to do as many correct squat thrusts as possible within a 10 second time limit. The teacher gives the starting signal, "Ready, — Go!" On "Go" the pupil begins. The partner or teacher counts each squat thrust. At the end of 10 seconds, the teacher says "Stop."

*Rules*:

The pupil must return to the erect position of attention at the completion of each squat thrust.

*To Pass*:

Boys, ages 10-17, 4 squat thrusts in 10 seconds.
Girls, ages 10-17, 3 squat thrusts in 10 seconds.

Squat Thrust

# OREGON MOTOR FITNESS TEST BATTERY

Directions for Administering the Girls' Test Battery
(Grades 4, 5 and 6)

## Hanging in Arm-Flexed Position

*Equipment*: A horizontal bar or similar support parallel to the floor; a stop watch, or a watch with a second hand; a stool or bench.

*Starting Position*: The student stands on a stool or table placing the hands shoulder width apart, palms outward on a one-inch standard horizontal bar or ladder with elbows flexed to permit chin to be level with the bar.

*Action*: The support is removed. The student holds her chin at the level of the bar as long as possible.

*Rules*: The legs should remain extended throughout.

*Scoring*: The number of seconds the student is able to maintain some flexion in the elbow, preventing the upper arm from straightening.

## Standing Broad Jump

*Starting Position*: A take-off line is drawn on the floor or mat. At a distance that all can jump, additional lines are drawn parallel to the take-off line and two inches apart to a point exceeding the farthest jump anticipated. The first line should be an even number of feet from the take-off line. The student toes the take-off line with both feet, but with feet slightly apart, prior to each jump.

*Action*: Taking off from both feet, the student jumps as far as she can. In jumping, she crouches slightly and swings the arms to aid in the jump.

*Rules*: The student must take off from both feet and land on both feet. The start must be from a stationary position.

*Scoring*: The distance to the nearest inch from the take-off line to the closest heel position. If the student falls back, she should re-take the test. Record the best of three trials.

## Crossed-arm Curl-ups

*Starting Position*: The student assumes a lying position on the back with knees bent at approximately a right angle, soles of the feet flat on the floor, arms folded and held against the chest. The feet of the student tested should be held down firmly by a partner. The feet are hip width apart.

*Action*: The student rises to an erect sitting position and returns to a back lying position as many times as possible without stopping.

*Rules*: The feet must remain on the floor throughout the test. The elbows must be kept down, and the arms are not used to help the body sit up. Bouncing from the floor is not permissible. Resting during any phase of the performance is not allowed.

*Scoring*: The number of times the student raises herself correctly to a sitting position.

## OREGON MOTOR FITNESS TEST SCORE CARD—GIRLS GRADES 4, 5, AND 6

NAME _____

SCHOOL _____   COUNTY _____

| DATE | Month Sept. 19 | | | Month 19 | | | Month 19 | | | Month 19 | | | Month 19 | | | Month 19 | | | Month 19 | | | Month 19 | | |
|---|---|---|---|---|---|---|---|---|---|---|---|---|---|---|---|---|---|---|---|---|---|---|---|---|
| | Test Score | Rat-ing | Std. Pts. | Test Score | Rat-ing | Std. Pts. | Test Score | Rat-ing | Std. Pts. | Test Score | Rat-ing | Std. Pts. | Test Score | Rat-ing | Std. Pts. | Test Score | Rat-ing | Std. Pts. | Test Score | Rat-ing | Std. Pts. | Test Score | Rat-ing | Std. Pts. |
| GRADE | | | | | | | | | | | | | | | | | | | | | | | | |
| AGE | | | | | | | | | | | | | | | | | | | | | | | | |
| HEIGHT | | | | | | | | | | | | | | | | | | | | | | | | |
| WEIGHT | | | | | | | | | | | | | | | | | | | | | | | | |
| OBJECTIVE TESTS | | | | | | | | | | | | | | | | | | | | | | | | |
| Hanging in Arm-Flexed Position | | | | | | | | | | | | | | | | | | | | | | | | |
| Standing Broad Jump | | | | | | | | | | | | | | | | | | | | | | | | |
| Crossed-Arm Curl-Ups | | | | | | | | | | | | | | | | | | | | | | | | |
| TOTAL STAND-ARD POINTS | | | | | | | | | | | | | | | | | | | | | | | | |

## RATING NORMS FOR GIRLS GRADES 4, 5, AND 6

| TEST ITEMS | Superior | Good | Fair | Poor | Inferior | Grade |
|---|---|---|---|---|---|---|
| Hanging in Arm-Flexed Position | 30-Up | 20- 29 | 5- 19 | 1- 4 | 0 | |
| Standing Broad Jump | 65-Up | 58- 64 | 49- 57 | 39- 48 | 0- 38 | 4 |
| Crossed-Arm Curl-Ups | 66-Up | 50- 65 | 26- 49 | 2- 25 | 0- 1 | |
| Hanging in Arm-Flexed Position | 31-Up | 22- 30 | 10- 21 | 2- 9 | 0- 1 | |
| Standing Broad Jump | 75-Up | 68- 74 | 57- 67 | 46- 56 | 0- 45 | 5 |
| Crossed-Arm Curl-Ups | 68-Up | 52- 67 | 28- 51 | 4- 27 | 0- 3 | |
| Hanging in Arm-Flexed Position | 37-Up | 27- 36 | 12- 26 | 1- 11 | 0 | |
| Standing Broad Jump | 73-Up | 66- 72 | 55- 65 | 44- 54 | 0- 43 | 6 |
| Crossed-Arm Curl-Ups | 71-Up | 55- 70 | 31- 54 | 1- 30 | 0 | |
| TOTAL STANDARD POINTS | 204-Up | 180-203 | 144-179 | 112-143 | 111-Down | |

## DIRECTIONS FOR RECORDING AND SCORING TESTS

1. Record the actual test score for each item in the column marked "Test Score" on this side of the score card.
2. Using test score, check rating norms and record superior, good, fair, poor, or inferior for each test item in the rating column.
3. Find standard point score corresponding to each actual test score in the "Scoring Table" on the back of the card and record in column marked "Standard Points."
4. Add "Standard Points" for all test items and record total at bottom of card in -space on line marked "Total Standard Points."
5. Using total standard points, check rating norms to determine fitness rating of superior, good, fair, poor, or inferior. Record this rating in the space provided at the bottom of the rating column. Below-standard individuals should be tested more frequently.
6. Repeat the test at the end of the school year. It is recommended that a mid-year test also be given.

43

## SCORING TABLE
## FOR GIRLS GRADES 4, 5, AND 6

| Std. Pts. Based on T-Score | Arm-Flexed Hang in Seconds | | | Standing Broad Jump in Inches | | | Number of Crossed-Arm Curl-Ups | | |
|---|---|---|---|---|---|---|---|---|---|
| | 4th | 5th | 6th | 4th | 5th | 6th | 4th | 5th | 6th |
| 100 | 69 | 65 | 77 | 91 | 104 | 102 | 130 | 120 | 149 |
| 98 | 66 | 63 | 75 | 89 | 103 | 101 | 126 | 117 | 145 |
| 96 | 64 | 61 | 72 | 87 | 101 | 99 | 122 | 114 | 140 |
| 94 | 61 | 59 | 70 | 86 | 99 | 97 | 118 | 110 | 136 |
| 92 | 59 | 56 | 67 | 84 | 97 | 95 | 114 | 106 | 131 |
| 90 | 57 | 54 | 62 | 83 | 95 | 93 | 110 | 103 | 127 |
| 88 | 54 | 52 | 62 | 81 | 93 | 91 | 106 | 99 | 122 |
| 86 | 52 | 50 | 60 | 79 | 92 | 89 | 102 | 95 | 118 |
| 84 | 49 | 48 | 57 | 78 | 90 | 87 | 98 | 92 | 113 |
| 82 | 47 | 46 | 55 | 76 | 88 | 85 | 94 | 88 | 109 |
| 80 | 44 | 44 | 52 | 75 | 86 | 84 | 90 | 84 | 104 |
| 78 | 42 | 42 | 50 | 73 | 84 | 82 | 86 | 81 | 100 |
| 76 | 40 | 40 | 47 | 71 | 82 | 80 | 82 | 77 | 95 |
| 74 | 37 | 38 | 44 | 70 | 81 | 78 | 78 | 73 | 91 |
| 72 | 35 | 35 | 42 | 68 | 79 | 76 | 74 | 70 | 86 |
| 70 | 32 | 33 | 39 | 67 | 77 | 74 | 70 | 66 | 82 |
| 68 | 30 | 31 | 37 | 65 | 75 | 72 | 66 | 63 | 77 |
| 66 | 27 | 29 | 34 | 63 | 73 | 70 | 62 | 59 | 73 |
| 64 | 25 | 27 | 32 | 62 | 72 | 68 | 58 | 55 | 68 |
| 62 | 23 | 25 | 29 | 60 | 70 | 67 | 54 | 51 | 64 |
| 60 | 20 | 23 | 27 | 59 | 68 | 65 | 50 | 48 | 60 |
| 58 | 18 | 21 | 24 | 57 | 66 | 63 | 46 | 45 | 55 |
| 56 | 15 | 19 | 22 | 55 | 64 | 61 | 42 | 41 | 51 |
| 54 | 13 | 16 | 19 | 54 | 62 | 59 | 38 | 38 | 46 |
| 52 | 10 | 14 | 17 | 52 | 61 | 57 | 34 | 34 | 42 |
| 50 | 8 | 12 | 14 | 51 | 59 | 65 | 30 | 30 | 37 |
| 48 | 5 | 10 | 12 | 49 | 57 | 53 | 26 | 27 | 33 |
| 46 | 3 | 8 | 9 | 47 | 55 | 51 | 22 | 23 | 28 |
| 44 | 1 | 6 | 7 | 46 | 53 | 50 | 18 | 19 | 24 |
| 42 | | 4 | 4 | 44 | 51 | 48 | 14 | 16 | 20 |
| 40 | | 2 | 1 | 42 | 50 | 46 | 10 | 12 | 16 |
| 38 | | | | 41 | 48 | 44 | 6 | 8 | 11 |
| 36 | | | | 39 | 46 | 42 | 3 | 4 | 6 |
| 34 | | | | 38 | 44 | 40 | 1 | 1 | 1 |
| 32 | | | | 36 | 42 | 38 | | | |
| 30 | | | | 34 | 41 | 36 | | | |
| 28 | | | | 33 | 39 | 35 | | | |
| 26 | | | | 31 | 37 | 33 | | | |
| 24 | | | | 30 | 35 | 31 | | | |
| 22 | | | | 28 | 33 | 29 | | | |
| 20 | | | | 26 | 31 | 27 | | | |
| 18 | | | | 25 | 30 | 25 | | | |
| 16 | | | | 23 | 28 | 23 | | | |
| 14 | | | | 22 | 26 | 21 | | | |
| 12 | | | | 20 | 24 | 19 | | | |
| 10 | | | | 18 | 22 | 18 | | | |
| 8 | | | | 17 | 20 | 16 | | | |
| 6 | | | | 15 | 19 | 14 | | | |
| 4 | | | | 14 | 17 | 12 | | | |
| 2 | | | | 12 | 15 | 10 | | | |
| 1 | | | | 11 | 14 | 9 | | | |

## GENERAL INSTRUCTIONS TO TEACHERS

1. The motor fitness tests are to be taken by only those individuals who are physically able to participate in the regular program of physical education.
2. In no instance should pupils be permitted to perform any test more than is necessary to get one hundred points. Performance should be stopped on any test if, in the opinion of the instructor, the pupil is overtaxing himself.
3. Individuals should be acquainted with the tests in advance of the testing period and sufficient practice should be allowed for thorough understanding of the execution of the tests.
4. Time should be provided for a few minutes warm-up at the beginning of each test period.
5. All equipment and facilities necessary for the administration of the tests should be prepared before the testing period begins.
6. Establish a policy of strictly enforcing all rules and regulations in scoring and administering the test.

## OREGON MOTOR FITNESS TEST BATTERY

Directions for Administering the Boys' Test Battery
(Grades 4, 5, and 6)

### Push-ups

*Starting Position*: The pupil assumes a front-leaning rest position with the body supported on hand and toes. The arms are straight and at right angles to the body.

*Action*: The pupil dips or lowers the body so that the chest touches or nearly touches the floor, then pushes back to the starting position by straightening the arms, and repeats the procedure as many times as possible.

*Rules*: The chest, no other part of the body, must touch or nearly touch the floor with each dip. The arms must be completely extended with each push-up. The body must be held straight, with no bend in the hips, throughout the exercise.

*Scoring*: The number of times the body is correctly pushed up. If the body sags, if the hips rise, or if the pupil does not push completely up or go completely down, no credit is given for each push-up.

### Standing Broad Jump

*Starting Position*: A take-off line is drawn on the floor or mat. At a distance that all can jump, additional lines are drawn parallel to the take-off line and two inches apart to a point exceeding the farthest jump anticipated. The first line should be an even number of feet from the take-off line. The pupil toes the take-off line with both feet, but with feet slightly apart, prior to each jump.

*Action*: Taking off from both feet, the pupil jumps as far as he can. In jumping, he crouches slightly and swings the arms to aid in the jump.

*Rules*: The pupil must take off from both feet and land on both feet. The start must be from a stationary position.

*Scoring*: The distance to the nearest inch from the take-off line to the closest heel position. If the pupil falls back, he should re-take the test. Record the best of three trials.

### Knee-touch Sit-ups

*Starting Position*: The pupil lies on his back on the floor, knees straight, feet approximately 12 inches apart, with hands clasped behind head. A scorer kneels on the floor and holds the soles of the feet against his knees, pressing firmly.

*Action*: The pupil performs the following movement as many times as possible: (a) Raise the trunk, rotating it somewhat to the left, and bend forward far enough to touch the right elbow to the left knee. (b) Lower the trunk to the floor. (c) Sit up again, but rotate the trunk to the right and touch the left elbow to the right knee. (d) Again lower the trunk to the floor.

*Rules*: The knees may be slightly bent as the subject sits up. The pupil must not pause during the test; the movement must be continuous either when leaning forward to touch the knee or when lowering the trunk to the floor. Bouncing from the floor is not permissible.

*Scoring*: One point is given for each complete movement of touching elbow to knee. No score should be counted if the subject unclasps hands from head, rests on the floor or when sitting, or keeps knees bent when lying on the back or when beginning the sit-up.

## OREGON MOTOR FITNESS TEST SCORE CARD—BOYS GRADES 4, 5, AND 6

NAME _____

SCHOOL _____ COUNTY _____

| DATE | Month Sept. 19 | | | Month 19 | | | Month 19 | | | Month 19 | | | Month 19 | | | Month 19 | | | Month 19 | | | Month 19 | | |
|---|---|---|---|---|---|---|---|---|---|---|---|---|---|---|---|---|---|---|---|---|---|---|---|---|
| | Test Score | Rating | Std. Pts. | Test Score | Rating | Std. Pts. | Test Score | Rating | Std. Pts. | Test Score | Rating | Std. Pts. | Test Score | Rating | Std. Pts. | Test Score | Rating | Std. Pts. | Test Score | Rating | Std. Pts. | Test Score | Rating | Std. Pts. |
| GRADE | | | | | | | | | | | | | | | | | | | | | | | | |
| AGE | | | | | | | | | | | | | | | | | | | | | | | | |
| HEIGHT | | | | | | | | | | | | | | | | | | | | | | | | |
| WEIGHT | | | | | | | | | | | | | | | | | | | | | | | | |
| OBJECTIVE TESTS | | | | | | | | | | | | | | | | | | | | | | | | |
| Standing Broad Jump | | | | | | | | | | | | | | | | | | | | | | | | |
| Push-Ups | | | | | | | | | | | | | | | | | | | | | | | | |
| Sit-Ups | | | | | | | | | | | | | | | | | | | | | | | | |
| TOTAL STANDARD POINTS | | | | | | | | | | | | | | | | | | | | | | | | |

## RATING NORMS FOR BOYS GRADES 4, 5, AND 6

| TEST ITEMS | Superior | Good | Fair | Poor | Inferior | Grade |
|---|---|---|---|---|---|---|
| Standing Broad Jump | 69-Up | 62- 68 | 52- 61 | 42- 51 | 12- 41 | 4 |
| Push-Ups | 25-Up | 18- 24 | 7- 17 | 1- 6 | 0 | |
| Sit-Ups | 64-Up | 47- 63 | 22- 46 | 1- 21 | 0 | |
| Standing Broad Jump | 73-Up | 66- 72 | 56- 65 | 46- 55 | 16- 45 | 5 |
| Push-Ups | 22-Up | 16- 21 | 7- 15 | 1- 6 | 0- 1 | |
| Sit-Ups | 70-Up | 52- 69 | 22- 51 | 2- 21 | 0- 1 | |
| Standing Broad Jump | 77-Up | 70- 76 | 59- 69 | 49- 58 | 18- 48 | 6 |
| Push-Ups | 24-Up | 18- 23 | 9- 17 | 4- 8 | 0- 3 | |
| Sit-Ups | 75-Up | 55- 74 | 25- 54 | 1- 24 | 0 | |
| TOTAL STANDARD POINTS | 204-Up | 180-203 | 144-179 | 112-143 | 111-Down | |

### DIRECTIONS FOR RECORDING AND SCORING TESTS

1. Record the actual test score for each item in the column marked "Test Score" on this side of the score card.
2. Using test score, check rating norms and record superior, good, fair, poor, or inferior for each test item in the rating column.
3. Find standard point score corresponding to each actual test score in the "Scoring Table" on the back of the card and record in column marked "Standard Points"
4. Add "Standard Points" for all test items and record total at bottom of card in space on line marked "Total Standard Points"
5. Using total standard points, check rating norms to determine fitness rating of superior, good, fair, poor, or inferior. Record this rating in the space provided at the bottom of the rating column.
6. Repeat the test at the end of the school year; it is recommended that a mid-year test also be given. Below-standard individuals should be tested more frequently.

# SCORING TABLE
## FOR BOYS GRADES 4, 5, AND 6

| Std. Pts. Based on T-Score | Standing Broad Jump in Inches | | | Number of Push-Ups | | | Number of Sit-Ups | | |
|---|---|---|---|---|---|---|---|---|---|
| | 4th | 5th | 6th | 4th | 5th | 6th | 4th | 5th | 6th |
| 100 | 97 | 100 | 106 | 55 | 43 | 39 | 131 | 153 | 158 |
| 98 | 95 | 99 | 104 | 53 | 41 | 37 | 127 | 148 | 153 |
| 96 | 93 | 97 | 102 | 51 | 40 | 36 | 123 | 143 | 147 |
| 94 | 91 | 95 | 100 | 50 | 39 | 35 | 118 | 138 | 142 |
| 92 | 90 | 94 | 98 | 48 | 37 | 34 | 114 | 133 | 137 |
| 90 | 88 | 92 | 97 | 46 | 36 | 33 | 110 | 128 | 132 |
| 88 | 86 | 90 | 95 | 44 | 34 | 32 | 106 | 123 | 127 |
| 86 | 85 | 88 | 93 | 42 | 33 | 30 | 102 | 118 | 122 |
| 84 | 83 | 87 | 91 | 40 | 32 | 29 | 97 | 113 | 117 |
| 82 | 81 | 85 | 90 | 38 | 30 | 28 | 93 | 108 | 112 |
| 80 | 80 | 83 | 88 | 36 | 29 | 27 | 89 | 103 | 107 |
| 78 | 78 | 82 | 86 | 35 | 27 | 26 | 85 | 98 | 102 |
| 76 | 76 | 80 | 84 | 33 | 26 | 25 | 81 | 93 | 97 |
| 74 | 74 | 78 | 83 | 31 | 25 | 23 | 76 | 88 | 92 |
| 72 | 73 | 77 | 81 | 29 | 23 | 22 | 72 | 83 | 87 |
| 70 | 71 | 75 | 79 | 27 | 22 | 21 | 68 | 78 | 81 |
| 68 | 69 | 73 | 77 | 25 | 21 | 20 | 64 | 73 | 76 |
| 66 | 68 | 72 | 75 | 23 | 19 | 19 | 60 | 68 | 71 |
| 64 | 66 | 70 | 74 | 22 | 18 | 18 | 56 | 63 | 66 |
| 62 | 64 | 68 | 72 | 20 | 16 | 16 | 51 | 58 | 61 |
| 60 | 63 | 66 | 70 | 18 | 15 | 15 | 47 | 53 | 56 |
| 58 | 61 | 65 | 68 | 16 | 13 | 14 | 43 | 48 | 51 |
| 56 | 59 | 63 | 67 | 14 | 12 | 13 | 39 | 43 | 46 |
| 54 | 57 | 61 | 65 | 12 | 11 | 12 | 35 | 38 | 41 |
| 52 | 56 | 60 | 63 | 10 | 9 | 10 | 30 | 33 | 36 |
| 50 | 54 | 58 | 61 | 9 | 8 | 9 | 26 | 28 | 31 |
| 48 | 52 | 56 | 60 | 7 | 6 | 8 | 22 | 23 | 26 |
| 46 | 51 | 55 | 58 | 5 | 5 | 7 | 18 | 18 | 21 |
| 44 | 49 | 53 | 56 | 3 | 4 | 6 | 14 | 13 | 16 |
| 42 | 47 | 51 | 54 | 1 | 2 | 5 | 9 | 8 | 11 |
| 40 | 46 | 49 | 53 | | 1 | 3 | 5 | 4 | 6 |
| 38 | 44 | 48 | 51 | | | 2 | 1 | 1 | 2 |
| 36 | 42 | 46 | 49 | | | 1 | | | |
| 34 | 41 | 44 | 47 | | | | | | |
| 32 | 39 | 43 | 45 | | | | | | |
| 30 | 37 | 41 | 44 | | | | | | |
| 28 | 35 | 39 | 42 | | | | | | |
| 26 | 34 | 38 | 40 | | | | | | |
| 24 | 32 | 36 | 38 | | | | | | |
| 22 | 30 | 34 | 37 | | | | | | |
| 20 | 29 | 33 | 35 | | | | | | |
| 18 | 27 | 31 | 33 | | | | | | |
| 16 | 25 | 29 | 31 | | | | | | |
| 14 | 24 | 27 | 30 | | | | | | |
| 12 | 22 | 26 | 28 | | | | | | |
| 10 | 20 | 24 | 26 | | | | | | |
| 8 | 18 | 22 | 24 | | | | | | |
| 6 | 17 | 21 | 23 | | | | | | |
| 4 | 15 | 19 | 21 | | | | | | |
| 2 | 13 | 17 | 19 | | | | | | |
| 1 | 12 | 16 | 18 | | | | | | |

## GENERAL INSTRUCTIONS TO TEACHERS

1. The motor fitness tests are to be taken by only those individuals who are physically able to participate in the regular program of physical education.
2. In no instance should pupils be permitted to perform any test more than is necessary to get one hundred points. Performance should be stopped on any test if, in the opinion of the instructor, the pupil is overtaxing himself.
3. Individuals should be acquainted with the tests in advance of the testing period and sufficient practice should be allowed for thorough understanding of the execution of the tests.
4. Time should be provided for a few minutes warm-up at the beginning of each test period.
5. All equipment and facilities necessary for the administration of the tests should be prepared before the testing period begins.
6. Establish a policy of strictly enforcing all rules and regulations in scoring and administering the test.

# SUGGESTIONS FOR TESTING

1. Tell the class about the test several weeks before it is given. Tell, or show, the class how they are to be tested. A moderate amount of practice on the test items will not affect test scores.

2. On the bulletin board post information about the test including the scoring and ranking procedure.

3. Prepare all necessary items for giving the test such as timing watch, score sheets, etc. Score sheets can be run off on a ditto or mimeograph machine.

SAMPLE CLASS SCORING SHEET

Teacher _____     School _____

Grade _____     Date _____

BOYS -- Ages 10-13

| Names of Pupils | Pull-ups 1 | | | Sit-ups 14 | | | Squat Thrust 4 | | | Remarks |
|---|---|---|---|---|---|---|---|---|---|---|
| | 1st test | | Re-test | 1st test | | Re-test | 1st test | | Re-test | |
| | Pass | Fail | | Pass | Fail | | Pass | Fail | | |
| 1. | | | | | | | | | | |
| 2. | | | | | | | | | | |
| 3. | | | | | | | | | | |
| 4. | | | | | | | | | | |
| 5. | | | | | | | | | | |
| 6. | | | | | | | | | | |
| 7. | | | | | | | | | | |
| 8. | | | | | | | | | | |
| 9. | | | | | | | | | | |

SAMPLE INDIVIDUAL SCORE SHEET OR CARD. Can be kept in separate file or in child's accumulative folder.

| | Date _____ First test | | Date _____ Second test | | |
|---|---|---|---|---|---|
| Name _____ Age _____ | | | | | |
| Grade _____ School _____ | | | | | |
| Test Items | Pass | Fail | Pass | Fail | |
| 1. Pull-ups | | | | | |
| 2. Sit-ups | | | | | |
| 3. Squat Thrust | | | | | |
| Remarks: | | | | | |

A third type of score sheet is one on which a pupil's fitness test scores can be recorded for more than one year. The score sheet should be a part of the material in the pupil's accumulative folder and go with him from grade to grade or school to school. This has some advantage in that the pupil's record on fitness tests can be compared from year to year.

## PHYSICAL FITNESS RECORD

Name _____     Sex _____

| | Grade 4 Age 10 Date | | Grade 5 Age 11 Date | | Grade 6 Age 12 Date | | Grade 7 Age 13 Date | |
|---|---|---|---|---|---|---|---|---|
| Test Items | Pass | Fail | Pass | Fail | Pass | Fail | Pass | Fail |
| 1. Pull-ups | | | | | | | | |
| 2. Sit-ups | | | | | | | | |
| 3. Squat Thrust | | | | | | | | |
| Comment: | | | | | | | | |

4. On the days designated for testing, work with a small group of pupils while the remainder of the class plays. Scores will be better, and you will lessen the possibility of strain or overexertion, if you do not give any one child the whole test on the same day. For example, do all pull-ups one day, all sit-ups the next day, etc.

5. Pupils should be dressed in gym clothes if possible; if not, have girls wear shorts or slacks. Gym shoes are almost mandatory.

6. Be sure the test is done correctly and the scoring is accurate. Encourage the children to do their best.

7. Fifth or sixth graders and older children may be able to test each other, in partners, but younger children need to be tested individually by the teacher for accurate results. Sometimes it is possible for two teachers to work together. One may conduct the tests while the other supervises the children not being tested. The following day, jobs could be alternated.

8. After testing is completed:
   a. Post on bulletin board names of those who passed the test and discuss test results with the class.
   b. Report results to the principal.
   c. Note those who did not pass the test or who made low scores. Discuss it with them and make plans to help them improve their scores on the next test.
   d. Notify parents of test results. This notification may be sent home with the report card.

SAMPLE PARENT NOTIFICATION SLIP --

REPORT ON PHYSICAL FITNESS TEST given on _____(date)

Name_____     School_____

Your child passed   failed   the physical fitness test recommended by the President's Council on Youth Fitness.

We hope you will encourage your child to participate in vigorous play activities after school and on weekends. Experts recommend three to four hours of vigorous play every day for growing children. We, at school, through the physical education program, will do all we can to increase his physical fitness.

Signed_____
                           Teacher

## SUMMARY ON FITNESS

There is no doubt about the value of physical fitness as a necessary ingredient of the physically and emotionally healthy individual. Further, there is no doubt that physical fitness can be achieved and maintained only by some type of regular and consistent physical activity.

A physical education curriculum can justify its use of school time and its place in the school program *only* of it contributes to the physical fitness of boys and girls. Teachers have the responsibility to plan and to work toward this goal and, if they do, they can be assured that they are contributing to the lifelong health of their pupils and to the strength and vitality of the nation.

### OTHER EXERCISE (CALISTHENIC) SERIES

1. Royal Canadian Air Force Exercise Plans for Physical Fitness. 1962. Secure from This Week Magazine, P. O. Box 77-E, Mt. Vernon, New York. 80 pages, $1.00. (Primarily for men and women but may be used for children. A progressive program. Good.)
2. Youth Physical Fitness. Compiled by the President's Council on Physical Fitness. 1967. Secure from Superintendent of Documents, U. S. Government Printing Office, Washington, D. C. 20402. 108 pages, 40 cents. (A school centered program. Very good.)
3. Steinhaus, Arthur. "How To Keep Fit and Like It." Secure from Dartnell Corporation, Chicago 40, Illinois. 70 pages, about $1.00. (Good.)
4. Physical Conditioning, Technical Manual No. 21-200. Secure from Department of the Army, Washington, D.C. 574 pages. (Teacher would need to make selection from many activities included.)
5. Logan, Gene A. and Wallis, Earl L. "Exercises for Children." Prentice-Hall, Inc., Englewood Cliffs, N. J., 1966. 65 pages. (An interesting, at times somewhat detailed, explanation of a theory about exercises for children. ". . . the muscular system and the demands upon it . . . pull along the development of fitness of all the other systems of the body." A series of exercises. Good section on strength development. Illustrations.)

Information about calisthenic series can also be obtained from the following:

6. State Departments of Education.
7. Local, state and national associations for health, physical education and recreation. Write to American Association for Health, Physical Education and Recreation, 1201 16th Street, N.W., Washington, D.C.
8. Physical education departments in colleges and universities.

SOME RECORDS FOR EXERCISES

1. *Fifteen for Fitness*
   Boyd Pexton
   Windsor Records, WLP 3-06, Temple City, Calif.
   Three warm-up exercises, six fundamental exercises, seven additional exercises. Each exercise done quite a long time.
   Some 'hoedown' type of music.
2. *Kimbo Educational Records*
   Send for catalog.
   Kimbo Educational Records, P. O. Box 55, Deal, New Jersey 07723
3. *Primary Modern Dynamic Physical Fitness Activities*
   Instructed by Ed Durlacher, Album 14.
   Send for catalog.
   Square Dance Associates, Freeport, New York
4. *Institute for Physical Fitness, Inc.*
   Materials and records by Bonnie Prudden.
   112 Central Park South, New York, N. Y. 10019

# 3

# Responsibilities of
# the School Administration

The classroom teacher, with the best of intentions to provide her pupils with a physical education program, must rely on the school administration for moral support and for supplying certain essentials such as facilities. The school administration owes this support to the conscientious teacher and to the parents and pupils it serves who, in reality, are its employers. In turn, school administrators may be supported in their efforts to provide physical education facilities by state departments of education and by professional organizations which set standards for school planning and construction. It is possible to carry on some sort of a physical education curriculum in classrooms and halls but such situations set up obstacles that no teacher should have to surmount.

It is not the purpose of this book to provide detailed information about the planning and construction of physical education facilities. This material is available to school administrators and to architects from more expert sources; however, certain minimum suggestions are not out of place here. The term "physical education facility" means a place for physical education activities — a gymnasium, play shed or playroom, and outdoor play space. The facilities necessary depend, to a large extent, on the climate prevalent in a particular area. In areas where pupils can play outside most of the year, indoor space may not be necessary. In our nation, however, most schools need some kind of a sheltered space in which to conduct the physical education program and in which children can play in inclement weather.

## MINIMUM INDOOR SPACE NECESSARY FOR AN ADEQUATE PHYSICAL EDUCATION PROGRAM

A gymnasium or indoor play space at least 50' x 70'. Consideration should be given to the following:

1. Floor — A wooden floor is preferable as it is resilient and thus easier on feet and legs; it also makes injuries less severe than on a tile, cement or asphalt floor. A tooth will break if a child falls and knocks it against a hard floor. On a wooden floor, the tooth will likely remain intact and the wood will be dented! Disadvantages of wood floors are that they are often more expensive than those constructed of other materials, and maintenance is more difficult. Regardless of the type of material used for the floor, it should not be slippery. If wax is used on the floor, it should be of the nonskid variety such as used in hospitals.
2. Walls should be nonreflecting, and of a type that do not cause injury (splinters) if a pupil brushes against the wall or runs into it.
3. Ceilings should be covered with acoustical tile or similar material.
4. The room should be well lighted and ventilated. Windows are not necessary if artificial lighting is adequate and ventilation is sufficient. Windows add to the original cost of the building and present a maintenance problem.
5. There should be several electric outlets on each wall.
6. Lines for games should be painted on the floor, not just for basketball but for other games as well.
7. The room should be attractive and colorful.
8. Adjoining the gymnasium there should be storage closets for supplies and, if possible, dressing and shower rooms.

The multi-use or multi-purpose room has been used a great deal in recent years. The main, and only, advantage of the multi-purpose room is that the lunchroom, auditorium and gymnasium can be combined into one room, and this costs less than two or three large rooms. The disadvantages include difficulty in scheduling and interruptions of classes for special events such as rehearsals, programs, films and community or parent meetings. The school administrator must establish priorities for the use of the room, keeping in mind that the school exists for the purpose of teaching children, and not for any other reason.

## MINIMUM OUTDOOR SPACE NECESSARY FOR AN ADEQUATE PHYSICAL EDUCATION PROGRAM

The extent and type of area needed depends upon the climate in the area where the school is located. Assuming that about half of the physical education curriculum is best taught out of doors (in the fall and spring) there should be outdoor ground space equal to one football field, plus a hard surfaced area (blacktop or asphalt preferred) where playground equipment such as chinning bars, horizontal ladders and swings can be located.

Ground space should:

1. Be located, in relation to the school building, so that it can be easily supervised and used by children and adults in out-of-school hours. If the school is located next to, or near, a city park area, joint use can be made of the area.
2. Preferably be grass covered.
3. Be level and free from holes, rocks, trees, stumps and other hazards that might cause injury.

Hard surface area should:

1. Be located, in relation to the school building, so that it can be easily supervised and used in out-of-school hours.
2. Have a blacktop or asphalt surface. Cement is more expensive and not necessary.
3. Be level, but sloped slightly for proper drainage.
4. Be at least 50' x 50' for the average enrollment school.
5. Have painted lines and circles for games.
6. Have protecting or guard lines around playground equipment for safety purposes.

## MINIMUM EQUIPMENT AND SUPPLIES FOR AN ADEQUATE PHYSICAL EDUCATION PROGRAM

Equipment is generally considered to mean those items which last for several years such as chinning bars, tumbling mats and basketball baskets. Supplies refers to those items, such as balls, which are usually reordered every year.

Minimum Equipment:

2 chinning bars at different heights or adjustable. May be located in the gymnasium or on the hard surface area.

Sample layout of space and equipment on hard-surfaced area

SCHOOL BUILDING

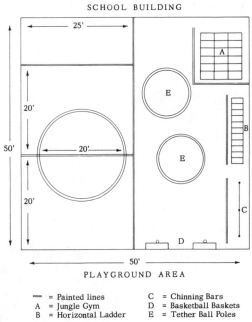

PLAYGROUND AREA

| — | = Painted lines | C | = Chinning Bars |
| A | = Jungle Gym | D | = Basketball Baskets |
| B | = Horizontal Ladder | E | = Tether Ball Poles |

## GAME LINES PAINTED ON HARD SURFACED AREA

'Double' Four Square

Cirles and Lines

Four Square

Hopscotch

Jungle Gyms
Climbing Apparatus

Horizontal Ladder

3 Level Chinning Bar

Turning Bar

Having all playground equipment located on one part
of the playground makes for easier supervision.

Tether Ball Pole
(anchored in cement in old tire)

Tether ball pole may be set in hard surfaced area.

Playground equipment may be set over a mulch
material to make for softer landings.

1 horizontal ladder — located either in the gymnasium or on hard surface area.

4 tumbling mats — size 4' x 6' or 5' x 10', 2" thick, plastic covered.

2 or more basketball baskets, some installed at less than the official height (for high school and adults) of 10' from the floor. Located on hard surface area, or in the gymnasium.

Some means of putting up a net for net games.

Softball home plates and bases

1 ball pump to inflate balls

Exercise routines can be developed
using war surplus parachutes.

1 softball backstop

1 record player with amplifiers, microphone and adjustable speed mechanism. (Should be kept on a movable cart so that it can be stored without opening and closing every time it is used, thus jarring the machine.)

Swings, jungle gyms and slides are desirable but not necessary equipment. Money should not be spent on merry-go-rounds, as they provide little physical activity and are dangerous.

Minimum Supplies:

20 beanbags
20 single jump ropes
5 long jump ropes
4 soccer balls — rubber
4 volley balls — rubber
4 basketballs — rubber,
   junior size
4 footballs — rubber,
   junior size
12 softballs — rubber
   covered

6 softball bats
2 softball catcher's masks
20 rubber balls, 6" and 8"
12 Indian clubs or tenpins
24 sticks about 18" long (dowling)
50 records for rhythms — see
   list in rhythms unit
Very desirable additions
   fleece balls
   tether balls

It should be kept in mind that this list of equipment and supplies is a minimum list for a school of about 200 pupil enrollment.
There should be sufficient equipment and supplies so that, in physical
education classes, every child can have what he needs and not have to
waste time and learning opportunity by waiting. The total cost of this
list of physical education supplies would come to about $400, or
slightly more than $2.00 per child per year. Many of these items will
last and will not have to be replaced each year. Some items such as
beanbags and jump ropes may be furnished by the children themselves.

Equipment and supplies may be improvised by the innovative
teacher or custodian. Weighted quart milk cartons or bleach bottles
may be used as targets or markers; wooden squares or filled gunny
sacks may be used for bases, and tetherball poles, turning bars, etc.,
may be made from pipe.

## STORAGE AND CARE OF SUPPLIES

The two most popular methods of storing physical education
supplies are (1) to have all supplies kept in a central storage room,
and (2) to have supplies divided and kept in the individual classrooms. Method (1) has the advantage of making supplies available
to all teachers in the school and has the disadvantage of being more
inconvenient in that the teacher or a pupil must go to the storage
room and get what is needed. Storing supplies by Method (2) makes
them more easily available to the teacher and the pupils but limits
the number of balls, etc., which can be used. Where supplies are
plentiful, there can be a combination of the two methods. When
supplies are kept in central storage, someone on the staff should have

the responsibility for keeping an inventory and making any minor repairs that are necessary. Balls and other supplies should be marked so that they are easily identified as belonging to the school. Children should be taught to care for all physical education supplies so that they will not be damaged and will last as long as possible. Only soccer balls and footballs should be kicked. Balls should not be sat on or used where they are likely to be cut or punctured.

REFERENCES ON FACILITIES, EQUIPMENT AND SUPPLIES

1. NEILSON, N. P., VAN HAGEN, WINIFRED AND COMER, JAMES L. *Physical Education for Elementary Schools*. Third Edition. Ronald Press Co., New York, N. Y. 10016. 1966.
2. The Athletic Institute, 805 Merchandise Mart, Chicago, Illinois. *Planning Facilities for Health, Physical Education and Recreation*, Revised edition. Designed primarily for community, college or high school but adaptations can be made for the elementary school.
3. *Sources of Equipment and Supplies for Athletics, Health Education, Physical Education, Outdoor Education and Recreation*. Directory published by American Association for Health, Physical Education and Recreation, 1201 Sixteenth Street, N. W., Washington, D. C. 20036.

## SCHEDULING

The scheduling of physical education classes is an administrative responsibility because all classes must use the same facilities. A way must be found to give all classes an opportunity to use these facilities. The larger the school enrollment, the greater the problem of scheduling. If the characteristics of children of elementary school age and the objectives of physical education are understood, certain limitations or guiding principles concerning scheduling become apparent. These principles are:

A. A daily period of physical education for every child is necessary.

B. The physical education class should not be less than twenty minutes nor more than thirty minutes long. The amount of time for physical education is usually considered to equal from 10 per cent to 15 per cent of the total school day. This may or may not include health instruction, depending upon school policy and the curriculum in health education. In the five hour day that is customary for the primary grades, 10 per cent of the time would be thirty minutes. For the fourth, fifth and sixth grades, 10 per cent of the time would be 33 minutes. This block of time refers only to that spent in activity and does not include dressing or showering time.

C. If children change clothes for physical education, 10 or 15 minutes more must be allowed.

D. If possible, physical education classes should be scheduled to provide a break or a change from classroom activities.

E. If the best use is to be made of the physical education period, classes or rooms should not be combined for physical education any more than for any other subject. If the only objective of physical education were exercise in the form of calisthenics, large groups would be justifiable. Though exercise is one of the most important objectives of physical education, it is not, by any means, the only one. The classroom teacher should have only her own class so that she can provide each child with opportunities and experiences and observe and give individual attention to each child.

F. There is no good reason why, if boys and girls have experienced the same physical education curriculum, they should be divided into separate classes for physical education. Depending upon the maturity and skill of the boys and girls, there may be some sports activities in the fifth and sixth grades that are best played by boys alone or by girls alone. The conscientious teacher can provide for this within her own class. Generally speaking, there is something to be gained by both sexes by participating together in physical education activities in the elementary school.

In a two, three-or four-room school the scheduling of physical education classes is no problem. The most suitable time for physical education is the middle of the morning or the middle of the afternoon. This is desirable for all elementary age children, but is particularly true for those pupils in kindergarten and the primary grades. Scheduling physical education in midmorning or midafternoon allows a block of time before and after physical education class which is long enough, and not too long, for the five to eight year old youngster to work on classroom subjects.

In a larger school, if a daily period of physical education is to be provided for each child, use must be made of the other hours in the school day. It has been found by experience that children and teachers, particularly from the fourth grade up, do not object to having physical education the first thing in the morning or the last thing in the afternoon. There is, in fact, no physiological or psychological reason why physical education cannot be scheduled for any time in the school day. Perhaps the least desirable time is that immediately after the lunch period. This time of day defeats the purpose of providing a break in classroom activities but there is no other logical objection. It used to be considered harmful to exercise immediately following a meal, but this has been largely disproved. Of course, it is not a good health practice, especially for an adult, to do strenuous exercise following a heavy meal. The school lunch is a comparatively light meal, however, and the healthy child plays after meals. The administrator can be assured that there is no harm in scheduling a physical education class immediately following the lunch period if this is the only time available in the day.

If the administrator is aware of the characteristics of children and convinced of the value of physical education and fitness, he will not schedule the physical education period in a two or three times a week block for a period of 40 minutes or more. By all that is known about the development of fitness and the laws of learning, two or three times a week is not often enough for physical education for children and 40 minutes is too long a period for the average elementary age youngster. If the class is as well planned as it ought to be, the child becomes too fatigued and more often than not — because children lose interest due partially to faitgue — time is wasted.

There are situations where it is impossible, of course, because of school plant or other factors, to provide the suggested amount of time for physical education. The school administrator should then allot the maximum possible time for each class. This writer believes that if any grades must sacrifice their daily period in the gymnasium or the multi-purpose room, it should be the lower grades, starting with the first. Activities for these grades are more easily adapted to the classroom or other limited space, albeit this is far from ideal or even satisfactory. Most teachers, sad to say, are used to making adjustments. This situation can be somewhat relieved if teachers alternate or rotate their turns in the gymnasium at the end of a month or a term.

The writer also believes that when facilities or equipment or supplies are limited, it is the professional responsibility of teachers and administrators to make this fact known to their superiors and to parents. Parents want a good physical education program for their children and administrators are anxious to provide one. Sometimes a school superintendent or a school board needs the support of, and even a certain amount of tactful agitation from, teachers to help them achieve their educational goals.

Some comment might be made here regarding playground scheduling chiefly as it applies to the noon hour. Again, a small school situation presents fewer problems than a large school. In the small school, there usually is room for all of the children to be on the playground at the same time with no difficulty. In larger schools, the lunch hour and the following free time on the playground may need to be scheduled to avoid waste of time and crowding that may lead to accidents and injuries. Following is a sample schedule showing a staggered noon hour:

11:10 — 11:30 — 1st and 2nd grade lunch
11:40 — 12:00 — 1st and 2nd grade playground
12 — 12:20 — 3rd and 4th grade lunch
12:20 — 12:50 — 3rd and 4th grade playground
12:40 — 1:00 — 5th and 6th grade lunch
1:00 — 1:30 — 5th and 6th grade playground

If the school is large, a schedule such as this makes for a more relaxed noon hour for teachers, children and lunchroom personnel.

## SAMPLE PHYSICAL EDUCATION SCHEDULE

12 teacher school — 1 multi-purpose room

A.M.   9 — 9:25 — 4th grade — 25 minutes
9:25 —   9:50 — 4th grade — 25 minutes
9:50 — 10:10 — 1st grade — 20 minutes
10:10 — 10:30 — 1st grade — 20 minutes
10:30 — 10:50 — 2nd grade — 20 minutes
10:50 — 11:10 — 3rd grade — 20 minutes

Lunch

P.M.   1 — 1:30 — 5th grade — 30 minutes
1:30 — 2:00 — 5th grade — 30 minutes
2:00 — 2:20 — 2nd grade — 20 minutes
2:20 — 2:40 — 3rd grade — 20 minutes
2:40 — 3:10 — 6th grade — 30 minutes
3:10 — 3:40 — 6th grade — 30 minutes

A schedule as tight as this requires the teacher to be prompt. Also, changing shoes and/or clothes must be completed before the scheduled time.

If the physical education space is not used for lunch, the time between 11:10 and 12 o'clock can also be scheduled.

# 4

# Planning the Physical Education Curriculum

There should be a planned, progressive curriculum for physical education as there is for any other subject taught in the school. A teacher could not teach arithmetic or spelling or art without being guided by a planned progression for the school year — not if she expected to have her pupils achieve their goals and be at grade or age standard at the end of the school year.

The school system as a whole preferably should have a planned and written curriculum for physical education so that there will be progression from grade one through grade twelve. If such a curriculum does not exist, an individual school might adopt or adapt a curriculum from another source. If there is sufficient knowledge among the school staff members they may plan their own physical education curriculum, though this is a time and energy consuming process. In any case, the individual teacher must have a plan for the year based on the characteristics and purposes of children and the objectives of physical education. Within the framework of the facilities, equipment and supplies available and the time alloted for physical education, the activities can be selected and a general plan for the year outlined. This book provides the teacher with a planned, progressive curriculum in physical education.

Before and while planning the physical education curriculum, the teacher must have a general knowledge of the characteristics of the age group in her class and the health status of the individual members. While activities selected to be taught should be those which a normal, healthy six or eight or ten year old should be able to do, some allowance may be necessary for the physically immature or inferior child as well as the physically superior child.

Each teacher must know the health status of every child in her class. Most school systems now have a health record of some kind that goes with the child from grade to grade. If these health records are properly filled out and maintained, they will reveal to the teacher, at a glance, the children who have physical or health problems or defects. In order to be aware of limitations or restrictions, the teacher should question each child (or parent or previous teacher depending upon the age of the child) who has a record of frequent absences, allergies, asthma, operations or who has an obvious physical defect. Provisions for handicapped children can be met in the physical education curriculum, but the teacher needs to know that these problems exist so that there is no injury or worsening of the condition.

There are several types of activities that should be included in the well-balanced physical education curriculum. They are:

1. *Games and Sports* — includes circle games, tag games, small and large group games, team games, games played with two players, sports. Includes skills necessary for games and sports.
2. *Relays* — a special type of team activity where "one group strives to complete a pattern of activities before opposing groups complete the same pattern."[1]
3. *Rhythms* — includes creative and free rhythms, singing games, folk dancing and marching.
4. *Self Testing activities* — includes stunts, tumbling, combatives, individual skills such as running, skipping, track events, calisthenics and fitness testing.
5. *Aquatics* — (swimming) in the rare cases where facilities are available.

Not included in the classification is creative activities, or movement exploration or self-direction activities, but inherent in each of the foregoing types of activities are situations where these needs of the child can be met. Movement exploration or movement education would probably be classified as a 'self testing' activity rather than any other type of activity. Also not included is free play or supervised play (see Chapter 10). This may or may not be considered a part of the physical education curriculum, though there is some justification for including it if it is properly organized and evaluated by

---

[1]Physical Education in Oregon Elementary Schools, Oregon State Department of Education, Salem, Oregon, 1953, Page 19.

the teacher. Free play is defined as a type of play organization where each child decides what he is going to play. This is in contrast to the usual physical education class where the decision of what to do is made by the teacher and where the class as a whole participates in the same activity. Several children may wish to play the same game or activity. For best results, the free play period should be planned before the class goes to the playground or gymnasium and should, of course, be supervised by the teacher. There are times when, because of the pressure of classroom work or examinations, the free play period provides needed release from tension for both the children and the teacher. In addition, the free play period gives the teacher a good opportunity to observe the progress of the class in a situation that is largely self-controlled and self-directed.

A Pupils' Choice Day can be scheduled from time to time. This is when the class as a whole chooses the activity to be played that day.

Where it is possible to give children experience in aquatic activities, this opportunity should of course be eagerly seized. Most often

Amount of Time To Be Spent on Each Type of Activity
(Percentage of Physical Education Time)

| Activity | Grades 1, 2, 3 | | Grades 4, 5, 6 | |
|---|---|---|---|---|
| | % | Approximate number of lessons | % | Approximate number of lessons |
| Games & Sports | 30% | 54 | 35% | 63 |
| Relays | 5% (3rd grade) | 9 | 5% | 9 |
| Rhythms | 30% | 54 | 25% | 45 |
| Self-Testing | 40% -- 1st & 2nd 35% -- 3rd | 72 63 | 35% | 63 |
| Aquatics | | | | |
| Totals | 100% | 180 | 100% | 180 |

this means transferring the children to a pool or lake, but this should not deter the teacher from taking advantage of the chance to give children a start in the wonderful world of water sports.

The good physical education curriculum is well balanced and includes a variety of activities with no one type emphasized to the point where another is omitted or given only cursory attention. On the other hand, the foregoing figures should be considered relative as there is overlapping in some cases, due to difficulty in classifying an activity as one type or another.

Translating these percentages into actual amount of time to be spent on the activities in the elementary physical education curriculum, it can be seen that:

Over 1/3 of the total time is devoted to self-testing activities,
About 1/3 of the time is spent on games and sports,
Over 1/4 of the time is for rhythms,
The least amount of time is for relays.

A factor to be considered in planning the physical education curriculum is that certain activities are considered seasonal. Football or soccer type games are played in the fall; basketball type activities in the winter months; and baseball or softball type games in the spring. Most track activities are scheduled in the spring months also, though some can be taught and performed during other parts of the year in the gymnasium or playroom.

During the winter months the physical education class will be held indoors most of the time. This fact influences curriculum planning also. The teacher should try to complete work on indoor activities by the first of April so that children can be outside for the remaining days of good weather.

While a teacher's plan or schedule should be followed the majority of the time for satisfactory results, it should be flexible enough to be changed for good reasons. One of these is a desire to correlate some activity in the classroom with a physical education activity. If, for example, a pioneer unit is being studied, it should be possible for the children to play a game or learn a folk dance that was used by the pioneers. The teacher should feel free to make such adjustments if they are beneficial to the education of the pupils.

The writer believes that far more learning takes place if activities are taught in units rather than being scattered throughout the year. Most rhythms (except perhaps in the first and second grades) thus should be taught in the eight to ten week period during the winter months. The wise teacher will, of course, sense when a class gets bored or tires of an activity and will change to another type for a lesson or part of a lesson.

The ordinary school year is thirty-six weeks long. An outline of the year's curriculum can be divided into nine week periods although some teachers may feel that they would prefer to work with six week periods. The following suggested programs assume that the physical education class is at least twenty minutes long in the primary grades and thirty minutes long in the fourth, fifth and sixth grades, exclusive of the time spent changing shoes and/or clothes and getting the class to and from the play area. These programs also assume that the minimum facilities, equipment and supplies suggested heretofore are available to the teacher and the pupils.

One last word about curriculum planning. The teacher following a progressive, sequential curriculum should not use activities from the next grade level for her class. This defeats the purpose of a progressive curriculum, and also defeats the teacher following who, when she presents a new activity, hears the class say, "Oh, we had that last year!" If a class is above average and learns quickly, it is better to broaden the curriculum and add a game or activity on the same level rather than using material from the next grade.

## FIRST GRADE
### Suggested Yearly Program

| First 9 weeks | Second 9 weeks | Third 9 weeks | Fourth 9 weeks |
|---|---|---|---|
| Walk, run, gallop — with or without music A series of calisthenics or stunts at the beginning of each class period. | Continue | | |
| Fitness testing | | | Fitness testing |
| Self testing using horizontal ladder and chinning bar. | Stunts Rhythms including 'free' rhythms, marching and simple folk dances. | | Horizontal ladder review |
| Games | Skills with bean bags | Ball skills | Games Rope jumping |
| | Occasional game for variety or on a regular once a week schedule. | | Informal racing |

## SECOND GRADE
### Suggested Yearly Program

| First 9 weeks | Second 9 weeks | Third 9 weeks | Fourth 9 weeks |
|---|---|---|---|
| A run and a series of calisthenics at the beginning of every class period. Vigorous self-testing activities such as stunts can be used instead of calisthenics. | Continue ⟶ | | |
| Fitness testing | | | Fitness testing |
| Review first grade games especially circle games, Mickey Mouse, Run for Your Supper and group games, Hill Dill. | Rhythms — including review of first grade rhythms, 'free' rhythms and marching. Stunts ⟶ Ball Skills ⟶ | | Continue ball skills  Games — not yet taught Bat Ball or Home Run |
| Games | Occasional game for variety, or on a regular once-a-week schedule. | | Rope Jumping |
| Self testing using horizontal ladder and chinning bar. Also running, skipping. | | | |

## THIRD GRADE
### Suggested Yearly Program

| First 9 weeks | Second 9 weeks | Third 9 weeks | Fourth 9 weeks |
|---|---|---|---|
| A run and a series of calisthenics at the beginning of each class period. | Continue − − − − − ⟶ | | |
| Fitness testing | | | Fitness testing |
| Horizontal ladder review | Floor Stunts and Mat Stunts | | Review Bat Ball from Second grade Kick ball |
| | Marching and Rhythms − − − − ⟶ | | |
| Review second grade games, i.e. Hill Dill Cat and Rat Come Along Line ball Tag games Rope jumping | Beanbag and ball skills  Dodge Ball and other games at least once a week. | Relays | Rope jumping  Informal racing and track type contests |

## FOURTH GRADE
### Suggested Yearly Program

| First 9 weeks | Second 9 weeks | Third 9 weeks | Fourth 9 weeks |
|---|---|---|---|
| A run and a series of calisthenics at the beginning of every class period | Continue | | |
| Fitness testing | | | Fitness testing |
| Review of third grade games and relays, especially<br>Dodge Ball<br>Steal the Bacon<br>Line Ball | Stunts and tumbling<br>Marching<br>Start on rhythms latter part of the period | Continue and emphasize Rhyhms<br><br>Basketball type games<br>Ball skills | Review Kick Ball from Third grade<br>Softball type games, skills and strategy<br>Throw It and Run |
| Circle games | Ball games and skills<br>Prison Dodge Ball<br>Octopus | Relays using ball skills | Track events<br>Running<br>Jumping<br>Throwing |
| Line Soccer<br>skills of line soccer and strategy | Other games<br>Stealing Sticks | | |

## FIFTH GRADE
### Suggested Yearly Program

| First 9 weeks | Second 9 weeks | Third 9 weeks | Fourth 9 weeks |
|---|---|---|---|
| A run and a series of calisthenics at the beginning of each class period | Continue | | |
| Fitness testing | | | Fitness testing |
| Review Line Soccer from Fourth grade<br>Simple Soccer<br>Tag games<br>Net Ball | Stunts, tumbling and combatives<br>Marching<br>Review selected Fourth grade rhythms | Marching and rhythms<br><br>Basketball lead-up games and skills | Softball<br><br>Track events |
| Rope jumping | Bombardment<br>V-B-B | | |

### SIXTH GRADE
Suggested Yearly Program

| First 9 weeks | Second 9 weeks | Third 9 weeks | Fourth 9 weeks |
|---|---|---|---|
| A run and a series of calisthenics at the beginning of each class period. | Continue — — — — — — — — — — — — — — — → | | |
| Fitness testing | | | Fitness testing |
| Review Soccer | Stunts, tumbling and combatives. | | Softball |
| Flag Football | Review rhythms and marching. | Rhythms | Beater Goes Round |
| Last Couple Out | Volleyball Corner Dodge Ball | Basketball lead-up games | Track events |

Once the teacher has the year's curriculum in physical education in mind and has a general plan (preferably on paper!) of activities throughout the year from September to May, the planning of the daily lesson is simplified.

The daily lesson should start in a more or less routine way, with the same formation every day. This saves time for the teacher and the children. If every lesson begins with a run and a series of calisthenics, the teacher can be certain that the pupils have had a good warm-up for succeeding activities and have had activities that contribute to their physical fitness.

It is well to start any new activity with a review of it from the previous grade level. How fast new activities can be presented will depend, of course, upon the pupils' previous experiences in physical education and their level of fitness. The teacher should try to teach the activities for her grade level during the time allotted to them in the year's plan.

Following are several sample lesson plans:

# SAMPLE DAILY LESSON PLANS

Grade 2

Rhythms

20 Minutes

| | | |
|---|---|---|
| 1. | Warm-up run and calisthenics | 3 to 5 min. |
| 2. | Marching, skipping, galloping to music | 3 min. |
| 3. | Review previous rhythm A Hunting We Will Go | 5 min. |
| 4. | Teach new rhythm Seven Steps | 8 to 10 min. |

Grade 4

Self-Testing Stunts and Tumbling

30 Minutes

| | | |
|---|---|---|
| 1. | Warm-up run and calisthenics | 5 min. |
| 2. | In partners -- Twister Hand Push | 10 min. |
| 3. | In squads -- 1 mat to each squad<br>a. Forward roll<br>b. Forward roll with hands on knees<br>c. Forward roll with crossed legs<br>d. Jump and roll over rope | 15 min. |

Grade 5

Games and game skills

30 min.

| | | |
|---|---|---|
| 1. | Warm-up run and calisthenics | 5 min. |
| 2. | In squads, practice passing and catching basketballs; chest pass, bounce pass, dribbling. | 10 to 12 min. |
| 3. | Play Three against Three; then Five against Five Keep-Away | 15 min. |

**Part** $\boxed{\text{II}}$

# The Curriculum:
# Self-Testing Activities

# 5

# Self-Testing Activities

## THE TEACHING OF SELF-TESTING ACTIVITIES

A large group of physical education activities are included in the classification which, for want of a better name, is called *self-testing activities*. These are activities that are participated in by the individual rather than by a team or a group. To a large extent, they permit the individual to test himself against others in the class or to test his present against his previous performance. The words "see if you can do this" or "can you do this" are appropriate, especially in the primary grades. This group of activities includes the following:

1. Calisthenics and fitness testing. (Chapter 2)
2. Stunts, including those performed on the floor and those performed on a piece of equipment such as the horizontal ladder.
3. Tumbling, performed on a mat.
4. Combatives, partners testing strength and skill with each other.
5. Locomotive skills, run, walk, skip, gallop, etc.
6. Skills in ball handling, throwing, catching, bouncing.
7. Traditional track events, running, throwing, jumping.
8. Rope jumping.
9. Movement exploration.

In Chapter 4, "Planning the Physical Education Curriculum," it was stated that 40 per cent of the total time alloted to physical education in the first and second grades and 35 per cent of the total time in the third, fourth, fifth and sixth grades should be spent in self-testing activities. This is over one-third of the total physical education time or approximately 65 full lessons in a school year of 180 days. Of course, these figures are general and should be used as a guide only, for there is some overlapping in the classification of activities. When the class does calisthenics to music, or a warm-up consisting of locomotive skills done to music, these activities are combinations of self-testing and rhythms. It will be noted from the sample year plans and sample lesson plans in Chapter 4 that a four to five minute warm-up of calisthenics and running should start every class period. The teacher may, on occasion, substitute certain rhythms and/or stunt type activities for the calisthenics. The writer believes, however, that every class period should start more or less the same way, in the same formation and with a run and calisthenic type exercises.

Self-testing activities have great appeal to both boys and girls. The activities are challenging and fun. As the elementary age youngster is keenly competitive and anxious to show what he can do, he wants to try new stunts, tricks and skills to see if he can do them. When a new stunt or skill is accomplished, the child's personal satisfaction is something to behold.

Self-testing activities contribute to the development of fitness. They produce increased strength, coordination, flexibility and balance. Most of these activities also contribute to the development of courage, confidence and poise. While it is true that children are curious, adventuresome and eager to try new things, there is also often a fear of failure that is very strong. Teachers may need to encourage children to try new things. The achievement of a new skill or a new stunt provides great motivation for the succeeding activity.

As in any other subject in the curriculum or in any other physical education activity, there is great individual variation in the ability to perform some self-testing activities, especially stunts and tumbling. The overweight child has a distinct disadvantage. Often he cannot support his own weight and, because of the additional weight, is less flexible than the thinner child. Here again the teacher needs to offer encouragement and must set the scene so that the child will not be embarrassed and thereby become even more reluctant to participate. The desire to do certain stunts and tumbling activities may be sufficient motivation for older children to try to lose weight.

The curriculum herein presented for stunts, tumbling and combatives (no combatives for first and second grades) is a progressive curriculum with the activities increasing in difficulty and in the need for strength and coordination as the pupil goes from one grade to the next. Activities for the first and second grades are simple but challenging to the six and seven year old youngsters. The organization of the class in the first and second grades may be more informal with added emphasis on the locomotive skills and the use of playground apparatus. Tumbling on the mats begins in earnest in the third grade with the introduction of the forward roll, a basic fundamental to more advanced tumbling. Throwing and catching skills begin in the first grade and continue throughout the sixth grade though perhaps in a different form and with different motivation. While racing is included in the primary grades, traditional track events begin with the fourth grade. Rope jumping should be done in all grades.

It is almost a necessity for the pupils to wear gym shoes for stunts and tumbling. If this is not possible, socks should be worn for mat work and no street shoes allowed. Ideally all should wear shorts. If this is impossible, girls should bring slacks or play clothes from home. A girl cannot think about a stunt while she is worrying about her skirt flying over her head.

Many teachers fear to teach stunts and tumbling, thinking that this is a dangerous activity, one in which children may get hurt. This is not true if proper safeguards and procedures are established and observed. Many running games and ball games are far more dangerous than self-testing activities. The following should be strictly observed:

1. There must be good discipline in the class. Children must listen to and follow directions.
2. No horseplay should be allowed. This is more likely to happen when pupils have to wait for their turn. The teacher should organize the class so that things move fast and each child gets as many turns as possible.
3. The lesson should always begin with a warm-up. Muscles and joints work better when they are warmed up; strains and sprains thus are not likely.
4. While the teacher will need to encourage children to try new stunts, she should not force a child to do a stunt particularly if there is some doubt that he has the strength or coordination for it.
5. The writer strongly believes that teachers *should not lift or support* a pupil. This is dangerous for the teacher as well as for the child. The child must learn to support and control his own body. Some-

times just placing a hand on the child will give him a feeling of
security. This can be done without lifting or supporting the
youngster.

## Planning the lesson

The self-testing activities included in one lesson should be varied.
The teacher's aim is to help each child achieve success in as many
of the activities as possible, and to plan the lesson so that each child
gets the maximum possible amount of physical activity within the
time limits of the class period. Activities must be repeated — or
practiced — in order to be perfected, but care must be taken to
avoid monotony and boredom. It will be necessary to give some
children individual help. Try to provide activity for the remainder
of the class while helping one pupil. Unfortunately, there is no "seat
work" in the gymnasium or on the playground!

## Sample lesson plans

First Grade
1. Locomotive skills with or without music ............ 5 minutes
2. Calisthenics .... .................................................. 4 minutes
3. Review — Human Rocker
   Rabbit Hop ...................................................... 5 minutes
4. Present "Blast Off"
   Bear Walk .... ................................................... 6 minutes

Second Grade
1. Locomotive skills ......... .......... .... .................... 5 minutes
2. Calisthenics ..... ................................................ 4 minutes
3. Ball Skills ...................................... ................11 minutes
   Bounce, bounce, bounce, catch — with or with-
   out music
   Bowling

Fourth Grade
1. Warm-up run ........ .... ..................................... 3 minutes
2. Calisthenics ......... ....... ............................... ...... 5 minutes
3. Review floor stunts ............................. ............ 5 minutes
   Coffee Grinder
   Pike Jump

    4. Mats ............................................................................... 15 minutes
       Review forward roll
       Review jump and roll
       Present jump and roll over rope

### Sixth Grade

    1. Warm-up run .................... ........................... ...... 3 minutes
    2. Calisthenics ................... ........................... 5 minutes
    3. Floor Stunts — partners ................................. . 6 minutes
       Boys and girls separate — Churn the Butter
       Hand Slap
    4. Mats ........................... ...................................15 minutes
       Review — Backward roll with leg extension
       Review — Jump and roll
       Review — Jump and roll over mat
       Present — Dive over one person

In introducing a stunt or an activity, the following procedure is generally observed:

1. Name the stunt and describe it vocally.
2. Let the class try it.
3. Spot a child who is doing the stunt well and have him demonstrate it in front of the class.
4. Let the class try again.
5. Select others to demonstrate.
6. Let part of the class perform the stunt while the others observe.

If the teacher herself can demonstrate the activity, so much the better. Even then, the teacher may want to follow the foregoing procedure most of the time.

The importance of review cannot be emphasized too much. Physical skills cannot be learned, by the average child, by trying them only once or twice. To become efficient, the child must practice the skill (especially from the third grade up) and with *thinking*. The child must *think* as he does the activity.

If a third, fourth, fifth or sixth grade class has had little previous experience or practice with these skills, it will be necessary for the teacher to present activities from the previous grade or grades. When the pupils can do those activities with a fair degree of skill, proceed to the activities for the next grade level. Accidents and injuries may

occur when children are asked to do skills for which they are not
ready and which are too difficult for them. Also, the pupils will
become frustrated and will develop a dislike for the activity rather
than enjoying it.

Children should be expected to do the activities well and high
standards of performance should be set by the teacher. At the same
time, consideration must be given to the poor performer. Develop, on
the part of the class members, a feeling of tolerance for those who,
though they sincerely try, are unable to do the activity well. No
doubt they have other talents which compensate for their lack of
ability in this area. An important step in the development of self-
esteem — necessary for good mental health — is the acceptance of
the fact most people cannot do *everything* well, and equally important, that most people can do *some* things well.

### Squad Organization

The teacher will find that it saves time and energy to have the
class organized into squads or teams. This is true when the lesson is
to be on self-testing activities, relays and/or team games. The class
can be divided into squads in one of several different ways. If the
teacher is aware of the mental health of her pupils, she will *not* have
the class choose squads by having the leaders choose their team
members, calling out their names. The same children — the poorer
performers — will naturally always be the last chosen. It is not fair
to any youngster in any subject to make his poor position in the
class so obvious. Methods for choosing squads follow:

1. The most objective way is to have the class line up and count
   off. If four squads are wanted, count off by 4's. The numbers 1
   become one team, 2's another, etc.
2. Before class, the teacher can divide the class into squads, writing
   the names down and making the squads as even in ability as
   possible.
3. A committee of the class can select squads with or without the
   assistance of the teacher. This should be done before class also.

There should be six to eight persons on a squad. The captain
or leader can be elected by the team or appointed by the teacher.
Through the year, each pupil should have the opportunity of being

a squad leader. Squads should be changed at least at the end of each month.

## Suggestions for Using Equipment Such as Horizontal Ladder or Chinning Bars

1. Work with a small group of children (six or eight) while the remainder of the class participates in some other activity such as rope jumping or ball bouncing. Do not have a long line of pupils waiting for their turn. This is a waste of physical education time and also creates behavior problems.
2. Be sure that children waiting their turn stand back from the equipment so that they will not be kicked by the performer and so that the performer has sufficient space. Do not crowd around the equipment.
3. Stand beside the performer to offer encouragement, to provide instruction and to be ready to assist if necesary.
4. Do not lift a child to the bar. Let him step up to the bar or climb up.
5. Give each pupil two or three turns on the bar. Hands will get sore, before they are toughened, if hanging is done too long at one time or too frequently.
6. Be sure that children drop from the bar in proper form: knees bent, and on balls of the feet, with a slight bounce.

## Suggestions for Teaching Floor Stunts — (Those Stunts Performed on the Floor Without Equipment)

1. Line up in a single line, facing the teacher. If there are 20 or more in a class, a double line is preferred. Lines may stand one behind the other or facing each other. Be sure there is adequate room between lines and between individuals so that each child can work without interference.
2. Some stunts, such as the seal walk, can be done in circle or scattered formation.
3. The teacher should position herself so that she can see all members of the class.
4. Children should learn the name of the stunt at the same time they learn how to do it.

## Class Organization for Mat Stunts — (Those Performed on a Mat)

1. Divide the class into as many groups as there are mats available, or use squads already selected. The activity to be performed and the experience of the class will also partly determine the number of groups. If there are only one or two mats and the class is large, take only a part of the class to the mats while the other pupils do some other

activity. Do not have long lines of children waiting for their turn on the mat.

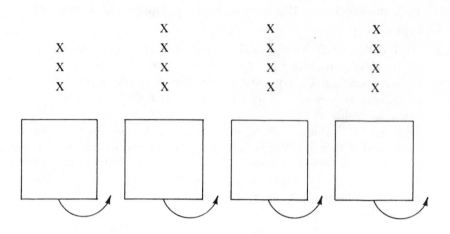

2. The teacher should position herself so that she can observe all mats. There will be times when she will want to go to one mat to help an individual pupil.
3. Be sure there is adequate room around the mats so that children will not interfere with each other and that there are no hazards near the mats such as pianos, chairs or a wall.
4. Line leaders should be responsible pupils who will help to maintain the proper formation.
5. Rules for the use of the mats should be strictly observed; Pupils should
   a. Never interfere with a person on the mat, not touching him or talking to him.
   b. Stand back about three feet from the end of the mat until it is their turn to do the stunt. It is helpful to have a line drawn on the floor for this purpose.
   c. Return to the end of the line as indicated in the illustration, and without interfering with other boys and girls.

## Stunts and Tumbling for Demonstrations

Stunts and tumbling provide a good activity for use in exhibitions or demonstrations. At the end of a stunts and tumbling unit, another class, or parents, can be invited to observe.

To be effective, the program must be planned and organized by the teacher and/or a group of the pupils. The following points should be considered:

1. Every child in the class should participate.
2. All equipment such as mats should be ready and easily available.
3. Children should know what activities they are going to do.
4. The order of the program should be established ahead of time. It is well to have a pupil or the teacher announce the name of the stunt before it is performed.
5. The program should start with the usual warm-up.
6. The program should be varied and include as many activities as the class does well.
7. Events should follow each other in quick sequence.
8. The program should not be too long. Thirty minutes is probably long enough for both the participants and the audience.

## BALL SKILLS — PROGRESSION

**First Grade**

*Rolling ball to a partner*
*Bounce and catch*
*Bounce to partner*
*Bounce hard to self — catching ball as it comes down*

**Second Grade**

*Overhead throw to wall*
*Toss overhead and catch*
*Combinations*
*Roll ball to target (bowling)*

**Third Grade**

*Bounce ball while walking forward*
*Underhand throw*
*Combinations*
*Kicking the ball*
*Ball Day*
*O'Leary*

**Fourth Grade**

*Kicking for distance and direction (fall of the year)*
*Ball Day*
*Seven Up*
*Bounce while dog trotting — dribbling (winter)*
*With fleece ball or soft ball — Underhand throw*
  *(spring)          Overhand throw*

## FIRST GRADE SELF-TESTING ACTIVITIES

1. Calisthenics and Fitness Testing

   See Chapter 2

2. Individual and Floor Stunts
   1. *Line walking*
   2. *Human rocker*
   3. *Rabbit Hop*
   4. *Jump and click heels*
   5. *Balance on one foot*
   6. *Blast Off*
   7. *Toe Touch*
   8. *Bear Walk*

3. Horizontal Ladder
   1. *Drop off*
   2. *Travel*

4. Locomotive Skills
   1. *Walk, run*
   2. *Gallop, skip*
   3. *Hop, jump*
   4. *Slide*

5. Stunts with Beanbags

6. Throwing the Beanbag

7. Ball Skills

2. Floor Stunts

1. *Line Walking*

   Use a line on the gymnasium floor, draw a chalk line or place masking tape on the floor about 15 feet in length. Walk across the line, arms outstretched to help maintain balance. Try not to fall off the line.

   ❖     ❖     ❖

   TEACHING SUGGESTIONS

   1. Have several lines so that children do not have to wait too long for their turn.
   2. Pretend to walk on a tight rope as a circus performer.
   3. Variations
      a. Walk to center of line, do deep knee bend with both feet on the line; continue to end of line.
      b. Walk backwards on the line.
      c. Walk, raising knees to waist level on each step.
      d. Walk to center of line, bend over and touch the line without losing balance. Continue to end of line.
      e. Pupils may devise various ways to walk along or over a piece of rope stretched out on the floor or playground.

   ❖     ❖     ❖

2. *Human Rocker*

   Lie on stomach, grasp feet with both hands. Hold head up. Rock back and forth. (As this stunt involves bending the spine backward, follow it with a stunt that bends the trunk forward, such as the Rabbit Hop.)

How many ways are there to get over the rope?

3. *Rabbit Hop*

Squat position, hands touching the floor in front of, and closer together than, the feet. Leap forward by pushing with the feet. Land on hands, bringing feet up quickly to position outside of the hands. Continue.

❀   ❀   ❀

TEACHING SUGGESTIONS

a. Have the class in line or circle formation.
b. Explain the stunt and have the class try it.
c. Select a pupil — or pupils — who can do the stunt well and let these children demonstrate for the class. "Do you think this is a good rabbit?"

4. *Jump and Click Heels*

From a standing stride position — feet comfortably apart — jump up and click heels together. Land in stride position on balls of feet and with knees bending slightly.

5. *Balance on One Foot* (sometimes called the Stork Stand)

Place hands on hips and put left foot on inside of right knee. Close eyes and try to stand on one foot for 10 seconds. Repeat on the other foot.

6. *Blast Off*

Stand erect, feet slightly apart and arms stretched over head. While counting downward from ten, the pupil moves slowly to a full squat position. Head should be down between the knees, arms circling the knees tightly. Class count out loud. When the signal is given, "Blast Off," the children leap as high as possible, landing in the starting position.

7. *Toe Touch*

From a standing position bend forward, keeping the knees straight, and touch the toes. Hold this position for three seconds before returning to original position.

8. *Bear Walk*

Bend over and place hands on the floor. Walk forward, moving right arm and right leg at the same time, then left arm and left leg.

## 3. Horizontal Ladder

1. *Drop Off*

Drop from the ladder correctly — Hang with both hands from rung of ladder. Drop to the ground relaxed — look at the ground, let go with both hands at once, bend knees upon landing.

2. *Travel*

Travel forward under the ladder — in sequence.

a. In steps, right hand leading. Grasp bar with right hand, bring left hand up to right. Continue. Same with left hand leading.
Children should grasp bar with thumb around the rung.

b. Travel along one side of the ladder, hand to hand. (If the side of the ladder is made of a large pipe or board, it may be too large for the child to grasp securely.)

c. Travel forward with one hand on each side of the ladder.

*            *            *

TEACHING SUGGESTIONS

1. Be sure the pupil grasps the rung with his thumb around the rung and not alongside the fingers. Palms of hands should be forward.

2. Children must learn how to drop correctly from the ladder before trying to travel across it.

3. Do not hold the pupil or support him. Stand to one side of the child, ready to help him if he needs it. Give vocal encouragement.

4. Give each child about three turns on the ladder and no more the first day. Hands will get sore if you work on this too long.

5. If you have a reluctant learner — usually a child who is overweight — let him try every day, but do not force him to do it if he is afraid. Some overweight children will not be able to support their own weight.

6. The "drop" can be practiced from a chinning bar instead of from the horizontal ladder.

                ✿     ✿     ✿

4. **Locomotive Skills** (sometimes considered a part of the rhythms unit)

1. *Walking* — "How many different ways can you walk?"
   a. Forward, sideward, backward.
   b. On toes, on heels, pigeon-toed.
   c. Walk on outside edges of feet.
   d. Walk with giant strides; with baby steps.

2. *Running*
   a. With long steps
   b. With short steps
   c. Backward
   d. With knees high
   e. Slow and fast
   f. In place

3. *Galloping* — The same foot is forward all the time during the gallop.

4. *Skipping* — Feet alternate in being forward.

5. *Hopping* — On one foot. Land on ball of foot. May hold other foot with one hand.

6. *Jumping* — On both feet. Land on balls of feet with a bounce. Land lightly, quietly.

7. *Sliding* — Moving to the side. Same as a gallop except that the direction is sideways instead of forward.

                ✿     ✿     ✿

TEACHING SUGGESTIONS

1. Skills may be done with or without music.

2. Children should learn the terminology and be able to name each skill. Point out that galloping and sliding are similar. "How are a skip and a gallop different? Try them and see."

3. If a child needs help with some skill, stand beside him, take his hand and help him with the rhythm of the skill.

4. Most first graders are able to skip. A few may need individual help.
5. Children stand in a circle, or in scatter formation. IT walks around saying, "One, two, what can you do?" pointing at one person who answers, "I can jump," (or hop or skip or any locomotor skill.) IT then says, "Jump until I say stop" and all the children in the group jump until IT says stop. The second child then becomes IT and the game continues.
6. Running is excellent exercise and children love to race. For races, divide the class into groups of six or eight children. Let each group race; then the winners of each group can compete. Be sure that there are no hazards on the "race course." Have the race end by crossing a line, NOT by hitting a wall of the gymnasium.

✿      ✿      ✿

## 5. Stunts with Beanbags

1. Place beanbag between the ankles. Jump and land correctly (with bounce) without losing the beanbag.
2. Place beanbag on floor behind legs. Without moving feet, reach around right leg and pick it up. Repeat, reaching around left leg.
3. Place beanbag on head. Lean backwards, drop the beanbag. Reach through legs and pick it up without moving feet.
4. Throw the beanbag up into the air as high and straight as possible. Catch it if you can.
5. Throw the beanbag as far as possible. Run and pick it up.

✿      ✿      ✿

TEACHING SUGGESTIONS

1. Each child should have a beanbag. At least, there should be one beanbag for every two children. A beanbag 4" or 5" square is the best size. Sometimes children can make or furnish their own beanbags.
2. Organize the class in a single line or in parallel lines.
3. Good discipline should be maintained. Children should follow directions.

✿      ✿      ✿

## 6. Throwing the Beanbag

1. Throw the beanbag across a line or into a circle marked on the floor. Distance should be 8 to 10 feet.
2. Children stand 8 or 10 feet apart in partners. Lines marked on the floor are helpful. Throw the beanbag so that your partner will be able to catch it.

TEACHING SUGGESTIONS

1. A beanbag is easier to hang on to and to catch than a ball, so it is wise to start practice in throwing and catching with a beanbag.
2. First grade children will usually throw and catch with both hands.
3. Do not be too concerned with how they throw, but emphasize catching the beanbag with *both* hands in front of the body. "Give" to the catch. Arms should be relaxed, not stiff.
4. Tell children to aim at their partner's chest.
5. After some experience in throwing, most children will begin to throw with their dominant hand instead of with both hands. When the majority of the class is able to throw the beanbag fairly accurately with one hand, emphasize the correct stance or position, as follows:

    Stand in a relaxed forward-backward stride position. Right-handed children should have their *left* foot forward. Left handed children will have their *right* foot forward. The correct stance is a basic necessity for learning how to throw correctly.

* * *

7. **Ball Skills** (use beanbags before using balls)

    1. Partners sit on the floor 7' to 8' apart, facing each other and with legs spread. Roll ball back and forth, using both hands to roll it (push the ball) and both hands to stop, or catch, the ball.
    2. Individuals standing. Bounce the ball once and catch it. Use both hands. Push the ball to the floor, do not "slap" it. Count one for each successful bounce and catch. See which child can get the highest count.
    3. Bounce the ball twice or three times and catch. Bounce, bounce, bounce, catch.
    4. When pupils can do #2 and #3 fairly well, proceed to bouncing the ball to a partner. Partners stand 7' to 8' apart. Push the ball toward the partner. The ball should bounce near the player who is to catch it. Caution about bouncing the ball too hard. Count one for each successful bounce and catch. Count out loud. Pupils should stand in stride position.

5. Bounce the ball as hard as possible and catch it when it comes down. Catch with both hands. Ball may be caught against the chest.

6. Children stand in a circle, 10 to 15 in a circle. One child, while walking, bounces the ball across the circle, stands in front of another, continuing to bounce the ball and says, "_____, keep the ball bouncing, please."

The player so addressed bounces the ball, approaches a third child and so the activity continues.

As skills improve, two or three balls might be used in one circle.

❋   ❋   ❋

TEACHING SUGGESTIONS

1. Preferably each child should have a rubber ball. (See supply list, playground balls.) All balls need not be the same size. If rubber balls are in short supply, use other balls — volleyballs, basketballs, etc. — though these are harder to bounce than rubber balls. If there are two children to a ball, organize the class so that half sits down while the other half is using the balls. Change frequently.

2. In order to avoid chaos and to save time, some method for distributing the balls should be established. All balls may be kept in a big sack or box and tossed out by the teacher or by a pupil. Another method of distributing them is to have children line up at a designated place where the balls will be passed to them.

3. The class may be in a circle or line formation.

4. When bouncing, it is helpful to have a leader in front of the class. Another aid is to have the teacher say "bounce, catch, bounce, catch," etc.

5. Pupils should be instructed to hold the ball or place it on the floor while instructions are being given.

6. Be aware of individuals. Be sure children push the ball and do not slap it. Help those who need it.

❋   ❋   ❋

## SECOND GRADE SELF-TESTING ACTIVITIES

1. **Calisthenics and Fitness Testing**

   See Chapter 2

2. **Floor Stunts**
   1. *Jump and Touch Heels*
   2. *Measuring Worm*

3. *Thread the Needle*
4. *Seal Walk*
5. *Jump 1/2 turn, right and left*
6. *Wring the Dishrag*
7. *Egg Roll*
8. *Bicycling*

3. **Mat Stunts**
   1. *Knee Walk*
   2. *Log Roll*
4. **Horizontal Ladder**
   1. *Review from first grade*
   2. *New ways of traveling on the ladder*

5. **Locomotive Skills**
   *Review from first grade*

6. **Throwing the Beanbag**

7. **Ball Skills**

8. **Rope Jumping**

❖     ❖     ❖

2. **Floor Stunts**

   1. *Jump and Touch Heels*
      Stand erect, feet slightly apart. Jump up, kick heels behind body and touch heels with hands. Land correctly with 'bounce' on balls of feet and knees bending. A 'quiet' landing.

   2. *Measuring Worm* (sometimes called Inch Worm)
      From a standing position, bend over forward placing weight on hands on floor with knees straight. Walk forward with small steps with hands, keeping knees straight and feet in place. When body is out straight, take small steps with feet until feet are near hands. Repeat.

   3. *Thread the Needle*
      Clasp the hands to form a low ring in front of the body. One foot at a time, step through the ring, and stand up. Hands will now be behind body. Repeat, stepping backward to return to original position.

Thread the Needle

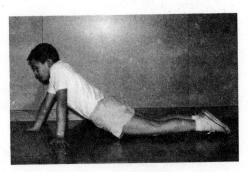

Seal Walk

4. *Seal Walk*

   Extend body along floor, elbows straight and toes dragging. Weight of the body is mainly on the arms. Child moves forward by taking small steps with the hands, pulling the body forward. Feet should be together. Feet and legs should drag along the floor, like the body of the seal.

5. *Jump half turn right and left*

   Stand on a line, feet slightly apart. Jump with both feet and land on both feet facing the opposite direction. Pupils should start and finish on the line. Be sure that take-off and landing are on both feet.

6. *Wring the Dishrag*

   Partners. Two pupils face each other, join hands and raise them overhead. Turn, No. 1 going under his left arm and No. 2 under his right arm, until they are back to back. Continue, turning in the same direction until they are face to face again. Do not let go of hands. Do several times. Repeat to opposite direction. Pupils of approximately the same height should be together.

7. *Egg Roll*

   Sit on floor with knees bent and heels close to buttocks, arms between legs and hands around in front of shins, grasping shins. Roll over to the left, then around to the back, to the right side and up again in front. Repeat to the right. A certain amount of momentum is necessary to do the stunt.

8. *Bicycling*

   Lie on back and lift legs to vertical position so that most of the weight is on the shoulders. Place hands under hips, elbows on the floor, to help support the body. Hold body up as straight as possible. In this position (called shoulder stand) move the legs as though pedaling a bicycle.

3. **Mat Stunts** (Pupils may prefer to do Egg Roll and Bicycling on mats instead of on floor.)

   1. *Knee Walk*

      Kneel on the mat. Grasp feet with hands behind the buttocks. Walk on knees the length of the mat .

   2. *Log Roll*

      Lie crossways the mat on one side with arms stretched over head along ears and hands clasped. In this position, roll like a log down the length of the mat.

                              ❖        ❖        ❖

TEACHING SUGGESTIONS

See pages 85 and 86 for organization of class for mat stunts.

## 4. Horizontal Ladder

*1. Review first grade activities as follows:*
   a. Drop from ladder correctly.
   b. Travel forward along one side of the ladder, hand to hand.
   c. Travel forward with one hand on each side of the ladder.

*2. New ways of traveling on the ladder:*
   Be sure pupils can do aforementioned before proceeding to the following:
   a. One hand on one rung of the ladder. First right hand, then left hand on next rung, etc. Body should swing from side to side.
   b. Travel backward by method b. in foregoing.
   c. Travel backward by method c. in foregoing.
   d. Are there any other ways to travel across the ladder?

      ❖     ❖     ❖

TEACHING SUGGESTIONS

See first grade, page 91.

      ❖     ❖     ❖

## 5. Locomotive Skills
Review and continue those from first grade.

## 6. Throwing the Beanbag

1. In partners 8′ to 10′ apart. Lines marked on the floor help children to keep proper spacing. Toss the beanbag with one hand to partner. Hold the beanbag in one hand, not by its corner. Let the arm swing past the hips before throwing (underarm throw). Aim at partner's chest. Catch with both hands in front of the body. Emphasize having arms relaxed, not stiff.

Children should learn proper stance as this is basic to learning how to throw well.

Stand in a relaxed forward-backward stride position. Those who throw with the right hand should have their *left* foot forward. Left handed children will have their *right* foot forward. Check individual children to be sure they are standing in correct position.

2. Throw and catch, with increased distance — about 15 feet — between partners.
3. Throw the beanbag as high as possible. Try to catch it.
4. Throw the beanbag as far as possible. Run and pick it up. Be sure all throw in the same direction so that no one gets hit.

❖   ❖   ❖

TEACHING SUGGESTIONS

1. Organize the class in two or four parallel lines for throwing to partner.
2. Random organization is all right for throwing as high as possible.
3. For distance throwing (as far as possible) it is best to have children in two or three lines (depending upon how many are in the class) all at one end of the gymnasium or playground. Let Line 1 throw and get their beanbags, then Line 2 and Line 3. Retrieve beanbags quickly.

❖   ❖   ❖

7. **Ball Skills** (Use beanbags for throwing before using balls)

   1. Review ball bouncing from first grade. Can be done with music.
      a. Bounce, bounce, bounce, catch. Push ball, do not slap it.
      b. Bounce ball hard and catch it as it comes down. Do with both hands, and with right and left hands separately.
      c. Bounce the ball to a partner 10′ away. Ball should hit floor nearer partner. Catch with both hands.
   2. Stand 10′ to 12′ away from a wall, facing the wall, in stride position; right-handed children should have left foot forward and vice versa. Hold the ball in both hands over the head and throw it against the wall (overhead throw). Catch it on the bounce as it comes back. Do not throw too hard. Count successful throws and catches.
   3. Toss ball up in the air — arms should be extended above head at the end of the throw, follow through. Catch it as it comes down or on the bounce. Be able to do both.
   4 Combinations, i.e.,
      Bounce, catch, throw, catch.
      Bounce, bounce, throw, catch.
      Hold the ball with both hands. Swing arms to make a big circle in front of the body, bounce, catch. "Swing, bounce, catch." Ask children if they can think of other combinations.

5. Rolling ball to a target (bowling). Stand in forward-backward stride position, right-handed children should have left foot forward; left-handed children should have right foot forward. Roll the ball, holding it with two hands, but rolling from the side of the body. Roll ball and try to hit target. Count successful hits in three or five trials.

If Indian clubs or duck pins are available, use them. If not, paper milk cartons can be used, or wooden blocks if they are not too heavy. Set up in threes in a triangle. Aim at #1.

As this is rather slow and time-consuming, have half the class working on some other skill while half is bowling.

* * *

TEACHING SUGGESTIONS. See first grade ball skills.

* * *

## THIRD GRADE SELF-TESTING ACTIVITIES

1. **Calisthenics and Fitness Testing**
   See Chapter 2

2. **Floor Stunts**
   1. *Cross leg sit and stand*
   2. *Crab Walk*
   3. *Different ways to walk*
   4. *Snail*
   5. *Heel Click two times*
   6. *Chinese Get Up*
   7. *Wheelbarrow*

3. **Mat Stunts**
   1. *Bridge*
   2. *Knee Jump*
   3. *Forward Roll*
   4. *Jump and Roll*

4. **Combatives**
   1. *Hand Tug-of-War*
   2. *Back to back push*

5. **Horizontal Ladder**

6. **Ball Skills**

7. **Rope Jumping**

2. **Floor Stunts**

   1. *Crossed Leg Sit and Stand* (sometimes called Turk Stand)
      Sit on the floor with legs crossed, knees bent and arms folded on chest. Raise up to a standing position keeping arms and legs

crossed. Repeat. The secret of this stunt is to lean forward slightly and put the weight on the outside of the feet as one starts to stand up.

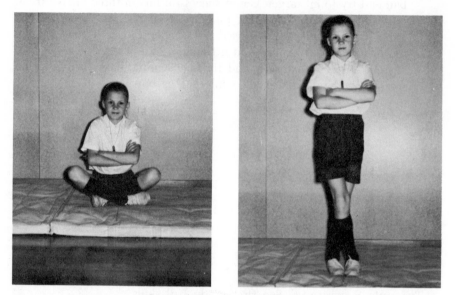

Crossed Leg Sit and Stand

2. *Crab Walk*

Sit on the floor, feet fairly close to buttocks. Place hands on the floor slightly behind shoulders. Raise body from floor until trunk is straight and parallel with the floor. Walk in this position. Walk forward, (towards head) backward, and sideways.

Crab Walk

Three Legged Walk

3. *Walking in different ways*

Let the pupils discover how many different ways they can walk on hand and feet, i.e.

a. Four legged walk — right arm and right leg together, left arm and left leg together.

b. Three legged walk — one arm and both legs, both arms and one leg.

4. *Snail* (may wish to do on mat)

Lie on back on floor. Raise legs and place feet on floor beyond head. Knees should be on the floor also. Arms remain alongside the body, palms down.

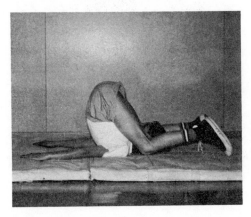
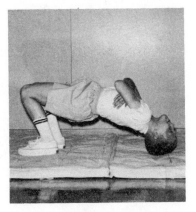

Snail                                          Bridge

5. *Heel Click two times*

From a standing stride position (feet comfortably apart) jump up and try to click heels together twice before landing. Land in stride position on balls of feet with knees slightly bent. May need to practice clicking heels once before trying to do it twice. Also, click heels to side: Cross right foot in front of left and step on it. Jump up and click heels together. Repeat to right side.

6. *Chinese Get Up*

Partners. Pupils stand back to back with elbows hooked. There should be eight to ten inches between the partners' heels. In this position, lower the body and sit on the floor. Raise to standing position without losing position. Partners should be of approximately the same height and build. To do this stunt, it is necessary to lean or push slightly against the partner's back.

7. *Wheelbarrow*

Partners. No. 1 supports himself on his hands and feet, elbows straight, body straight and facing the floor. No. 2 steps between No. 1's. legs and lifts No. 1's legs by grasping them at the knee or slightly above the knee. No 1 then walks with his hands and No. 2 pretends he is wheeling the wheelbarrow. *Walk, do not run.* Do not drop partner's legs. Do not grasp partner's legs below the knee. Rotate positions.

Methods of organizing class for mat stunts —

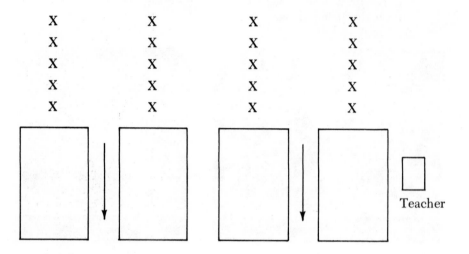

If only two mats, use the following method: Children do stunt to opposite side of the mat. When everyone has had a turn, go back the other way.

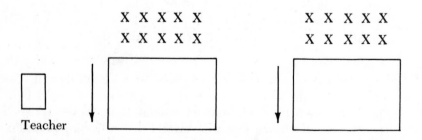

### 3. Mat Stunts

#### 1. *Bridge*

Pupil lies on back on the mat. Place feet flat on floor up comfortably close to the buttocks. Fold arms on chest. Lift body, rolling up on top of head. Body is supported by feet and head. Keep neck tense.

#### 2. *Knee Jump*

Kneel on mat with feet flat, not turned under. Using a strong pull with the arms, jump up to a standing position. Do not rock back on feet.

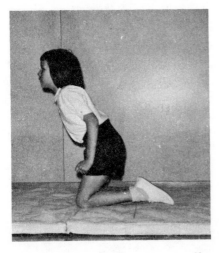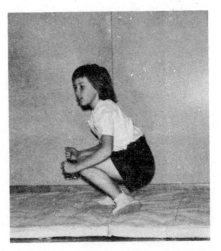

Knee Jump

Start                                        Finish

#### 3. *Forward Roll*

This is the first real tumbling stunt in this curriculum. It is important that the forward roll be done correctly as it is the basis for many tumbling activities in later grades.

The pupil squats on the mat with his hands on the mat slightly ahead of the feet. Arms are between the knees — or "inside" the knees. The head should be down, buttocks up, chin on the chest and the back rounded.

The pupil gives a slight push with his feet and rolls forward. Do not push the child. If the head stays down in the proper position, only the back of it will touch the mat. Part of the weight should be taken on the hands and part on the back.

TEACHING SUGGESTIONS

1. When first presenting this stunt, the teacher should check each child's starting position to be sure that it is correct. If the teacher stands to one side of the row of mats, she can see all pupils in starting position. Say, "Ready," and quickly glance to see that all are in correct position; then "go" or "roll."

2. The child must curl up like a ball. The back must be rounded to complete the roll. If the pupil touches, or lands on, the top of his head, he is not "curling" enough. Emphasize "chin on chest" and hold this position throughout the roll.

3. As soon as the class has achieved the proper starting position and the idea of the roll, teach the proper finish of the roll as follows:

   a. Tell pupils to reach forward with their arms as they come out of the roll. This will help to bring them to a standing position at the end of the roll. Say "Reach!" as the pupil starts to roll.

   b. Equally effective in achieving a proper finish is to grasp the shins just below the knees when coming out of the roll. Try both a. and b.

   c. For variation — but not till a. and b. have been learned — come to a standing position with crossed feet.

✿      ✿      ✿

Forward Roll

Start                    "Reach" Finish              Grab Shins Finish

### 4. *Jump and Roll*

Draw or tape a line on the floor about two feet from the starting end of the mat. Pupil stands on the line, jumps with both feet to the edge of the mat, places hands on the mat and rolls as before. Come to correct standing position at end of roll.

❀　　❀　　❀

TEACHING SUGGESTIONS

1. Pupils should start and finish the jump on the floor, not on the mat. Hands, however, are placed on the mat.
2. The jump must be with *both* feet.
3. This is an excellent way to develop a little more momentum in the roll, and a necessary step before more advanced forward rolls can be done.

❀　　❀　　❀

## 4. Combatives

In partners of approximately equal height and weight. If there is considerable difference between the strength of boys and that of girls, have boys pair off and girls pair off.

### 1. *Hand Tug-of-War*

Pupils stand on opposite sides of a line. Grasp right hands. When the signal "go" is given, each tries to pull his partner across the line. When either is entirely across the line, the contest is over. Repeat with left hands.

### 2. *Back to Back Push*

Partners sit on floor, back to back, with feet braced flat on the floor. Arms are folded on chest. At the signal "go," each tries to push his partner across a line drawn three feet in front of the feet. May also be done with hands on the floor and using hands to help push.

❀　　❀　　❀

TEACHING SUGGESTIONS

1. In order to avoid too much roughness, combatives must be done on signal as indicated.
2. A class champion may be determined by having winners go against winners.

❀　　❀　　❀

## 5. Horizontal Ladder

Review all first and second grade activities as follows:
1. Drop from the ladder correctly.
2. Travel along one side of the ladder — to the right and to the left.

3. Travel with one hand on each side of the ladder — forward and backward.

4. Travel rung by rung, one hand on each.

ADDITIONAL

1. Hang from ladder. Raise both knees to chest and hold for three seconds or longer.

2. Travel rung by rung, as in #4, while turning.

* * *

TEACHING SUGGESTIONS

1. Sometimes a child's gain in strength does not keep up with his gain in weight. He may be unable to do the activities on the horizontal ladder that he was able to do in the first or second grades.

2. Do not hold or support the pupil. Stand to one side to be ready to help him if needed. Give vocal encouragement.

3. If there is only one horizontal ladder, work with a group of six to eight children while the remainder of the class participate in some other activity. Change frequently. Do not let pupils practice to the point where their hands get sore.

* * *

## 6. Ball Skills

1. Review all ball skills from first and second grades including:
   a. Bounce and catch
   b. Bounce to partner
   c. Overhead throw against the wall
   d. Toss into the air and catch
   e. Rolling to a target
   f. Combinations of foregoing.

2. *Individual bouncing while walking.*

   Pupil will need to bounce the ball (push it) a little ahead of his feet. Right-handed pupils will feel most comfortable bouncing the ball ahead of their right foot, or a little to the right of their right foot. Left-handed children will bounce to their left. Try about 10 consecutive bounces while walking. Most should be able to bounce the ball with one hand. Pupils may do a slow run, or "dog trot" instead of walking.

3. *Underhand throw to partner.*

   There should be 10′ to 12′ between partners. Each stands in a forward-backward stride position, right-handed children with left foot forward; left-handed with right foot forward. Hold ball with both hands. Right-handed children should bring ball back past right hip (raising right elbow) throw forward and release ball about waist to chest height. Left handers bring ball back past left hip. Aim at partner's chest. Count each consecutive catch.

This is an important basic throw. Be sure all children have correct stance. Provide for sufficient practice — each child should have at least 20 throws at any one time. Help individuals.

4. *Combinations*

Make figure eight with ball, held in both hands, bounce, catch, or figure 8, toss ball up, bounce, catch. Create new combinations.

5. *Kicking the ball.*

In the spring of the year, third graders play Kick Ball, a lead-up game to softball. Along with throwing and catching the ball, this game requires kicking the ball. Only *soccer* balls should be kicked. Take a group of six to eight children and have them practice kicking a ball lying on the ground. Pupil (right-handed) should stand in a forward-backward stride position with the left foot forward. Swing right leg and kick the ball with the *top of the foot* — not the toe. This means that the ankle must be extended. Next, kick a moving ball. One pupil may stand 20' in front of the kicker and roll the ball toward him.

6. *"Ball Day."*

This is a free play lesson, in the gymnasium. Each child has a ball. Pupils may do anything they wish with the ball as long as they do not interfere with other children. Safety rules are important so that no one gets hit by a ball. Such a lesson gives the teacher an opportunity to move around and give extra help to those children who need it. Playing catch with a child often gives the teacher an opportunity to see what the pupil is doing wrong and to make corrections.

❖     ❖     ❖

TEACHING SUGGESTIONS

1. Use as many balls as are available. They do not all have to be the same size. Rubber balls are best for primary age children, but volleyballs, soccer balls, basketballs, etc. may be used. If there are two children to a ball, have half the class sit down while the other half is using the balls (or play some other activity). Change frequently.

2. Some method must be established for distributing the balls. All balls can be kept in a large sack or box. Pupils can line up, walk past the ball box and be handed a ball.

3. The class may be in circle or line formation.

4. Pupils should be instructed to hold the ball or place it on the floor while instructions are being given.

5. Pupils must learn to look before they throw in order to avoid hitting another child.

✿    ✿    ✿

### 7. *Ball Bouncing Skills* (O'Leary)

The child sings to the tune of "One Little, Two Little, Three Little Indians" the following words: "1-2-3 O'Leary; 4-5-6 O'Leary; 7-8-9 O'Leary; 10 O'Leary Postman."

The player pushes the ball with the flat of the hand to "1-2-3" during the prescribed movement, each time at the word "O'Leary" letting the ball bounce higher by hitting it harder. To "10 O'Leary Postman" he gives one bounce and catches on "Postman." The ball is never caught until the last.

Exercise 1. Swing right leg outward over ball on saying, "O'Leary."

Exercise 2. Swing left leg outward over ball on saying, "O'Leary."

Exercise 3. Swing right leg inward over ball on saying, "O'Leary."

Exercise 4. Swing left leg inward over ball on saying, "O'Leary."

Exercise 5. Grasp edge of skirt with left hand and upon saying, "O'Leary," make the ball pass upward between the arm and skirt.

Exercise 6. Same as Exercise 5, but let ball pass through from above.

Exercise 7. Grasp right wrist with left hand forming circle with arms, and make the ball pass through from below saying, "O'Leary."

Exercise 8. Same as Exercise 7, letting the ball drop over from above.

Exercise 9. Touch forefingers and thumbs together when saying, "O'Leary," and through circle formed let ball drop from above.

Exercise 10. To the words "1 O'Leary, 2 O'Leary, 3 O'Leary" and so on to "10 O'Leary Postman," bounce ball alternately to right and left of right foot. (The foot may be moved from side to side.)

Exercise 11. Bounce ball to same words as in Exercise 10, standing absolutely still.

Exercise 12. To same words as in Exercise 10, bounce ball throwing right leg over at every bounce.

Exercise 13. Same as Exercise 12, throwing right leg inward over ball.

Exercise 14. Same as Exercise 13, throwing left leg outward at every bounce.

Exercise *15*. Same as Exercise 14, throwing left leg inward at every bounce.

Exercise *16*. To the words, "Jack, Jack, pump the water; Jack, Jack, pump the water; Jack, Jack pump the water; So early in the morning," go through the same movements of bouncing ball three times, then giving it a stronger push on the word "water"; make a complete turn left.

Exercise *17*. Same as Exercise 16, making a complete turn right.

In the tournament a player is permitted to play as far as he can without a miss.

## FOURTH GRADE SELF-TESTING ACTIVITIES

1. **Calisthenics and Fitness Testing**

   See Chapter 2

2. **Floor Stunts**

   *1. Cartwheel*
   *2. Jump full turn*
   *3. Coffee Grinder*
   *4. Mule Kick*
   *5. Pike Jump*
   *6. Walk Through*
   *7. Twister*

3. **Mat Stunts**

   *1. Shoulder Stand*
   *2. Forward Roll and Variation*
   *3. Jump and Roll — variations*
   *4. Backward Roll*
   *5. Frog Stand*
   *6. Simple pyramids*

4. **Combatives**

   *1. Hand push*
   *2. Hand wrestle*

5. **Ball Skills**

6. **Track Events**

7. **Rope Jumping**

2. **Floor Stunts**

   *1. Cartwheel*

   The pupil stands erect, right foot sideward and right arm extended over head. Lean to the right, placing right hand on the floor, then left hand as the left leg is kicked up, followed by the right leg. Return to starting position.

   The sequence is right hand, left hand, left leg and right leg. Arms and legs remain extended — elbows and knees straight — throughout. Head should be held up, and the trunk should be straight.

   ❋　　❋　　❋

TEACHING SUGGESTIONS

1. It is helpful to have pupils do the cartwheel along a line, placing hands and feet on the line.

2. If pupil is unable to do the cartwheel, it may be due to lack of ability to support body weight on the arms.

3. Be sure each child has adequate room so that no one gets kicked.

✿     ✿     ✿

2. *Jump Full Turn*

    Stand with feet 10″ to 12″ apart. Jump into the air and make a complete turn before landing in original position. Use arms to help pull body around. Land with knees bent and on balls of the feet. Have pupils stand on a line.

3. *Coffee Grinder* (or pivot)

    The body is out straight, one side towards the floor, supported on one arm with elbow straight. Walk, in a circle, around hand. Repeat with other arm.

<table>
<tr><td>Coffee Grinder</td><td>Mule Kick</td></tr>
</table>

4. *Mule Kick*

    Place both hands on the floor. Kick the legs up into the air, keeping knees bent. Head should be up. Then bring feet sharply back to the floor and stand. The down "snap" is important as a lead-up to more advanced stunts.

5. *Pike Jump*

From a standing position with feet slightly apart, jump into the air, stretching legs out to the diagonal front to form a "V." Keep knees straight. Try to touch toes with hands.

6. *Walk Through*

Hands and feet on the floor, body supported in prone (push-up) position. Toes should be turned under and elbows straight. Walk forward, through arms, until body is fully outstretched. Walk backward between arms. Some pupils may be able to kick legs through the arms with feet together.

Walk Through

Start                                    Finish

7. *Twister*

Partners. Partners stand facing each other. Grasp right hands. No. 1 puts his right leg over the clasped hands, thus turning so that his back is toward his partner. No. 2 does the same, but using his left leg. Partners are now back to back with hands still joined. To get back to original position, No. 1 puts his left leg over, followed by No. 2 with his right leg.

## 3. Mat Stunts

1. *Shoulder Stand*

Pupil lies on back on the mat. Raise legs until body is vertical, resting on shoulders and head. Place hands under hips for support, elbows resting on mat. Hold position with toes pointed.

**Shoulder Stand**

2. *Forward Roll and variations*

   Review third grade forward roll. See description and illustrations on page 103-4. Be sure pupils have correct starting position and do the roll correctly.

3. *Repeat jump and roll*

   a. Jump and roll over a rope.

      Two people hold a jump rope over the end of the mat nearest the performer, about 18″ to 2′ high. Pupil jumps and rolls over the rope, ending in good position. Pupils must put hands *over* the rope, and place them on the mat on the other side of the rope. It is helpful to make a chalk mark on the mat where hands should be placed. Hands should be placed on the mat fairly close in to the rope.

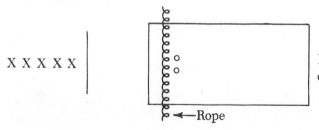

Hands should land on mat at ○ ○.

b. If plastic hoops are available, do jump and roll through the hoop.

c. Do continuous rolls, ending in good position.

d. Do rolls to music.

e. Combinations — i.e. — Jump, roll, full jump turn, roll and stand. Jump, roll, several knee jumps, roll and stand.

4. *Backward Roll*

Pupil squats facing end of the mat. The body is curled, chin on chest and hands are placed *palms up* just above the shoulders. Rock back and forth several times to gain momentum and then roll over backward. As the hands hit the mat, push with the arms to lift body over head. Finish roll standing on feet.

✿    ✿    ✿

Teaching Suggestions

1. The important points are to keep the head down and to push with the hands. As the pupil starts the roll, say 'Push.'

2. The roll should be smooth and continuous. As the pupil gains speed, the roll will be easier.

3. Pupils should finish the roll in good position, and not just fall off the mat.

4. As pupils learn how to push with the hands, they will be able to straighten the legs to a greater extent as they roll over.

✿    ✿    ✿

Backward Roll                              Frog Stand

Start                        Finish

5. *Frog stand* — preliminary to the head stand.

Pupil kneels on the edge of the mat. Place hands, palms down about shoulder width apart and place *forehead* ahead of and between the hands to form a triangle. Gradually transfer the weight to the head and arms. Place knees on elbows. Regain position by placing feet back on the mat.

❈    ❈    ❈

TEACHING SUGGESTIONS

1. The hands and head must form a triangle in order to maintain balance.
2. The forehead should be placed on the mat so that, as the weight is transferred, the pupil will be standing on the front part of the head. Most frequent error is to put top of head instead of forehead on mat.
3. When pupils can do frog stand well, they may go down by rolling forward as in a forward roll. This involves pulling the chin into chest so that back will be rounded.

❈    ❈    ❈

6. *Simple Pyramids*

A pyramid is a combination of stunts put together to form a symmetrical whole. Following are some illustrations of simple pyramids that can be done by fourth graders.

*Pyramid A.*

No. 1 kneel on hands and knees. Knees should be spread.
No. 2—prone (push-up) position. Backs straight and heads up.
No. 3—Stands on the No. 1's.

Count 1—No. 1 and No. 2's take positions on the mat. 2—No. 2's go up to position; No. 3 steps up. 3—All go down and stand behind the mat.

*Pyramid B.*

No. 1 Stands erect with arms outstretched.
No. 2's do shoulder stands.
No. 3's do snails.

Count 1—All take positions on mat. 2—Shoulder stands (No. 2's) go up. No. 1 may help, if needed. 3—Snails assume positions. 4—All go down and stand behind the mat.

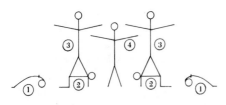

*Pyramid C.*

No. 1's do bridge.
No. 2's kneel on hands and knees.
No. 3's step on No. 2's.
No. 4 stands erect, arms out.

Count 1—No. 1, 2 and 4 take positions on the mat. 2—No. 3's step up and No. 1's make Bridge. 3—No. 3's step down and bridges come down. 4—All step behind mat.

*Pyramid D.*

No. 1's kneel on hands and knees.
No. 2 kneels on No. 1's.
No. 3's do frog stand.

Count 1—No. 1's and 3's assume positions on the mat. 2—No. 2 goes up and 3's do frog stands. 3—No. 2 and 3's go down. 4—All stand behind the mat.

❖        ❖        ❖

TEACHING SUGGESTIONS

1. Pupils who assume a kneeling position, such as No. 1's in Pyramid A and No. 2's in Pyramid C should get a good stable position by spreading the knees and hands at least 12″ to 15″ apart.

2. Pupils who stand on another person such as No. 3 in Pyramid A and No. 3 in Pyramid C should ALWAYS put their feet on the base's shoulders or pelvic (hip) bones — never on the small of the back, nor directly on the spine.

3. When kneeling on another person, as No. 2 in Pyramid D, pupil should place his fingers over the base's shoulders. His knees should go on the hip bones of the bases.

4. An extra person — called a "spotter" — should stand behind the group to assist those who step or climb up on another.

5. To be most effective, pyramids should be done to counts. All should start standing behind the mat in their respective positions. All should finish in the same position.

### 4. Combatives

*1. Hand Push*

Partners of approximately equal height and weight face each other. Brace feet by placing one forward and one somewhat back. Place palms of hands against partner's palms. At signal "go" push partner's hands. The winner is the one who makes his partner move his feet first.

*2. Hand Wrestle*

Partners face each other, standing in a forward stride position, the outside of the right feet touching. Clasp right hands. On the signal "go" each attempts by pulling, pushing, turning and twisting the hands to unbalance his partner. Free hand cannot touch the floor. When one partner is forced to move his feet, the other is the winner. Repeat with left hands.

✿          ✿          ✿

TEACHING SUGGESTIONS

1. The contest should have a definite starting time indicated by the signal "go" or a whistle.
2. Winners may compete against winners until a class champion is determined.
3. If there is considerable difference between the strength of boys and girls, have the boys compete against boys and girls against girls.

✿          ✿          ✿

### 5. Ball Skills

*1. With large balls*

Rubber balls, volleyballs, basketballs, etc. — review third grade skill, i.e., Underhand throw, Overhead toss, Bouncing ball while walking forward.

*2. Kicking the ball* — Only soccer balls should be kicked. In the fall of the year, fourth graders play Line Soccer, a lead-up game to Soccer. Kicking is the major skill. Balls should preferably be kicked out of doors. If necessary to practice in the gymnasium, balls should be somewhat deflated.

*Review third grade skills* — kicking a stationary ball, kicking a moving ball.

Emphasize — a.  Good leg swing.
            b.  Meet the ball with the top of the foot (instep) not the toe.
            c.  Leg should follow through in direction the ball is to go.

  d. Ball should stay fairly close to the ground.

  e. Increase distance.

*Kicking for direction* — When kicking to the right swing right leg from the hip, across the left leg, and meet the ball with the outside of the right foot. Follow through in direction ball is to go.

Kicking to the left, ball should be kicked by the inside of the right foot.

Reverse for left-footed pupils.

*Soccer dribbling* — advancing the ball by a series of small kicks while the body moves forward.

Contact the ball with the instep, not the toe. Kick with alternate feet. Keep ball close — about a foot in front of the body — so as to maintain control. This is a difficult skill which will not be mastered without much practice.

3. *Ball Day* — See third grade, page 107.

4. *Seven Up*

  A ball game played by one person. Targets 2′ wide and 3′ long and about 2 1/2′ from the floor can be painted or taped on a wall in the gymnasium or on an outside wall where there is a hard surface on the ground. Draw or tape a line on the floor, or blacktop, about 10′ away from the wall.

  a. The pupil stands behind the line and throws the ball against the wall in the target. Catches it on the bounce. Do seven consecutive times without a miss.

  b. Repeat #1 and clap hands before catching the ball. Do seven consecutive times without a miss.

  c. Repeat throw and touch the floor before catching the ball. Seven consecutive times without a miss.

  d. Repeat throw and turn around before catching the ball. Seven consecutive times without a miss.

The game is won if all 28 throws are completed without a miss. If a player makes an error, he must start all over from the beginning. This is a good game to use when the teacher wishes to work with a part of the class.

5. *Dribbling*

  Bouncing the ball while doing a slow run or dogtrotting.

  Emphasize — a. Pushing the ball down to the floor, not slapping it.

b. Keep ball slightly ahead and to the right (right-handed pupils).

c. Speed is not the most important thing at this point. Concentrate on correct skill and controlling the ball. Dribble the ball half the length of the gym floor, turn and return to place. Dribble around a circle with the ball on the outside.

6. *Throwing fleece or softball underhand and overhand*

Fourth grade boys and girls should be familiar with the general technique of the underhand throw and have a fair degree of skill. They should be ready to do the underhand throw with a smaller ball — the softball.

The school and the teacher should make every effort to provide soft softballs — now available on the market — or better yet, fleece balls — a wool center with a soft leather cover.

Although a softball is softer than a baseball hard ball it is still hard, and difficult to catch with unprotected hands. Most high school and adult softball players use a mitt or glove for catching. It is unreasonable to expect elementary age children to catch with their bare hands, and it is nearly impossible to teach correct catching form if the pupils are afraid the ball will hurt their hands.

Points to emphasize on the underhand throw —

a. Stance — forward backward stride position with opposite foot (from throwing hand) forward.
   OR start from position with feet together and step forward on opposite foot as the ball is thrown.

b. Grip — the ball with fingers (instead of 'palming' it) if the hand is large enough. Hold ball with both hands in front of the body.

c. To throw — throwing arm swings back, past the right hip, and then forward.

d. Release — ball at about waist height.

e. Follow through in direction ball is to go. Throw should end with hand pointing at target.

f. Ball should travel a course more or less parallel to the ground.

g. Catching — with both hands. "Give" to the ball at contact — bend elbows and allow ball to come in close to the body. Fingers should be relaxed.

Points to emphasize for overhand throw — (right-handed players)

a. Stance — Stand with feet together, left side toward target. Step, with left foot toward target as ball is released.

Hold ball with the fingers and thumb.

Fielding a ground ball — little fingers together.

Follow through at end of overhand throw. Hand should point at target.

Catching a fly ball — thumbs together.

b. Grip — ball with fingers. Do not palm it. Hold ball with both hands in front of body.

c. To throw — The throwing arm moves back with the hand slightly above the shoulder, elbow slightly bent. Left arm will naturally come up to counterbalance the right arm. Propel ball toward target, stepping on left foot and end facing the target.

d. Get 'snap' in the throw as though whipping a rope against a wall or fence.

e. Release ball at shoulder height.

f. Follow through with hand pointing at the target at the end of the throw.

g. Ball should follow a course more or less parallel to the ground.

h. Catching — should be done with both hands. "Give" to the ball at contact. Fingers should not be stiff. To catch balls above waist — thumbs should be together. To catch ball below waist — little fingers should be together.

✿      ✿      ✿

TEACHING SUGGESTIONS

1. Do not give pupils too much "talk" or too much explanation at one time. Emphasize correct starting position and follow through.

2. Have the class line up in parallel lines with partners facing each other about 20' apart. Players in line #1 each have a ball. Check the starting position and grip. #1's throw and #2's catch. Check the form of individuals.

3. If there are insufficient balls, work with a part of the class while the remainder do some other activity.

4. "Teacher and Class" formation for practicing throwing:
Six or seven pupils in a group, team or squad. One child stands in front of the group at a specified distance, facing the group. He throws to each one in the line. He then takes Number 5's place and Number 1 takes his place. The line moves up. Continue until all have had a turn to be "teacher" or leader. Can also be played so that the "teacher" retains his position until he misses the ball. This can be used in a circle formation with the leader in the center of the circle.

If each group has a dependable leader, the teacher of the class is free to move around and help those individuals who need it.

1   2   3   4   5<br>X   X   X   X   X

6<br>X

## FIFTH GRADE SELF-TESTING ACTIVITIES

1. **Calisthenics and Fitness Testing**
   See Chapter 2

2. **Floor Stunts**
   1. *Jump the stick*
   2. *Leap Frog*
   3. *Crab Run*
   4. *Greet the Toe*
   5. *Through Vault*
   6. *Centipede*

3. **Mat Stunts**
   1. *Forward Roll and variations*
   2. *Backward Roll and variations*
   3. *Side Roll*
   4. *Frog Stand*
   5. *Head Stand*
   6. *Partner Balances*
      a. *Horizontal Balance*
      b. *Sitting Balance*
      c. *Sitting Mount*
   7. *Pyramids*

4. **Combatives**
   1. *Rooster Fight*
   2. *Knee Slap*

5. **Ball Skills**

6. **Track Events**

7. **Rope Jumping**

2. **Floor Stunts**

   1. *Jump Through the Stick*
      Hold a stick 2′ to 3′ long in front of the body with both hands, palms down. Try to jump over the stick without letting go. Several preliminary light jumps in place are helpful. The pupil needs to swing the stick back quickly as he jumps over it. Bring knees high up to chest level. Jump back and forth over the stick. (Broom handles do nicely.)

   2. *Leap Frog*
      Partners of approximately equal height. No. 1 bends forward, knees straight, hands on shins, or knees, head down. No. 2 places his hands on No. 1's back and with legs in straddle position, leaps over No. 1. A short preliminary run is helpful. Rotate positions.

   3. *Crab Run*
      In Crab Walk position (see Grade 3) back to the floor supported by hands and feet, and with trunk straight (horizontal to the floor) run forward toward head, run backwards, run sidewards.

   4. *Greet the Toe*
      Stand on left foot. Hold right foot with both hands in front of body. Bend forward and try to touch the right foot to the forehead. Repeat with left foot.

   5. *Through Vault*
      In groups of three. No. 1 and No. 2 stand in a stable position — small stride, one foot forward and one foot back — join inside hands at hip level. No. 3 places hands on inside shoulders of No.

1 and No. 2 and jumps over the joined hands. After preliminary practice, No. 3 can start with a short run and attempt to vault over the joined hands, thrusting legs out in front, as straight as possible. Rotate positions.

6. *Centipede*

Partners. No. 1 leans forward and places hands on the mat. No. 2 stands in front of No. 1, fairly close. No. 2 places hands on mat, slightly in front of hands of No. 1, and lifts legs on top of No. 1's back. No. 2 should cross feet and bend knees to get a secure grip. Walk in this position calling out loud, "right, left, right, left," etc. This can be done with three or four persons as well as with two.

## 3. Mat Stunts

1. *Forward Roll and variations*
   a. Review forward roll from third and fourth grades, being sure that all pupils have correct starting and finishing positions.
   b. Review jump and roll.
   c. Combinations — Leap frog and forward roll. Jump, roll, 1/2 turn jump, backward roll.
   d. Review jump and roll over rope from 4th grade.
   e. Jump and roll over rolled-up mat. Place a rolled-up mat at the starting edge of the mat. Pupil jumps and rolls over the mat without touching it. Hands are placed on the *opposite* side of the mat. Place chalk mark or tape mark on mat where hands should be placed. Hands should be placed close to the mat on the opposite, or far, side. Finish in good position.

2. *Backward Roll*
   a. Review backward roll from fourth grade, being sure that all pupils have correct starting position and use hands to lift body over head.
   b. Do backward roll with leg extension. Push hard with the hands and straighten body so that legs are extended above head. Land on feet in good position.

3. *Side roll* (or shoulder roll)

Kneel crossways on the mat, supporting body on hands and knees. Drop the left shoulder (if rolling to the left) tuck left arm and left knee under body and roll to the left, finishing in original position. Repeat to right.

After this roll has been learned, pupils may approach it with a slight run and attempt to land on feet.

4. *Frog stand* — review from fourth grade

5. *Head Stand*

Assume the same starting position as for the frog stand, hands and head forming a triangle on the mat. Be sure forehead is placed on the mat and not the top of head. Pupil gradually "walks up" till weight is on head and hands. Slowly straighten legs up till they are above head. Point toes. Return to original position by lowering legs.

**Head Stand**

✿      ✿      ✿

TEACHING SUGGESTIONS

1. In this stunt, it is well to have another pupil stand in front of the performer so that he does not fall over forward. Beware of being kicked.
2. The back should be arched slightly. By stretching the legs upward, balance is more easily maintained. The teacher may hold her hand above the performer's feet and say "touch my hand."

✿      ✿      ✿

6. *Partner Balances*
   a. Horizontal Balance

Base — Lie on back, knees flexed in a comfortable position, feet flat on the mat, 10″ to 12″ apart.

Top — Stand at base's head, facing base's knees, feet on either side of base's head. Lean forward and place hands over base's knees elbows straight.

Base grabs top's ankles. At a signal, top springs upward as base lifts top's legs until base's arm are straight. Top balances on base's knees as base holds top's legs.

Top descends as base bends her elbows and lowers top's feet to the mat.

**Horizontal Balance**

b. Sitting Balance

Base — Lie on mat, arms along side body, legs raised in a vertical position with knees slightly bent.

Top — Place feet on either side of base's hips and sit on base's feet, facing away from base's head.

When top has a good "seat," base straightens knees and lifts top. Top stretches out arms to help maintain balance.

Spotter should stand close to aid in achieving balance, but should not lift top.

**Sitting Balance**

c. Sitting Mount

Base — Kneels on one knee behind top and places his head between top's legs.

Top — Sits on base's shoulders, wrapping his legs around base's shoulders and behind base's back.

Base rises to standing position, keeping trunk over legs and head up in normal position. Both pupils stretch arms straight out to the side.

Base bends knees to lower top to mat.

The spotter should stand in front of the pair as they rise to position and descend to the mat, to be ready to assist.

Sitting Mount

❋    ❋    ❋

TEACHING SUGGESTIONS FOR PARTNER BALANCES

1. The base should be heavier, taller and preferably stronger than the top partner.
2. The heavier and perhaps the stronger pupil is needed as a base, in partner balance; the small, light pupil excels as a top.
3. A spotter, or assistant, should be assigned to each pair to assist in achieving balance. Spotters should not, however, lift tops to position. Divide the class into groups of three or four for partner balances.

4. In teaching a new partner balance, work with one pair or group while the remainder of the class observes. Explain where the spotters should stand and what they should watch for.

*          *          *

7. *Pyramids* (See fourth grade pyramids)

   A pyramid is a combination of stunts put together to form a symmetrical whole.

*          *          *

TEACHING SUGGESTIONS

1. To be most effective, pyramids should be done to count. All participants should start standing behind the mat, in their respective positions, and should finish behind the mat. A simple pyramid done well is far more effective than a more difficult pyramid done in a sloppy manner.
2. A spotter should be assigned to each pyramid to assist pupils in getting into position and to help if needed.
3. These suggested pyramids use partner and individual stunts which are included in the fifth grade curriculum. Other combinations can be created.

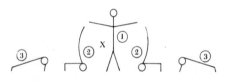

*Pyramid A.*

No. 1 stands erect, arms outstretched.

No. 2's do headstands.

No. 3's assume push-up position, trunk straight.

X is the spotter.

Count 1—All take positions on mat. 2—Head stands go up, No. 3's take positions. 3—No. 2's and 3's go down. 4—All stand behind mat.

(Illustration shows No. 3's doing 'Snail')

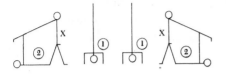

*Pyramid B.*

No. 1's do head stands.
No. 2's do horizontal balance.
X is the spotter.

Count 1—Take positions on mat, ready to go up. There should be a spotter for each horizontal balance. 2—All go up. 3—All come down. 4—Stand behind mat.

*Pyramid C.*

No. 1 — Sitting mount.
No. 2 — Stand erect, arms out to the sides.
X — Spotter.

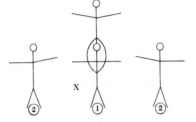

Count 1—Take positions on mat, arms of No. 2's at sides. 2—Sitting mount goes up, No. 2's stretch arms out to side. 3—Sitting mount comes down. 4—All stand behind mat.

*Pyramid D.*

No. 1, does headstand.
No. 2's do sitting balance.
X — Spotters.

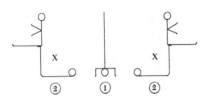

Count 1—Take positions on mat. 2—All go up. 3—All come down. 4—Stand behind mat.

❀        ❀        ❀

## 4. Combatives

### 1. Rooster Fight

Partners stand on their right feet within a six foot circle, facing each other. The left foot should be held behind the back by the right hand. The left arm is held against the chest, with fingers on upper right arm. On signal, each tries — by jumping and dodging — to cause his opponent to put his left foot to the ground, or to move out of the circle.

This can also be done between two lines, or without any lines; the aim, in this case, is to get the opponent to put his foot down.

2. *Knee Slap* (or Knee Tag)

Two partners stand facing each other four to five feet apart. On signal, each attempts to tag his partner's knees while at the same time protecting his own knees. Holding is not allowed. Contest can be terminated when one partner has three or five tags. Count out loud.

✿     ✿     ✿

TEACHING SUGGESTIONS

1. Partners should be boy and boy or girl and girl.
2. The contest should have a definite starting time, which should be indicated by the signal "go" or by a whistle.
3. Winners may compete against winners until a class champion is determined.

✿     ✿     ✿

## SIXTH GRADE SELF-TESTING ACTIVITIES

1. **Calisthenics and Fitness Testing**
   See Chapter 2

2. **Floor Stunts**
   1. *Bouncer*
   2. *Jump over leg*
   3. *Knee Dip*
   4. *Elbow Dip*
   5. *Churn the Butter*
   6. *Neck Spring*

3. **Mat Stunts**
   1. *Forward roll and variations*
   2. *Diving*
   3. *Backward roll with extension*
   4. *Headstand and roll down*
   5. *Handstand*
   6. *Partner Balances*
      a. *Chest stand*
      b. *Knee Shoulder balance*
   7. *Pyramids*

4. **Combatives**
   1. *Hand Slap*
   2. *Indian Leg Wrestle*

5. **Ball Skills** (with games)

6. **Track Events**

7. **Rope Jumping**

2. **Floor Stunts**

1. *Bouncer*

Pupil is in push-up position with body straight. Push off with hands and bounce on hands or fingers. Try clapping hands together when off the floor.

2. *Jump over Leg*

Hold right foot with left hand and jump through the loop, or over the right foot without letting go. Try jumping back again. Repeat with opposite foot.

3. *Knee Dip*

Hold right foot behind back with left hand. Bend left knee and touch right knee to floor (or mat) and stand up again. Repeat with other leg.

4. *Elbow Dip*

Pupil extends body out straight, right side to the floor and resting on right hand with elbow straight. Hand should be directly below shoulder. Left arm is along left side of body. Place a piece of paper (Kleenex) just next to right hand. Bend right elbow and pick up paper with teeth. Return to starting position.

❋   ❋   ❋

TEACHING SUGGESTIONS

1. Left arm can be used for balancing.
2. Best to do on a mat.
3. Dip down and up quickly.

❋   ❋   ❋

5. *Churn the Butter*

Partners of approximately equal height and weight. Boys with boys and girls with girls. Pupils stand back to back and hook elbows. No. 1 bends forward from the hips and lifts No. 2 on his back as No. 2 lifts his legs to right angles with his body. No. 1 straightens up, dropping No. 2 back to the floor. Repeat with No. 2 lifting No. 1 to his back.

6. *Neck Spring*

Pupil stands facing a wall, about half his height distance away from the wall. Bend forward from the waist and place forehead on wall. Stand up straight again without using hands against the wall. Bending knees is helpful. Pupil may stand closer to the wall until he is able to do the stunt, then move farther away.

3. **Mat Stunts**

1. *Forward Roll and variations*
   a. Review forward roll from fourth and fifth grade curricula. Emphasize take-off with jump (both feet) and correct finish, (standing on feet, arms at side in controlled position).
   b. Front Swan Roll — Hold arms out to the side while doing a forward roll. Start from a standing position without a take-off. Finish with arms out to the sides in good position.
   c. Review forward roll over rope and mat. See fourth and fifth grade curricula.

d. Forward roll combinations such as
   (1) Forward roll, jump full turn, forward roll.
   (2) Forward roll, pike jump, forward roll.
   (3) Combine forward and backward rolls.
   (4) Continuous forward rolls.
   (5) Forward rolls, or combinations, to music.

2. *Diving*

   A pupil kneels in tight tuck position (buttocks on heels, elbows pulled in to body, head down) on edge of mat. Performer, with jump take-off, (may precede with run) does a forward roll over the kneeling pupil. Hands should be placed on the far side of the kneeling pupil, but fairly close to him. Finish in good position. Those in the class who are capable (those who dive over one person with ease) may try to dive over two people kneeling on the mat. Those kneeling should be close together and in good tuck position. Caution: No diving should be permitted until pupil can do preceding forward roll over rope and mat *well.*

3. *Review backward roll with leg extension.* (fifth grade.)

4. *Head Stand and Roll Down*

   Perform a head stand as previously learned (grade 5). Instead of lowering feet to the mat by bending at hips, round the back and roll over, as in a forward roll, to a standing position.

❁      ❁      ❁

TEACHING SUGGESTIONS

1. Pupil should round the back, pull head under and push off with the hands.
2. Land on feet in good position.

❁      ❁      ❁

5. *Hand Stand*

   Place hands on the mat about shoulder width apart, elbows straight and fingers spread. One leg is bent under the body, supporting the weight, the other leg is straight. Shift forward until weight is on hands, kick up with straight leg, follow with other leg. Head should be up and back arched. To descend, bend the hips and drop legs, one at a time.

❁      ❁      ❁

TEACHING SUGGESTIONS

1. Place a mat against the wall and have pupils try a handstand against a wall, placing hands 12″ to 15″ away from the wall. When balance is achieved, bring the feet away from the wall.

2. Another pupil (or two) may stand in front of the performer to keep his legs from going over too far. Beware of being kicked. Do not pull the pupil's legs up into position.

3. Most common faults are kicking up too vigorously, thus throwing the legs too far forward, and failing to hold the head up or to arch the back.

✿   ✿   ✿

6. *Partner Balances* (See Teaching Suggestions, Grade 5)
   a. *Chest Stand*

   Base — Kneel on mat on hands and knees in a stable position, hands straight down from the shoulders, knees under hips, 15" to 18" apart. Head in normal position.

   Top — Stand at base's side. Place arms under base, across *chest*, with a firm hold. Lean across base's back with head on far side. Kick up, one leg at a time, and hold position with legs together, feet pointed. Descend one leg at a time.

   b. *Knee Shoulder Stand*

   Base — Lie on mat on back, knees bent, feet flat and about 15" to 18" apart. Raise arms, elbows straight, above shoulders.

   Top — Step between base's feet and place hands on base's knees, fingers pointing toward base's feet. Get a good grip. Lean forward and rest shoulders on base's hands. Kick up until legs are straight. Hold position with toes pointed. Descend by flexing hips and stepping down.

✿   ✿   ✿

TEACHING SUGGESTIONS

1. The base must have a good stable position. Arms should be extended directly above the shoulders.

2. When legs are up, the top should straighten elbows, hold head up, arch back and point feet.

✿   ✿   ✿

7. *Pyramids* (See fourth and fifth grade pyramids)

✿   ✿   ✿

TEACHING SUGGESTIONS

1. To be most effective, pyramids should be done to count. All participants should start standing behind the mat, in their respective positions, and should finish in the same way. A simple pyramid done well is far more effective than a more difficult one done in a sloppy manner.

2. A spotter should be assigned to each pyramid to assist pupils into position and to help if needed.
3. These suggested pyramids use partner stunts included in the sixth grade curriculum. Other combinations can be created.

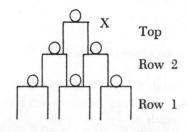

X    Top

Row 2

Row 1

*Pyramid A.*

Pupils kneeling on another, as in this pyramid, must put their knees on the base's hips. Grasp shoulder of base in order to maintain balance. Top man steps on hips of center man in Row 1 to get up to his position. All hold heads up. Pupils in Row 1 and 2 should be as close together as possible.
X — Spotter.

Count 1—Row 1 takes place on the mat. 2—Row 2 climbs on top of Row 1. 3—Top pupil steps on hips of middle man in Row 1 and climbs up to position. 4—Top man down. 5—Row 2 down. 6—All stand behind mat.

*Pyramid B.*

1. Head Stands.
2. Knee Shoulder Balances.
X — Spotters.

Count 1—All take positions on mat and bases for #2 go down. 2—Head stands go up. 3—Tops for #2 go up. 4—All down. 5—All stand behind mat.

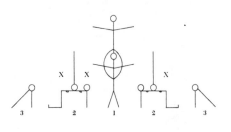

*Pyramid C.*
1. Sitting mount.
2. Chest balance.
3. Prone position, arms straight.
X — Spotters.

Count 1—Bases for #1 and #2 take places on the mat. 2—Top for #1 goes up. 3—Tops for #2 go up, #3 takes position. 4—#2's come down. 5—#1 comes down. 6—All stand behind mat.

❋   ❋   ❋

4. **Combatives** (May use other combatives from fourth and fifth grades)

   *1. Hand Slap* (or Hot Hands)
   Partners face each other about arm's distance apart. No. 1 holds hands out in front of body, palms up, and No. 2 places his hands on top of No. 1's. On signal, No. 1 withdraws his hands and tries to slap No. 2's hands in any way possible. Contest may continue for three or five slaps, or tags. Then start over with positions reversed.

   *2. Indian Leg Wrestle*
   Boys with boys, and girls with girls. Partners lie on the mat, side by side, their heads in opposite directions. Hook inside arms. Raise inside legs three times and on third time, hook legs with partner and try to force partner to roll over in a backward roll. Repeat with opposite legs.

## TRACK AND FIELD EVENTS

There has been increased nationwide emphasis on track during the past ten years. This has filtered down to the elementary school. Various athletic, fraternal and commercial organizations have sponsored community track meets thereby adding to the interest in this form of athletic competition. The Junior Olympics, sponsored by the Amateur Athletic Union, is one of these events. While it may or may not be the responsibility of the school to sponsor such community events, track activities can justifiably be included in the physical education curriculum. Competition in track events gives the pupil an opportunity to go "all out" and to test himself against local or national standards. In addition, this type of individual competition provides the pupil an opportunity to practice self-control, self-discipline and good sportsmanship. Track events, as individual contests, appeal to some pupils who do not care for team or group type activities.

In order to make the most efficient use of the class time, it is best to use a squad organization with the squads moving from one event to another during the class period. It is necessary to have dependable squad leaders. A good warm-up for the whole class should precede other activities.

Example:

|         | First 6 min. | 2nd period | 3rd period | 4th period |
|---------|--------------|------------|------------|------------|
| Squad 1 | dashes       | throw      | jump       | dog trot   |
| Squad 2 | throw        | jump       | dog trot   | dashes     |
| Squad 3 | jump         | dog trot   | dashes     | throw      |
| Squad 4 | dog trot     | dashes     | throw      | jump       |

Motivation for practicing track skills can be provided by planning a class, grade or school track meet; this event is usually held at the end of the school year. Following are a few suggestions for conducting such a meet:

1. All necessary facilities and supplies should be readied before the meet. Running distances should be marked off, throwing areas should be cleared, jump pits should be prepared. All running events can be run on dirt or grass or turfed areas.
2. Measuring tapes, or a substitute, stop watches and score sheets of some type will be needed.
3. It is preferable to have the participants sign up before the day of the meet so that they know what they are going to do and so that officials will have some idea of how many children expect to participate in each event. If the group is large, it may be necessary to conduct a preliminary meet. This can be done in classes, grades or rooms. Children should, of course, compete with their own age or grade level.
4. Participants should wear gym shoes for their own safety and protection. Where hard surfaced tracks are available, cleated shoes may be permitted.
5. Good officials are necessary — at least one to each event. Pupils who are not participating can assist officials.
6. While awards are not necessary, children love to take something home to show. First, second and third place ribbons can be given

(blue for first; red for second; white for third) or certificates can be presented stating that "John Smith won first place in the 25-yard dash."

## TRACK AND FIELD EVENTS — PROGRESSION

### Primary Grades

*Informal Racing*
*If third graders have sufficient maturity and skill, they may use the events listed for the fourth graders. They should, of course, compete against each other and not against older children.*

### Fourth Grade

*Twenty five yard dash or sprint with any starting position.*
*Standing Broad Jump*
*Softball Throw for Distance*
*Shuttle Relay*

### Fifth Grade

*Thirty yard dash with crouch starting position.*
*Standing Broad Jump*
*Running Long Jump*
*Softball Throw for Distance*
*Shuttle Relay*

### Sixth Grade

*Fifty yard dash with crouch starting position.*
*Running Long Jump*
*Softball Throw for Distance*
*Basketball Throw for Distance*
*Shuttle Relay*

### Fourth Grade

1. *Running*

    Running is a natural skill which most children have learned fairly well by the time they enter school. It is a very important skill in games and sports. Running is one of the best conditioners available in the average school situation. Children should have opportunity to run every day.

1. The body should lean forward slightly; elbows bent, but relaxed, at nearly a right angle. The arm swings forward with the opposite leg. Arms swing along the body and fairly close to it.
2. Chest and head should be up.
3. The feet should point straight ahead. Push off from the balls of the feet on each stride.

4. The body should move forward with all parts — feet, knees, hips and arms — in the same plane. If the feet toe out, or the knees or elbows are 'out of line', energy and time are lost. For the most efficient run, all parts of the body should move in a forward-backward plane and not sideways.

TEACHING SUGGESTIONS

1. In the elementary school it is not necessary to be concerned with the more technical aspects of the skill. It is not necessary to change a pupil's style of running unless he is doing something that is obviously and grossly incorrect, such as 'toeing out' or flailing with the arms. "Running need not be taught, and the less said about form the better. For the coach, it is well to remember that stride length is a function of running speed. The slower the run, the shorter the stride. The faster the run, the longer the step. Long runs at slow speeds will not result in the ability to run fast, desirable though this training may be in terms of developing general endurance."[1]

2. For a 25 yard run, there should be a straightaway of at least 30 yards. This area should be free of holes, bumps or other hazards.

---

[1]Fred Wilt, former U. S. Olympic Champion. From United States Track and Field Federation Record, Vol. 2 No. 2 — May-June, 1964. P. 4.

3. See Run-A-Mile, page 138.
4. For racing —
   a. Fourth graders may use any kind of a starting position behind the starting line. A forward-backward stride position gives the best leverage for a good start.
   b. The starting signal is "On your Marks" — pupils take positions. "Get Set" — prepare to start. "Go" — start.
   c. A warm-up run should precede a race. There should be sufficient rest between races.
   d. Teach pupils to finish the race regardless of their position. They should not slow up till they have crossed the finish line. Run *through* the line, rather than *to* it.
   e. Twenty five yards is a good racing distance for fourth graders.
   f. Five seconds is good time for 25 yards at this grade level. Girls will do approximately as well as boys.

Standing Start                Standing Start

## Fourth, Fifth and Sixth Grades

### 2. *Run-A-Mile*

Running, as stated previously, is one of the best conditioning activities. To motivate pupils to run increasingly longer distances, the Run-A-Mile program has been successful.

A chart is posted on the bulletin board, or kept by the teacher, with the names of the participants and a record of their running. In the gymnasium of usual size (50′ x 90′) 22 laps around the outside of the gym floor equals a mile. If there is room on the playground, a similar mile course can be designated there. A pupil may run as many laps as he wishes on any one day, e.g., six laps. He runs laps on subsequent days until the total adds up to 22 laps, or one mile. Some insignia, such as a red star, may be pasted on the chart to indicate that a mile has been completed. A pupil may run no more than 11 laps on any one day (half a mile).

      ✿    ✿    ✿

TEACHING SUGGESTIONS

1. Some means of counting laps is necessary. The runner cannot count his own laps. Another pupil or the teacher should count each lap as the runner comes around the floor.
2. No time limits are required. The object is to run a distance regardless of the time consumed.
3. This is a good activity to use at the beginning or the end of the class period, or in any lesson where part of the class can be doing some other activity.

      ✿    ✿    ✿

## Fourth and Fifth Grades

### 1. *Standing Broad Jump*

When done outside, pupils should land in a jump pit. The pit should be filled with wood shavings, sawdust, sand or some other soft mulch type material. When done in a gymnasium, landing should be on one or two mats.

1. Pupil stands with toes on — but not over — the starting line, feet slightly apart, in a semi-crouch position, arms back with half bent elbows. Head should be up and toes pointing straight ahead.
2. With a forceful arm swing, the pupil pushes off from balls of both feet and jumps as far as he can.
3. Landing should be on the balls of feet, with arms *forward*. The arms forward position aids in getting a good jump and also helps the pupil to fall forward instead of backward.

4. Measure is made from the take-off line to the spot that the pupil touches on the mat or pit nearest to the take-off line. In a good jump, measurement would be to the pupil's heels. If the child falls backward, measurement would be to where his hands or buttocks touch the mat or jump pit.

✿    ✿    ✿

TEACHING SUGGESTIONS

1. Pupils should land on the mat or in a jump pit. Do not have children land on the floor or hard ground, as this is injurious to the feet and legs.
2. Measuring may be facilitated if the mat is marked with lines at various distances or if markers are placed at various distances along the edge of the jump pit. These also serve to give the pupil a goal — or objective — for which to jump.
3. Measuring should be done with a measuring tape (50′) or, in the absence of a tape, a yardstick.
4. A forceful arm swing is necessary for a good jump. Pupils should reach forward with the arms as they jump.
5. Considerable practice should be allowed before an all-out effort is made.
6. A broad jump of 6′ is a good jump for fourth graders. Girls will do as well — or better — than boys. For fifth graders, 7′ is a good jump.
7. The broad jump is considered a good all-round measure of coordination and strength. In most cases, the youngster who does well on fitness tests will do well in the broad jump and vice versa.

✿    ✿    ✿

**Fourth, Fifth and Sixth Grades**

1. *Softball Throw for Distance*

See fourth grade Ball Skills Overhand throw. Should be done outside on a cleared area about 200′ long.

1. Pupil throws the ball from behind the take-off line. He may run up to the line if he wishes.
2. Pupil throws the ball as far as he can using an overhand throw. Some height on the ball aids in achieving distance.
3. Left side (for right-handed throwers) should be toward the target area when the ball is released.
4. At the end of the throw, weight should be on the left foot and the throwing arm should point toward the target. Follow through.

Teaching Suggestions

1. Measuring is done from the take-off line to the spot where the ball hits the ground.
2. Players should have a warm-up and several practice throws before attempting the throw for distance.
3. One hundred and twenty-five feet is a good throw for a fourth grader; 140' for fifth grades; 160' for sixth graders. Boys usually will do considerably better than girls.
4. Class organization — When throwing for distance, certain procedures are necessary for safety and to make most efficient use of time.

    a. All pupils should be out of the area where the ball is to land except those who are assisting.
    b. Spotters should be assigned to stand on the spot where the ball hits the ground and stay there until the distance is measured. Retrievers should be assigned to get the balls and return them to the starting line.
    c. With a group of six or eight pupils, each makes one throw; then each takes his second throw; then the third throw.
    d. At least three balls should be available.

                        ✿        ✿        ✿

2. *Shuttle Relay*
    This type of relay racing at the elementary level is more suitable than that which requires the use of a baton.
    1. There are four pupils on a team; two stand at the starting line and two at the other line.

    a. Fourth graders should run 100 yards — 25 yards each.
    b. Fifth graders should run 100 yards — 25 yards each.
    c. Sixth graders should run 200 yards — 50 yards each.
    2. No. 1 starts and runs to the other line where he touches the shoulder or hand of No. 2. No. 2 runs and touches off No. 3; No. 3 touches off No. 4, and No. 4 finishes.
    3. The touch off can be made by
        a. Touching the shoulder of the next runner. Do not push the runner as this will throw him off balance and delay his start. This method is best when a crouching start is used.
        b. Pupil waiting to run extends his hand and the runner touches his hand. Preferred method when standing start is used.

4. There must be sufficient space between teams to avoid collisions. Runners should know to which side (right or left) of their teammates they will run at the end of their lap.

5. Twenty-two seconds is good time for fourth graders for a 100 yard shuttle relay. Eighteen to twenty seconds is good time for fifth graders for a 100 yard shuttle relay. Twenty-nine seconds is good time for sixth graders for a 200 yard shuttle relay.

## Fifth and Sixth Grades

1. *Running*

    See fourth grade for running form.

Fifth and sixth graders may use the official starting position as follows:

1. "On your Mark" — Pupils crouch 5" to 6" behind the starting line, hands on the ground, fingers spread and pointing to the side. Weight is on the legs, one of which is somewhat back of the other. The knee of the rear foot should be up almost even with the front foot.

2. "Get Set" — Runner raises the hips so that the weight is moved forward toward the hands. Elbows are straight. Toes should have a good grip. Runner looks at the starting line.

3. "Go" — The runner pushes off as forcibly as possible and gradually raises head and body to an erect position.

If the runner starts before the "go" signal, the racers are called back and the start is done again. If the same runner again "jumps the gun," he is disqualified.

"On Your Mark"                    "Get Set"

Crouch Start

TEACHING SUGGESTIONS

1. A stop watch is very helpful. If one is not available, use an ordinary watch with a second hand to time the runners.
2. Thirty yards is a good racing, or dash, distance for fifth graders. Sixth grade pupils may race 50 yards.
3. Four and one-half seconds is good time for a fifth grader for 30 yards.
4. Seven seconds is good time for sixth graders for 50 yards. As girls at this grade level are maturing, they will not usually do as well as boys in the dash.

❖    ❖    ❖

2. *Running Long Jump*

Facilities as for the Standing Broad Jump. It is best to do this outside, landing in a jump pit. If done inside, landing on mats, it will be necessary to hold the mats to keep them from slipping forward on the floor.

1. Technique is generally the same as for the standing broad jump (see Grade 4) except that a run precedes the jump and longer jumps can be achieved.
2. The pupil takes a short run (25' is adequate) approaching the take-off mark. The take-off is from one foot instead of two as in the standing broad jump. Pupil must judge the length of his run so that the take-off foot will hit the take-off mark.
3. After the take-off, the pupil pulls the legs up into a semi-tuck position and pulls forward forcibly with the arms.
4. Landing is on both feet. Pupil should fall forward, if he falls at all.

❖    ❖    ❖

TEACHING SUGGESTIONS

1. Measurement of the long jump is the same as for the standing broad jump. See Grade 4.
2. Considerable practice should be allowed before an all-out effort is made. Preliminary warm-up should be a requirement before jumping.
3. A running broad jump of 12' is a good jump for fifth graders, 14' for sixth graders. Girls will do a little less than boys.

❖    ❖    ❖

## Sixth Grade

1. *Basketball Throw for Distance*

Draw a circle seven feet in diameter on the floor or ground. Mark the center point of the circle. Throwing area should be about 25' wide.

1. The contestant stands in the circle and throws the ball, attempting to throw it as far as possible. The ball may be thrown in any manner with one hand. The pupil must not step out of the circle until the ball has landed and until he has recovered his balance after the throw.

2. Pupil should stand with left side toward the target area. The ball lies on the hand of the throwing arm and may be partially supported by the other hand. The ball is propelled, after several preliminary swings, by a forward and upward swing of the throwing arm with a nearly straight elbow. Ball should leave the hand at about shoulder height.

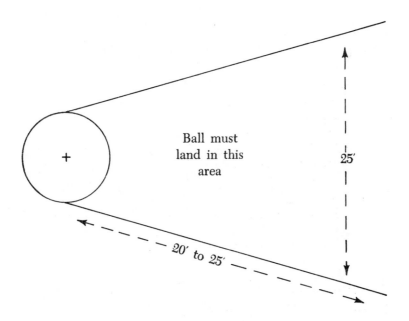

Ball must land in this area

25'

20' to 25'

TEACHING SUGGESTIONS

1. Pupil should throw as straight as possible. The throw is measured from the center of the circle to the spot where the ball hits the ground.

2. Pupils should have a warm-up and several practice throws before attempting the throw for maximum distance.

3. A 50' throw is a good throw for sixth graders. Boys as a rule will do considerably better than girls.

4. See organization suggestions for "softball throw for distance" under fourth grade.

# ROPE JUMPING

Rope jumping is a fine physical activity that should be a part of the curriculum at every grade level. It contributes to the development of fitness, especially of the respiratory and circulatory systems. It strengthens the legs and feet. It helps to develop and strengthen the sense of rhythm and aids timing and coordination. In addition, it is an activity which children enjoy and in which they can participate in out-of-school hours. Boys usually do not do as well as girls but this is largely because they have had less practice. With experience, they will enjoy jumping and will improve at a rapid rate. Rope jumping is by no means a sissy activity as it is used by many athletes — football and basketball players, boxers and others — as a part of their conditioning program.

Ropes may be made of 3/8″ or 1/2″ sash cord; the ends should either be knotted to prevent raveling, or tape may be wound around the ends of the rope. Wooden handles are not necessary and in fact present a hazard.[1] Short or individual ropes should be 8′ to 9′ long — long enough to reach the arm pits when a child stands on the middle of the rope. Long ropes should be about 20′ long.

Ideally, there should be one rope for each child. If the school cannot provide the ropes, children may bring them from home. There should be four or five long ropes available so that children do not have to wait too long for their turn to jump.

Rope jumping is a good activity to use for demonstrations or programs. The children may evolve a routine or sequence of rope jumping. This may be done individually, in partners or in groups. Routines are most effective when done to music.[2]

## ROPE JUMPING — PROGRESSION

1. Short Rope Progression
2. Long Rope Progression
3. Rope Tricks
4. Jump Rope Jingle.

### 1. Short Rope Progression

1. Hold both ends of the rope in one hand. Swing the rope forward in a circle, hitting the floor with the center of the rope. Keep the

---

[1]Various kinds of nylon and plastic rope are now available; skip ropes made of this material are colorful and wear better than ordinary rope.

[2]Some record companies have records for rope jumping. An example is "Rope Jumping and Ball Bouncing" from the Honor Your Partner Series by Ed Durlacher, Album 12. Square Dance Associates, Freeport, New York.

hands fairly close to the body. Swing the rope backward. All members of the class should hit the floor with their ropes at the same time.

2. Continue swinging the rope and jump in time with the rope. There should be two jumps for each rope swing; "jump, bounce;" or "big jump, little jump." Called 'rebound' step.

3. Take rope, one end in each hand, turning it forward. "Jump, bounce."

   a. Head up
   b. Body slightly bent forward
   c. Arms close to the body, hands about 12 inches from the body. Turn the rope with the wrists. Younger children may need more arm movement to get the rope around.
   d. Jump on balls of the feet, 'giving' in the knees as the feet touch the floor.
   e. Jump only high enough to clear the rope.
   f. Rope should touch the floor just in front of the feet.

           ❊     ❊     ❊

TEACHING SUGGESTIONS

1. It may be easier, for a child with no previous jumping experience, to jump with a long rope than to turn the rope himself as is done with the short rope.

2. It is imperative that the pupil get the rhythm of jumping. It helps at this point, to jump to music.

3. If a child has trouble getting the rhythm of the jump, another pupil or the teacher may take his hand and jump with him. This might be done with or without the rope.

4. Be sure that each pupil has ample room to swing his rope without hitting anyone.

After the pupils have the basic jump in good rhythm, the following may be tried:

1. Jump with both feet, keeping heels and toes together.
2. Jump on right foot, left foot held against ankle with toe extended downward. Same for left foot.
3. Alternating feet — Jumping on one foot and then the other alternately.
4. Forward-backward stride position — equal weight on both feet. Right foot forward. Left foot forward.
5. Straddle jump — Stride position, feet out to the side.
6. Cradle — Rope swings forward and backward, but does not go overhead.
7. Slips — Example:
   a. Pupil jumps with rope in both hands — 5 times.
   b. Continue jumping while transferring the rope to the right hand. Swing rope, in time, hitting the floor — 5 times.
   c. Regular jumps — 5 times.
   d. Transfer rope to left hand and continue jumping as the rope is swung — 5 times.
8. Combinations of foregoing.
9. Using any of the steps described, further variation can be added by
   a. Moving forward, backward and sideward.
   b. Turn rope with crossed arm swing.
   c. Jump with partner (1 rope) each turning one end of the rope, or partners face each other, with one person turning the rope.
   d. Jump with partner while partner bounces a ball.

**2. Long Rope Progression** — Two people turning the rope.

  *1.* Pupil stands beside the rope as it rests on the ground between the turners. Jump over the rope when it comes around using "jump, bounce" or "big jump, little jump." Face one of the turners.

❋    ❋    ❋

TEACHING SUGGESTIONS

1. Help the child who has trouble by saying "Jump!" as the rope is over his head.
2. Have the child stand away from the rope and jump in rhythm while another pupil jumps the rope.
3. Take a pupil's hand and jump with him to help him feel the rhythm.

❋    ❋    ❋

  *2. Running in*
  a. "Front Door" — Pupil runs in as the rope turns toward him from above. Run in as the rope hits the ground and start jumping immediately.
  b. "Back Door" — Running in as the rope is turned toward the pupil from below. Pupil jumps over the rope as it comes toward him and continues jumping. Start in when the rope is overhead.

❋    ❋    ❋

TEACHING SUGGESTIONS

1. It is easier if the pupil runs in from a position near the turners, i.e., diagonally instead of straight forward. This is also true for running out.
2. For variation use Jump Rope Jingles and perform the stunts suggested.
3. Rope jumping may be done to march music, for example RCA record LPM 2688 by the U.S. Navy Band. Another good record is Herb Alpert's Tijuana Brass, Volume 2, AM Records SP 103.
4. A good reference for rope jumping is the following: Rope Jumping by Paul Smith. Educational Activities, Inc., Freeport, New York 11520. 1969. Contains instructions, drawing, routines, dances, jingles, records and bibliography.

❋    ❋    ❋

**3. Rope Tricks** (for primary grades)

  *1.* Lay the rope out on the floor so that it makes a straight line.
  Can you —

  a. Jump over it?
  b. Jump over it with two feet?

    c. Hop over it?

    d. Run back and forth over it?

    e. Walk with one foot on each side of it?

    f. Do the Bear Walk over the rope?

    g. Do the Rabbit Hop over the rope?

2. Make a circle with the rope on the floor.
Can you —

    a. Get inside the circle?

    b. Crawl around the circle?

    c. Stoop down inside the circle and jump out?

    d. Go around the circle running, hopping, jumping?

    e. Go around the circle with one foot inside and one foot outside?

    f. Do the Bear Walk around the circle?

    g. Stand inside the rope, reach out and touch the floor?

3. Holding the rope with both ends in one hand,
Can you

    a. Swing it and make a circle by your right side?

    b. Make a circle on your left side?

    c. Make a circle over your head?

## 4. Jump Rope Jingles

Many verses and rhymes traditionally have been used in the playing of jump rope. Some of these call for specific actions or stunts to be combined with the jumping. In the following, the underlined word or syllables indicates where the jump should be made.

1. *Chickity Chop*

Chickity, chickity chop
How many times before I stop?
1 — 2 — 3, etc.

2. *Lady, Lady*

Lady, lady at the gate
Eating cherries from a plate
How many cherries did she eat?
1 — 2 — 3, etc.

3. *Jump the Fence*

I asked my mother for fifteen cents
To see the elephant jump the fence
He jumped so high he reached the sky
And never came back till the Fourth of July!

4. *The fly and the flea*

A fly and a flea got lost in a flue
They were both imprisoned and didn't know what to do
Said the fly, "Let us flee,"
Said the flea, "Let us fly,"
So they flew right out through a flaw in the flue!

5. *Teddy bear*

Teddy bear, teddy bear, turn around
Teddy bear, teddy bear, touch the ground
Teddy bear, teddy bear, show your shoe
Teddy bear, teddy bear, please skidoo!

6. *Around I Go*

Oh, In I run and around I go
Clap my hand and nod just so
I lift my knee and slap my shin
When I go out let ................... come in.

7. *Buster Brown*

Buster Brown, turn around
Buster Brown, touch the ground
Buster Brown, touch your shoe
Buster Brown, that will do.

8. *Johnny*

Johnny over the ocean and Johnny over the sea
Johnny broke a milk bottle and blamed it on me
I told Ma and Ma told Pa
Johnny got a spanking, ha, ha, ha.
How many spankings did he get
1 — 2 — 3 — 4, etc.

9. *Mother, Mother*

Mother, Mother, I am ill
Call a doctor over the hill
In comes the doctor, in comes the nurse
In comes the lady with the alligator purse.
I don't like the doctor, I don't like the nurse
I don't like the lady with the alligator purse.
Out goes the doctor, out goes the nurse
Out goes the lady with the alligator purse.

# MOVEMENT EDUCATION

Movement education is not a unit or a new program to be taught as such in the physical education curriculum, but rather it is a teaching approach—or technique—using the methods of exploration and problem solving. This approach is based on a high degree of pupil involvement, and emphasis is on the individual rather than on the group. Children are guided in learning experiences involving purposeful movement. Hopefully, these experiences make positive contributions to the child's knowledge of self and his understanding of a changing environment. These learning experiences involve work with the basic elements of movement—time, space, force and flow. Through these experiences, children develop skill in the use and manipulation of space, in the coordinated use of their own bodies, and in the use of objects and materials around them.

Movement education exposes children to a wide variety of motor activities. Children may explore and experiment with fundamentals such as walking, running, jumping, hopping, skipping, throwing, striking and climbing. They progress at their own individual rate in a non-competitive situation. Action is used to solve problems. Each child can analyze and work out a solution to a problem using his own unique mental and physical capabilities. Many different solutions to problems are encouraged. Each child is successful—there is no failure, because there is no one way that is totally correct. This helps children to accept their own adequacy and abilities and should give them confidence to approach other situations and attempt to solve other problems.

*        *        *

TEACHING SUGGESTIONS

1. *Class Organization*

Movement education stresses freedom of movement within a designated space. The child may have his own space, he may move in the total space, or he may move in his space and the space of others near by. Children are told to 'scatter' or 'spread out' and use the total space, finding a spot of their own where they can move comfortably, and can hear the teacher. The child must accept the responsibility for moving safely with regard for others in the class. He should have a space that lets him devote himself to solving the problem, and allows him to hear any additional directions. Class organization should develop in a child an awareness of his own body in relation to the space around him, and to the other children around him.

2. *Signals*

No productive work can begin until the teacher establishes certain signals with the class. She must be sure the signals are understood, and must watch closely in the first few moments to see that they are followed. A whistle is often successful to tell children to stop, look and listen. A verbal command, such as 'go' or 'begin' can be used to begin an activity. Sometimes a hand or body signal is helpful in showing children which way to move. Some children are confused by direction, and until all in the class can move at random without getting in each other's way, it is best for the whole class to move in the same direction. If, for example, children are to move in a large clockwise circle, the teacher should give verbal instructions, make a large arm sweep and also begin moving her own body in that direction.

3. *Challenging the Class*

Talking and discussion should be kept at a minimum with emphasis on movement. Lead-in phrases might be: "Who can . . .?," "Can you . . .?," "Show me . . . ," "How can you get the bean bag over to the box without using your hands?," "Show me some different ways to roll," "How many different ways can you . . .?" If some children do not respond to the challenge, different verbal suggestions should be tried. Teachers will want to plan problems and challenges to fit the abilities and needs of the children. There is no set formula for determining how long a class should explore a particular problem. The children will be the gauge for the length of the activity, depending on how strenuous it is, how appealing and how complex. The instructor must develop her own ability to judge signs of fatigue, lagging interest and the attention span of the group.

4. *Demonstration*

A teacher need not and should not be the one to demonstrate movement experiences. At appropriate times pupils may be given an opportunity to show what has been accomplished or to show creative work. When the teacher demonstrates, it limits the child's opportunity to be imaginative in his own response. The teacher's role is to develop her own ability to phrase challenges for the group.

5. *Safety*

Movement education shows, by its basic concepts, that it can be a very safe part of the total physical education curriculum. Much time should be spent helping children to become sensitive to the meaning of spatial awareness. They should learn how to move within their "own space" and within the total space around them that might be filled with other people and equipment. Another basic concept supporting the safety feature is that each child sets his own task or goal within the framework of his own ability. The child does not have to fear failing to meet a certain standard, and therefore he is less apt to overtax himself or to attempt difficult things for which he is not ready. Emphasis is also placed on self-direction by each child and the acceptance of personal responsibility for one's own actions.

6. *Evaluation*

Evaluation in movement education should be in terms of accomplishment of the individual child. Each child should be encouraged to improve his own performance. Each child is guided to learn about himself and how he moves and about his own physical abilities and limitations. Both teacher and pupil should share in evaluation. The child should be able to recognize how many activities he can do, and how well he performs them.

7. *Logical Progression*

As the teacher thinks of suitable challenges for her group, she also should consider the simple-to-complex order of various experiences she has planned. The size of the area available affects the choice of movements to be performed. An unrestricted area for the first moving lessons should precede performing in a smaller area. Doing the same skills (walking, running, etc.) in a smaller area requires greater skill.

The type of movement involved is also closely related to the size of the group. Size of the area and size of the group determine progression. As movement skills improve children may move in any direction they desire and change direction whenever they wish. Each child chooses his own direction but must anticipate the action and direction of everyone else.

Speed is also considered in progression. Group activities are first performed slowly, i.e., walking, and as good spatial awareness develops among the individual children, a fast walk is introduced. Running follows, as children display skill and personal control of their bodies.

8. *Some types of equipment that could be used in movement education are the following:*

|  |  |  |
|---|---|---|
| Balls | Scarves | Balance beams |
| Ropes | Hurdles | Stall bars |
| Bean bags | Mats | Climbing ropes |
| Wands | Stairs | Jump boards |
| Hoops | Stilts | Saw horses |
| Tires | Indian clubs | Chairs |
| Deck tennis rings | Tables |  |

9. *Suggestions for problems with bean bags*

Can you toss and catch the bean bag with one hand?

Can you do it just as well with the other hand?

Spread your feet apart for good balance and see if you can toss the bean bag just higher than your head from hand to hand.

How high can you throw the bean bag?

Can you toss the bean bag up and catch it with some other part of your body? *Let Children Experiment with This Idea for a While.* Then be *specific,* i.e.,

_____Can you toss it up and catch it on your back?

_____Can you toss it up and catch it on your shoulder?

_____Can you toss it up and catch it on your chest?

_____Can you catch it with your neck? Your knee? Your foot?

_____Can you catch it on your elbow?

Can you toss it up with one part of your body and catch it with another?

*No hands* used for throwing or catching. Let children create various patterns.

Make a shadow over the bean bag with some part of your body and then circle around bean bag. (For instance—holding foot above bean bag to cast shadow—then hopping around it with other foot.)

Cover the bean bag with some part of your body and circle around it.

\* \* \*

## PERCEPTUAL MOTOR TRAINING

Perceptual motor training is a relatively new approach in the attempt to solve some of the learning and personality problems of certain children. Experience with Head Start programs, and recent research on how children learn, point up the need for greater attention to the pre-school and early childhood years in the total development of the child.

Some school systems throughout the country are now planning and carrying out perceptual motor development programs as a joint effort of the physical education and special education departments. Many psychologists and educators feel that basic perceptual motor development has taken place by age five. Therefore, most programs of this nature involve pre-school and/or Head Start children, although some programs have helped older children who have learning problems. Screening and testing is carried out to locate children who, for a variety of reasons, do not seem to have the perceptual

What can you do with the

Beanbag?                    Balance Beam?

Wand?

Ball?

and physical skills and abilities that the educational curriculum assumes a child has when he enters school for the first time.

Perceptual motor training is, in brief, a plan (since this is, as yet, in the experimental stage, there are many different plans discussed in the literature) of physical or motor activities which are designed to improve strength, coordination, balance and a child's awareness of his environment including his own body. Concomitant with improvement in body awareness and motor skill is improved self-confidence and a more secure belief in one's worth.

The areas covered when working with these children might include body awareness, balance, laterality and directionality; eye, hand and foot dominance, eye tracking and control, spatial awareness; hand, eye and foot coordination, and combinations of these along with others. Many movement education activities and experiences can be incorporated into this program. So that a child can receive much encouragement, a variety of challenges for specific needs are given and praise for creative response is frequent. In this unthreatening setting, a youngster can be guided to develop coordinated skills that will make him more acceptable to his peers in other situations.

Perceptual motor training programs usually include no evaluation, success being achieved as 'no one fails' and all 'have fun trying.' No one could disagree with the concept that when a child feels good about himself, learning will be more successful.

Some studies have indicated degrees of success. Movement training may help children who have reading problems, perceptual acuity may be improved; learning readiness may be strengthened and behavior problems may be lessened as a child gains self-confidence.

Most perceptual motor training programs require a low teacher-student ratio, i.e., one to one, up to one to five. The use of student or parent aids is prevalent. A considerable amount of equipment is necessary, but much of this may be improvised by the instructor.

Classroom teachers who might be interested in further pursuing these theories and programs are advised to refer to the following bibliography for screening and testing devices and for practical activities for use with specific children.

BIBLIOGRAPHY

1. American Association for Health, Physical Education and Recreation. *"Approaches to Perceptual-Motor Experiences."* Washington, D. C., 1970.

2. American Association for Health, Physical Education and Recreation. *"Perceptual-Motor Foundations: A Multidisciplinary Concern."* Washington, D. C., 1969.
3. American Association for Health, Physical Education and Recreation. *"Feature on Perceptual-Motor Programs."* Journal of Health, Physical Education and Recreation, April, 1970, p. 30-48.
4. BRALEY, WILLIAM T., KONICKI, GERALDINE, AND LEEDY, CATHERINE. *"Daily Sensorimotor Training Activities,"* Educational Activities, Inc., Freeport, New York, 1968.
5. CRATTY, BRYANT J. *"Perceptual-Motor Behavior and Educational Processes.* Educational Activities, Freeport, New York, 1969.
6. GODFREY, BARBARA B., AND KEPHART, NEWELL C. *"Movement Patterns and Motor Education."* Appleton-Century-Crofts, New York, 1969.
7. ISMAIL, A. H. AND GRUBER, J. J. *"Motor Aptitude and Intellectual Performance."* Charles E. Merrill Books, Inc., Columbus, Ohio.
8. LEAVER, JOHN et al. *"Manual of Perceptual Motor Activities."* Mafex Associates, Inc., Jamestown, Pennsylvania.
9. Reading Research Foundation, Inc. *"Perceptual Motor Training."* 3849 W. Devon, Chicago, Illinois.
10. SUTPHIN, FLORENCE. *"Perceptual Testing and Training Handbook,"* Lions Publishing Co., Winter Haven, Florida.
11. Ventura County Board of Education. *"Training of Perceptual Motor Skills."* Ventura, California. 1969.
FILM—*"Thinking Moving Learning"* by Jack Capon.
Bradley Wright Films, 1 Oak Hill Drive, San Anselmo, California 94960. (Available for rental)

# The Curriculum

# Games and Sports

# 6

# Games and Sports

To those unfamiliar with the content of the physical education curriculum, games and sports *are* physical education, and vice versa. In the well balanced program, however, games and sports are only a part of the physical education curriculum. In the elementary school curriculum presented in this book, approximately one-third of the total physical education time is spent on games and sports. Many physical education curricula tend to overemphasize games and sports to the neglect of other activities in which children should have the opportunity to participate. Other skills and interests should be learned and developed. This overemphasis on games and sports no doubt results from the nationwide interest in sports, especially in the major sports of football, basketball and baseball. Teachers at the elementary level sometimes have to resist pressures to force an adult type program on children whose needs and interests are not met by adult type activities. Elementary age children can learn many game skills and concepts which lead up to the major sports so that, by the time they reach junior high school, they are ready and prepared to participate in the more complex team and individual sports of adults.

The games and sports in this curriculum combine to make a planned, progressive curriculum from grade one through grade six. Games are listed for each grade in approximate order of difficulty with exceptions for seasonal activities. If pupils have not had the previous year's curriculum, for best results it will be necessary to review the main activities of the previous grade. A class should accomplish the learning of the games and sports listed for its grade level sufficiently well to play with skill, satisfaction and enjoyment. Do not teach activities from the next or succeeding grade level. Rather than using activities from the next grade level if more activities are needed, vary the activities with different formations, different teams, tournaments, etc.

In the first and second grades, games are in circle or line formation and are group rather than team games. Children at this age level are individualistic and do not have the team concept. In most of these games the winner gets to be IT, in contrast to games for older children where the objective is *not* to be IT. Bat ball, in the spring of the second grade year, is the first game in this curriculum that might be called a team game. In the third grade, children are introduced to simple team games such as Steal the Bacon and Line Ball. In these games, although they are team games, individual expression and action are predominant. Kick Ball, in the spring, is a more formalized type of team activity.

Fourth grade team games include Line Soccer, Stealing Sticks, End Ball, Prison Dodge Ball and Throw It and Run. These are definite team games in which players assuming certain specific responsibilities for the good of the team. Even at this age level, however, children need and enjoy some games which are not team games such as Two and Three Deep and Octopus.

Fifth graders are ready for more complex team activities such as Soccer and Softball, and in the sixth grade these activities are further improved with the expectation that sixth graders will be capable of complete understanding of the rules and beginning elements of team strategy.

All ages of children like to review games they have learned in previous grades, especially those games of a recreational type including circle and group games.

To conform to, and take advantage of, the interest in different activities at certain times of the year, traditional seasonal games and sports should be taught at appropriate times of the year such as

> Soccer and Flag Football in the fall
> Basketball type games in the winter
> Softball type games in the spring

Games and sports contribute to the achievement of the objectives of physical education in many ways including the following:

1. Most games and sports involve running and other physical activities that contribute to fitness and physical development. In games where only a few children are active, the teacher must plan the lesson so that all will get physical exercise sometime during the class period. The teacher should see that all pupils get turns and that some do not spend the entire class period standing and watching others.

2. Skill development should and will take place in all games and sports. As in any other subject area, the teacher may need to give special attention to those children with poorer physical skills. If a teacher can assist a child to learn a skill — a skill that will allow him to achieve success and status in a game situation — the child will be eternally grateful. It is well worth the teacher's time and effort to give a child extra help and provide for extra practice if he needs it.

   The learning of skills is a long process with all but the most gifted pupils. The time spent in physical education class in learning to throw a ball, for example, is not sufficient to learn to become a good thrower. It is to be hoped that children will be sufficiently motivated to spend some of their out-of-school time in activities which will further the development of their skills. Children should learn how the skill *should* be done even though they have difficulty in performing it. They should learn to recognize good skills and poor skills. A fifth grader should know the elements of batting a ball correctly even though he may not be able to bat well consistently.

3. In games and sports, the opportunity to practice self-discipline and self-control is great. Games provide situations in which a person has to act and react quickly; things may go wrong or against one — and this with one's peers observing — where all can see one's failure. This is a tough situation for the elementary age child, or for any age, for that matter.

   The idea should be instilled in the child that one plays a game to *win*. Never say, "It doesn't matter who wins, does it?" It *does* matter who wins. Without trying to win, there is no game. Along with the concept of wanting to win, however, the idea must be developed that one wins within the rules of the game and within the rules of good sportsmanship. There is little satisfaction in winning if to do so one has to cheat or take undue advantage of an opponent. The games which are the most fun and the most satisfying are those in which both teams or both players try hard to win.

The development of those qualities included in the term sportsmanship is, like skill development, a long process. Some people, as we know, never do acquire these characteristics and qualities and they are no doubt the unhappy ones, the misfits in our society.

Teach children to be honest, whether or not the referee is looking. "There cannot be a referee for every player. Everyone is his own referee." "You are not playing the game if you don't observe the rules, as the rules make the game." Children will learn by experience that there is a great deal of personal satisfaction in doing something right just because it *is* right and not because someone else is checking on you.

Point out the correlation between, and the similarity of, rules and laws. Rules are like laws. Laws should be obeyed for the good of all (including the individual) whether a policeman is looking or not. The same is true of the rules for a game.

4. All healthy, normal children love to play games. The game is a challenge. It is exciting, it is fun. Some games are played just for fun, and that is sufficient reason. If a game is fun, the pupils will be motivated to want to play it again and again. This love of play, it is hoped, will carry over to their out-of-school life as children and as adults.

TEACHING SUGGESTIONS FOR GAMES AND SPORTS

1. Games and sports for a particular grade are listed more or less in order of difficulty with allowances made for seasonal activities. It is advisable to start in the fall of the year with a review of at least some of the activities from the previous grade level.
2. Discipline and order must be maintained if learning is to take place. Some agreed-upon signal — a whistle, a raised hand, for example — is almost necessary for the teacher in order to get attention or to stop the game in the midst of play.
3. Children should be given the opportunity to assist the teacher and thus assume some responsibilities for conducting the activities of the class properly. Even primary age children can help to get equipment ready, lead the class in calisthenics, etc.

4. Fourth graders and older children can help to officiate their games although the teacher should always be on hand to arbitrate any disagreements.

5. Time will be saved and much confusion eliminated if the class is divided into squads or teams when the activity is a team game. Four squads is the best organization for most activities. Teams should be determined before class time. The same teams may exist for from two to four weeks, depending upon the activity being stressed in the class and the pupils' satisfaction with the teams. Team leaders may be elected by the class or appointed by the teacher.

6. All lessons should start with a warm-up run and calisthenics. This part of the lesson can be done in a predetermined way and place so that time will not be wasted in getting started.

7. In the primary grades, it usually is wise to plan two games of different types — for example, a circle game and a line formation game — for one lesson. If interest is high in one game, however, do not stop the game and start another just because it is on the lesson plan.

8. In the fourth, fifth, and sixth grades, the usual lesson plan for games or sports would be as follows:
   a. Warm-up run and calisthenics.
   b. Introduction of new skills and skill practice.
   c. Play the game, using the skills.

9. A good culmination of a game unit is a tournament conducted among the teams in the class. See different kinds of tournaments, pages 344 to 349.

10. As motivation, announce at the end of the class period, a "Player of the Day," this being a pupil who has done especially well that day, or who has made good improvement over his previous performance. A "Sportsman of the Day" might be selected, this being the player who has demonstrated especially good sportsmanship during the lesson.

## FIRST GRADE GAMES

1. Magic Carpet
2. Follow the Leader
3. Drop the Handkerchief
4. Old Mother Witch
5. Brownies and Fairies
6. Run for Your Supper
7. Fire Engine
8. Trades
9. Mickey Mouse
10. Squirrels in Trees

## 1. Magic Carpet

Play area — Gymnasium or playground

Equipment — None. Several squares or circles drawn on the floor, representing magic carpets.

Formation — Single Line.

The children form a single line, with hands joined. A leader leads the line around the floor and across the Magic Carpets. When the line stops, those caught on the Magic Carpets are eliminated. The object is to see who will remain in the game the longest — not having been caught on a Magic Carpet.

TEACHING SUGGESTIONS

1. The line can be stopped in various ways: by blowing a whistle, saying "stop", or if music is used, when the music stops. Those caught on the carpets are eliminated.
2. The line may walk or skip.
3. Those eliminated by being caught on a carpet may start another game.
4. Ten or twelve in a line is a good number. If the class is large, have several groups playing at the same time.

## 2. Follow the Leader

Play area — Any unobstructed area.

Equipment — None.

Formation — Single line.

The children form a single line. The first person is the leader. The leader walks, runs, skips, turns, does various movements with arms, head, etc. All pupils in the line watch the leader and do everything that he does.

TEACHING SUGGESTIONS

1. This is a good activity with which to start or end a class period.
2. Give the leader suggestions if he runs out of ideas.
3. Change leaders frequently.

## 3. Drop the Handkerchief

Play area — Any unobstructed area large enough for a circle.

Equipment — Piece of cloth, beanbag or other object.

Children join hands to form a circle. Drop hands. One player is IT with the object to be dropped. He walks around the outside of the circle and drops the object behind another player. This player picks up the object and chases IT. If he catches IT before IT gets back to the place in the circle, the second player becomes IT. If he does not catch him, the same player is IT again.

TEACHING SUGGESTIONS

1. A circle painted on the floor or blacktop is most helpful.
2. If the same person is IT more than twice, have him choose some-one to take his place.

## 4. Old Mother Witch

Play area — Two parallel lines about 40 feet apart and long enough to accommodate the group.

Equipment — None.

Formation — Single line, with one child standing about 20′ in front of the line, facing the line.

The following chant is said,

Group — "Old Mother Witch, fell in a ditch,
    Picked up a penny and thought she was rich."
The Witch — "Whose children are you?"
Group — "The man in the moon's."
    Repeat first chant
Witch — "Whose children are you?"
Group — "Yours!"

When the group says "Yours" they run to the opposite line while the Witch tries to tag as many people as he can. Those caught become the Witch's helpers for the next game (starting at the opposite line). Continue until all have been caught. The last child to be caught becomes the Witch for the next game.

TEACHING SUGGESTIONS

1. Teach children the proper way to tag: just touch a player — do not push or grab him.
2. Honesty and good sportsmanship should be emphasized. Children must admit when they are tagged.
3. Children enjoy this game around Hallowe'en time.

## 5. Brownies and Fairies

Play area — Two parallel lines about 40 feet apart and long enough to accommodate the group.

Equipment — None.

Formation — Divide class into two groups.

One group is called the Fairies, the other the Brownies. Each group stands on one of the lines. One child is appointed to be the Look Out. The Fairies turn their backs to the Brownies who creep up quietly from their goal line. When the Brownies are fairly close to the Fairies, the Look Out calls "Here come the Brownies!" The Fairies then turn and try to tag as many Brownies as they can. All who are tagged become Fairies and join the Fairies' line. Game continues with the Fairies approaching the Brownies' line.

TEACHING SUGGESTIONS

1. The Look Out must wait until the children are close to the other line before calling "Here come the Brownies."
2. Children should try not to be caught. Praise those who did not get caught. "How many did not get caught?"
3. There must be adequate space for all to run without colliding.
4. Other terminology might be used, suggested by the children or the teacher, instead of Brownies and Fairies, such as cowboys, spacemen, dragons, cheerios, etc.
5. Lines marked in the gym or on the playground are almost a necessity for a good game. Lines can be made with chalk or tape.

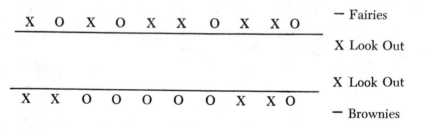

X   O   X   O   X   X   O   X   X   O        — Fairies

                                            X Look Out

                                            X Look Out

X   X   O   O   O   O   O   X   X   O

                                            — Brownies

## 6. Run for Your Supper

Play area — Circle 20' to 25' in diameter

Equipment — None.

Formation — Circle.

Children join hands to form a single circle, then drop hands. One player is IT. IT walks around outside of the circle, stops between two children and says, "Run for your Supper!" At this signal, the two children run in opposite directions around the circle, each one trying to get back to her original position in the circle before the other child gets there. Whoever wins is IT for the next time, and the first IT steps into the vacant place in the circle.

TEACHING SUGGESTIONS

1. Some regulations should be made to avoid collisions between the runners. Have children pass to their right.

2. If the two runners tie in getting back to the empty place, the teacher should quickly decide who will be IT for the next game.
3. IT may place his hand between the two children in the circle as he says "Run for your Supper."
4. The teacher should see that every child gets a turn.

## 7. Fire Engine

Play area — Two parallel lines about 40′ apart and long enough to accommodate the group.

Equipment — None.

Formation — Single line facing one leader, the Fire Chief.

The children line up along one line and count off by fours. One pupil is selected by the teacher to be Fire Chief. He stands in front of the group, facing them. The Fire Chief stands in the middle of the area between the two lines. The Fire Chief calls "Fire! Fire! Station No. 2" (or any of the four numbers.) Those with that number then run and touch the other line and return to touch the Fire Chief's hand. The first one to do so is the Fire Chief for the next game.

TEACHING SUGGESTIONS
1. The teacher should stand so that she can see the line to which the children are running and be sure that each touches the line before returning.
2. The Fire Chief should stand with his arms outstretched to the side.
3. If the same children are Fire Chief a number of times, have them choose someone who has not had a turn.

## 8. Trades (sometimes called New York)

Play area — Two parallel lines about 40′ apart and long enough to accommodate the group.

Equipment — None.

Formation — Two groups, each standing on one of the lines.

The first group chooses an activity that can be pantomimed. When the activity has been decided upon, the group advances toward the other line saying.

"Here we come,"
The other line says, "Where from?"
First side — "New York."
Second side — "What's your trade?"
First side — "Lemonade."
Second side — "Show us some."

The first side then pantomimes the activity which they have chosen. The second group tries to guess what the activity is by asking questions. When a player of the second group guesses the activity, all children of his group chase the first group, attempting to tag as many as possible before they get back to their goal line. Those caught must go to the other side. The second group then has a turn to choose an activity and pantomime it.

TEACHING SUGGESTIONS

1. Help the children decide on their activity. If it is very difficult, vocal cues may be given.
2. Groups must get up close enough to the other line to make tagging a possibility.
3. The space must be large enough so that children are not crowded and have room to run.

9. **Mickey Mouse**

Play area — Circle 20′ to 25′ in diameter.

Equipment — None.

Formation — Children join hands to form a circle, then drop hands.

Count off by three's around the circle. One child, Mickey Mouse, is in the center of the circle. Mickey Mouse calls a number — 1, 2, or 3 — and those pupils with that number run around the circle in a counterclockwise direction. The object is to get back to their places in the circle, turn in and touch the outstretched hands of Mickey Mouse. Whoever gets there first is the Mickey Mouse for the next game.

TEACHING SUGGESTIONS

1. Players must return to their own places or holes before turning into the center of the circle.
2. A runner may pass another runner on the outside or to the right.
3. Be careful of collisions when several runners get to Mickey Mouse at about the same time.
4. A circle painted on the floor or blacktop is a big help.

10. **Squirrels in Trees**

Play area — Any unobstructed area.

Equipment — None.

Formation — In groups of threes. Two of the children join both hands forming a tree. The third child, the squirrel, gets 'in the tree' standing inside the joined hands of the other two. Groups are scattered over the play space. There should be one or two squirrels without a tree.

At a signal (teacher claps hands, says 'change' or blows a whistle) all the squirrels must find a new tree home, while those without trees, try to find one. This will leave others without a tree home. Squirrels may not return to the tree they just left.

TEACHING SUGGESTIONS

1. There should be adequate space between the trees.
2. Change positions so that everyone has a turn at being a squirrel.
3. The trees must let squirrels come into their trees.

Squirrels In Trees

## SECOND GRADE GAMES

*Review from First grade —*
   *Fire Engine*
   *Mickey Mouse*

*Second grade games —*
1. Slap Jack ε.Ο.
2. Hill Dill

3. Boston and New York
4. Black Tom
5. Ring Call Ball
6. Cat and Rat
7. Come Along
8. Center Base
9. Bat Ball — spring

## 1. Slap Jack

Play area — Circle about 25' in diameter.

Equipment — None.

Formation — Single circle with one player on the outside of the circle.

IT runs around the circle and tags someone on the back. The one tagged immediately runs around the circle in the opposite direction. The object of each runner is to get back to the vacant place in the circle before the other runner gets there. The winner gets the place in the circle and the loser is IT for the next game.

TEACHING SUGGESTIONS

1. Game can be varied by having runners do a stunt when they meet while running around the circle: such as shake hands, jump three times, say "good morning" turn around, touch the floor, etc.
2. Encourage children to give everyone a turn.

## 2. Hill Dill

Play area — Two parallel lines 40' to 50' apart and long enough to accommodate the group.

Equipment — None.

Formation — All players, except one, line up on one line. IT faces the group.

IT calls out the following jingle:

> "Hill Dill come over the hill,
> Or else I'll catch you standing still."

All players then run to the opposite line while IT tries to catch them. Those caught become ITS helpers, and the game continues until all have been caught.

TEACHING SUGGESTIONS

1. Teach children to tag by just touching a player. Do not grab or push.
2. IT should tag as many children as he can, not just one.
3. Good sportsmanship and honesty can be taught by seeing that children admit being tagged.
4. IT should stand about half way between the two lines.
5. This is a good, vigorous game that appeals to children.

## 3. Boston and New York

Play area — Two parallel lines 40' to 50' apart and long enough to accommodate the group.

Equipment — None.

Formation — The class is divided into two groups, one called Boston and the other New York. They stand on opposing lines and each child extends one hand with the palm up.

A player from Boston goes across to the other side and slaps the hands of three players at random. The player whose hand is the third one slapped chases the slapper back to Boston. If he catches him before he reaches his home line, the slapper must go to the other side, i.e., join the New York team. Teams alternate in sending a "slapper" to the other side. The winning team is the one with the most number of players from the opposing team.

TEACHING SUGGESTIONS

1. The names of other cities may be used.
2. The game may be played by giving a point to the team that catches the slapper, and the slapper remains on his own team. The team having the most number of points at the end of the playing time is the winner.
3. In order that all get a turn, players may be numbered and become a "slapper" in sequence.

## 4. Black Tom

Play area — Two parallel lines 40' to 50' apart and long enough to accommodate the group.

Equipment — None.

Formation — All players line up on one line. IT stands facing the group about halfway between the two lines.

IT calls out a series such as "red tom, green tom, black tom, yellow tom, black tom, white tom, black tom." When he has said black tom three times, this is the signal for the group to run to the opposite line. While they are running, IT tries to tag as many as he can. Those tagged become ITS helpers. Game continues until all have been caught.

TEACHING SUGGESTIONS

1. This game is similar to HILL DILL, but adds a suspense element as the players do not know when the third black tom will be called.
2. See Teaching Suggestions for HILL DILL. Emphasize sportsmanship in admitting when tagged.
3. IT should tag runners by touching them — not push or grab.

## 5. Ring Call Ball

Play area — Circles of 8 to 10 children.

Equipment — One ball — rubber ball or volleyball — for each circle.

Formation — Circles, with 8 to 10 children in each circle. Or children may line up on outside lines of a four-square court.

The pupils in each circle are numbered consecutively from 1 to 8 or 10. A player stands in the center of the circle with the ball. He tosses the ball up into the air as he calls out one of the numbers. The child whose number is called tries to catch the ball in the air or on the first bounce. If he does, he replaces the person in the center and the game continues. If he does not catch the ball, he returns to his place in the circle and the original center player tosses the ball again, calling another number.

TEACHING SUGGESTIONS

1. Circles must be small enough so that children get frequent turns.
2. The center player must toss the ball in such a manner that it is possible for someone to catch it.
3. The game may be played with the center player calling names instead of numbers.
4. This game may be played as a group game as follows: A player tosses the ball into the air, another player catches it, and tosses it up again into the air. Each time someone catches the ball, the *number* of catches is called out. The purpose of the activity is to make as many consecutive catches—without a miss—as possible. Groups may compete with each other to see who can make the most catches.

## 6. Cat and Rat

Play area — Circle 20′ to 25′ in diameter.

Equipment — None.

Formation — Two players are selected to be Cat and Rat. The remainder of the group join hands and form a circle. Hands remain joined.

The Cat tries to catch the Rat. Circle players help the Rat by allowing him to go in and out of the circle under their joined hands. They try to hinder the Cat by not letting him through the circle. When the Cat catches the Rat each chooses a new player to take his place.

TEACHING SUGGESTIONS

1. Care must be taken that the Cat does not try to break through the circle in a manner that could injure the circle player's hands or arms.

2. If Cat and Rat run too long and are obviously fatigued, the teacher should stop the game and allow the Cat and Rat to choose others to take their places.
3. Do not permit the Cat and Rat to run too far away from the circle. Set boundaries.
4. See that all players get an opportunity to be Cat or Rat.

## 7. Come Along

Play area — Circle about 25′ in diameter.

Equipment — None.

Formation — Single circle, all facing center. One child, the leader, stands outside of the circle.

The leader walks around the outside of the circle, tapping several children (3 or 4) on the back as he says, "Come Along." Those tapped follow the leader and the vacant places in the circle are left open. The leader does various activities — skips, walks backwards, walks on tiptoes, arm movements, etc. — and all who are following him do the same. At any time the leader may say, "All run home!" At this signal, each child runs back to an open place in the circle, each attempting to get a spot. The first one there becomes the new leader and the game continues.

TEACHING SUGGESTIONS

1. Help the leader to think of different things to do if he runs out of ideas.
2. If a leader is leader two times in succession, have him choose someone to take his place or let the second child who gets back to an empty place be the new leader.
3. Be sure all children have a turn.

## 8. Center Base

Play area — Circles of 8 to 12 children.

Equipment — One ball (rubber ball or volleyball) for each circle.

Formation — Children in circles of 8 to 10 with one child in the center. Three to four feet between players in the circles.

The center player, IT, throws the ball to someone in the circle and starts to run. The person who caught the ball runs and places it on the floor in the center of the circle. He then chases IT and tries to tag him before IT can get back and touch the ball. If IT gets back to the ball before he is tagged, he remains in the center and throws to another child. If IT is tagged, the chaser goes to the center of the circle and IT takes that child's place in the circle.

Teaching Suggestions

1. This game is somewhat like Ring Call Ball except that the element of running and chasing has been added.
2. Keep circles small so that all get several turns. See that all get a turn to be in the center.
3. Runner and chaser should not go far from the circle. Set boundaries.
4. ITS throw must be accurate enough so that it is possible to catch the ball.

## 9. Bat Ball

Play area — A gymnasium, play room or an outdoor area equal to one softball diamond.

Equipment — A large rubber ball or volleyball.

Formation — Two teams with 8 to 12 players on a team.

One team is in the field, the other team at bat. The batter, standing at home base, throws the ball and then runs to second base, if played on a softball diamond. (If played in a gym, designate a place to which the players are to run.) He returns to home base. If he gets back home without being hit by the ball, he is safe and counts one point for his team. The fielding team can put the batter out by catching his ball on the fly (in the air before it hits the ground) or by getting the ball and hitting the batter with the ball below the hips. A team is at bat until three outs have been made, at which time the teams change places. The team with the highest score, after each team has had an equal number of times at bat, is the winner.

Teaching Suggestions

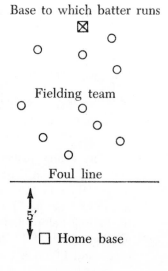

Base to which batter runs

Fielding team

Foul line

5'

☐ Home base

1. This is a lead-up game to kick ball (played in the third grade) and to softball. It is the first real team game in this curriculum.
2. Players should learn the following terminology and rules:
   a. An inning — when each team has had a turn at bat.
   b. Ways of making outs.
   c. Batting team and fielding team.
   d. Home base.
   e. Foul line and foul ball. When batter throws the ball, it must go across the foul line. If it does not, it must be rebatted.

f. Batting order — The batting team lines up near home plate. It is a good idea to give batters numbers and they bat in that sequence. At the start of an inning, begin with the batter next in line — not the first batter.

| 1 | 2 | 3 | 4 | 5 | 6 |
|---|---|---|---|---|---|
| X | X | X | X | X | X |

Batting team  X7
X8
X9
X10

3. If there are more players, have two games.
4. Teach members of the fielding team to throw the ball to a team-mate instead of running with it themselves. The game may be varied by making it illegal for the fielders to run with the ball.
5. Discuss good plays and poor plays. Encourage teams to figure out good strategy.
6. After the players have the idea of the game, the pitcher (one of the fielding team) can toss the ball to the batter, who then throws it; or the batter may kick the ball — in which case, use a soccer ball.
7. A variation of the rules may be used in which a team stays at bat until each team member has batted, regardless of the number of outs made.
8. The game may be played with two 'batters' running at the same time, instead of one.

## THIRD GRADE GAMES

Review from second grade —
Hill Dill
Cat and Rat
Mickey Mouse (first grade)
Third grade games — Best presented in this order
1. Chinese Wall
2. Steal the Bacon

3. Tag Games
4. Forest Look Out
5. Line Ball — fall
6. Dodge Ball
7. Crows and Cranes
8. Run the Gauntlet
9. Kick Ball — spring
Review Bat Ball — 2nd grade

## 1. Chinese Wall

Play area — Two parallel lines about 50′ apart.

Equipment — None.

Formation — All children line up on one line. One player, the Guard, stands in the center between the two lines. The space between the lines represents "the wall."

The Guard calls "Scale the Wall!" All players then run to the other line while the Guard attempts to tag as many as he can. Those tagged are eliminated. The object is for the Guard to tag as many children as he can in three (or four or five) trials. In other words, the Guard has three turns to tag as many people as he can. The teacher then selects another Guard.

TEACHING SUGGESTIONS

1. An area may be designated as a prison and all caught (tagged) go to the prison. When the Guard has had three turns, .count the number in prison. That is the Guard's score.
2. Be sure there is adequate room for the group to run without colliding.

2. **Steal the Bacon** (sometimes called Club Snatch)

Play area — Two parallel lines about 50′ apart.

Equipment — Beanbag or towel or Indian club.

Formation — Two teams, each lined up along one of the lines. Number the players of each team consecutively from one to however many children there are. The "bacon" is placed in the center of the area between the two teams.

X   X   X   X   X   X   X   X   X   X
1   2   3   4   5   6   7   8   9   10

☐ Bacon

10  9   8   7   6   5   4   3   2   1
O   O   O   O   O   O   O   O   O   O

The teacher (or a pupil) calls a number and the two players (one from each team) with that number run out to the center and attempt to Steal the Bacon and get back to their line without being tagged by the other player. If the player gets back to his line with the bacon without being tagged by the other player, he scores one point for his team.

TEACHING SUGGESTIONS

1. It is helpful to have a pencil and paper to write down the numbers called in order to be sure that all numbers are called during the game.
2. Players should try to get the opposing player off guard, or off balance, so that they can get the bacon.
3. If the two players do not pick up the bacon within three seconds (count out loud) they lose their turn.
4. After the pupils have the idea of the game, two or more numbers can be called at the same time.

## 3. Tag Games

Play area — Inside or outside, an area about 50′ square. Boundary lines are helpful.

Equipment — None.

Formation — One pupil is IT. The remainder are scattered at random in the playing area.

IT tries to tag another player by touching him. If he does, that person is IT, and he tries to tag someone else. No tag-backs are allowed, i.e., a player cannot retag a player who just tagged him.

TEACHING SUGGESTIONS

1. For most action, keep groups small.
2. Some restriction must be put on the playing area so that children do not run all over the playground while the rest of the group waits.
3. Variations include Stoop Tag, in which a player who is squatting is safe and cannot be tagged. Limit the length of time a player may stoop, and limit the number of stoops allowed in the game.
4. Tag games are good to use for a few minutes at the beginning or end of the class period. Children lose interest if the game lasts too long.

## 4. Forest Look Out

Play area — Circle about 25′ in diameter.

Equipment — None.

Formation — Two concentric circles, with the outside circle standing behind inner circle players. The outside players represent fire fighters and the inside players, trees. One player is chosen to be the Look Out and stands in the center of the circle.

Look Out calls, "Fire in the mountain — run, run, run" and at the same time claps his hands. On the last "run" the outside players start running around the circle counterclockwise. While the fire fighters are running, the Look Out quietly steps in front of one of the inner circle players. The runners who see the Look Out do this do likewise. The player who can find no tree becomes the new Look Out. Circle players have changed places with the former inside players now on the outside.

TEACHING SUGGESTIONS

1. A painted circle on the floor or blacktop is very helpful.
2. The Look Out should try to deceive the fire fighters as to the last command and also when he steps in front of a "tree."

**5. Line Ball** (sometimes called Boundary Ball)

Play area — Two parallel lines about 50′ apart with a center line. Lines should be long enough to allow some space between the players.

Equipment — Two rubber balls, volleyballs, or soccer balls.

Formation — Two teams, each in half of the playing area. Each team has a ball.

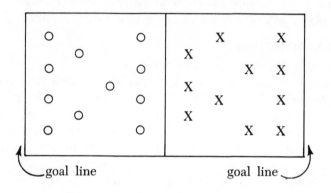

goal line                                   goal line

Each team tries to throw the ball so that it will cross the other team's goal line, waist level or below. Players may go anywhere in their half of the area but may not cross the center line. A score is made by the team that throws the ball (or rolls it) across the opponent's goal line.

TEACHING SUGGESTIONS

1. This game is a simple lead-up to more advanced games where the object is to get the ball across the opponent's goal line. Discuss with the class good strategy in placing their players so that some guard the goal line while others play forward in the court and attempt to throw the ball across the opponent's line.

2. Players may run with the ball, but should be encouraged to pass to someone near the center line where a more advantageous throw can be made.

3. If the game is played outdoors where the ball may get away, a few players from each team can be stationed on the sidelines to get the balls and return them to their team.

4. After the children have the idea of the game it can be played with three or four balls.

5. It is almost necessary to have one scorer stationed by each goal line.

6. Pupils should use an underhand throw or roll the ball.

## 6. Dodge Ball

Play area — A circle 25′ to 30′ in diameter.

Equipment — One rubber ball or volleyball.

Formation — Six to ten children in the center of the circle. The remainder stand on the circle.

Those on the circle attempt to hit the players in the center by throwing the ball and hitting the center players waist level or below. When a player is hit with the ball, he is eliminated. When all inside players have been hit, another group goes into the center.

TEACHING SUGGESTIONS

1. Dodge ball is a good game for children from the third grade up. Teach pupils to throw with an underhand throw. Hits above the waist do not count.
2. Circle players must be alert so if a ball comes to them they can quickly pick it up and throw it again. If a ball goes between two players, the teacher can quickly say the name of the player who should throw it. Do not let more aggressive players monopolize the game.
3. This game can be played by teams: give each team a certain period of time in the center of the circle and see how many players the team has left at the end of the time, or how many have been hit at the end of the playing time. Winners of each group (those left last in the center) can be permitted to go in the center to determine a "champion."
4. Pupils should be taught that if the ball goes out of the circle, they should get it quickly and throw it to someone on the circle who will then attempt to hit a player in the center.
5. If the group is large — more than 25 — have two games going at the same time.
6. The game may be played as follows: each time a player is hit below the waist, a point is recorded for the circle team. A player who is legally hit raises an arm to signal the scorekeeper to tally a hit for the circle team. He continue to play until time for the teams to change places. At the end of the game, the team who has been hit the least number of times is the winner.
7. Other variations are to count the total number of throws necessary to eliminate a team. (The team requiring the most throws to get all of its players out of the center is the winner.) Or an individual may go into the center of the circle, and count the total number of throws necessary to get him out.

Dodge Ball

### 7. Crows and Cranes

Play area — Two parallel lines about 50' apart. A center line is helpful.

Equipment — None.

Formation — Two teams, the Crows and the Cranes, line up with one foot on the center line, facing the teacher or the leader. The teacher stands to one side of the playing area, at the center.

The teacher, or a pupil leader, calls "Crows" or "Cranes". If "Crows" are called, the Crows chase the Cranes back to their line. If "Cranes" are called, the Cranes chase the Crows back to their line. Players caught (tagged) before they reach their line must go to the other team. Which ever team has the most number of players at the end of the game is the winner.

TEACHING SUGGESTIONS

1. Children should stand, when at the center, with one side toward the other group so that they are in a good position to run in either direction.
2. Be sure there is room enough so that children do not collide.
3. Teacher, or pupil leader, should attempt to fool the player by saying "C-r-r-r-ows" or "Cr-r-r-ranes." The teacher can also say "Crawfish" in which case no one runs.

### 8. Run the Gauntlet

Play area — Gym floor or equivalent.

Equipment — Four to six rubber balls or volleyballs.

Formation — Divide the class into three equal teams. Two teams line
up on each side of the gym and the third team at one end.

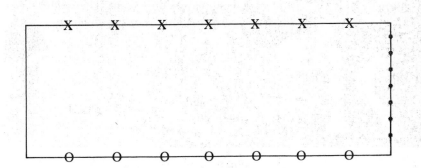

The third team, the *'s, run to the other end of the gym while
the X's and the O's attempt to hit them with a ball. Rules of dodge ball
apply, i.e., all hits must be waist level or below. Each team has three
turns to "run the gauntlet." When a player is hit, he is eliminated. The
object of the game is to see which team will have the largest number
left, or not hit, when they "run the gauntlet" three times. Teams on
the sides may go out into the center to get a ball, but must go back
to the side before throwing again.

TEACHING SUGGESTIONS
1. Each team on the sides should have an equal number of balls with
   which to start the game.
2. This game involves the skill of throwing at a player who is running.
   Teach the pupils to aim *ahead of the runner* in order to hit him.
3. Runners must run, but may run a zigzag course to try to avoid being
   hit.

9. Kick Ball

Play Bat Ball (second grade) before starting Kick Ball. Review
Bat Ball rules and terminology including:

a. Batting order. Players bat in order even though all do not get to
   bat in one inning.
b. Batting team and fielding team.
c. Inning.
d. When a team has three outs, it goes to the field and the fielding
   team comes to bat.

Play area — One softball diamond with bases 35′ to 45′ apart.

Equipment — One soccer ball.

Formation — Two teams of 7 to 10 players on a team. The fielding team assumes positions approximately as in the diagram.

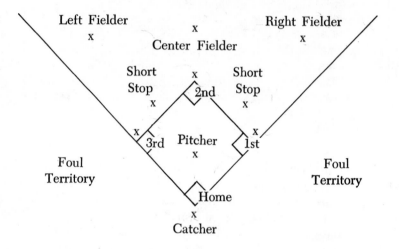

Kick ball is a lead-up game to softball and softball rules apply except that the pitcher rolls the ball and the batter kicks it.

The pitcher rolls the ball to the batter who kicks it and then runs to first, second, third base and home. He may stop on any base and advance to the next base on the next batter's kick.

The batter must kick a *fair* ball. If he kicks a foul ball — one that goes into foul territory — it counts as a strike, except on the third strike, and he bats again. The pitcher must pitch the ball so that it touches home plate. If it does not, it is called a "ball." Four balls entitle the batter to a "walk." He goes to first base without having to kick.

A score is made when the batter (base runner) gets around all the bases and crosses home plate without being put out. A run coming in on the third out does not count. A team is at bat until three outs have been made. Outs are made in the following ways:

1. A member of the fielding team catches a fly ball. (Fair ball or foul ball.)
2. A batter, when he is not on base, is touched with the ball in the hands of a member of the fielding team. (Runners are not put out by throwing the ball at them. Ball must be in the fielder's hands.)

3. A batter has three strikes. A strike is called when a batter attempts to kick the ball and misses it, or if the pitcher rolls a good ball across home plate, and the batter makes no attempt to kick it. A batter is never out on a foul ball.

4. If the base which a runner is approaching is touched with the ball by a fielder, or the fielder, holding the ball, steps on the base. Fielders may not hinder a runner's progress. Runners may not prevent a fielder from playing the ball.

No sliding is allowed. A player is out if he slides. No stealing is allowed. Base runners may leave their base and start toward the next base when the pitcher releases the ball but not before.

If there are questions concerning rules, see Softball rules for fifth grade.

TEACHING SUGGESTIONS

1. There are many interpretations of softball rules. Decide upon the rules to be used and don't fluctuate. Say, "We have agreed to use these rules." Some children confuse baseball rules with softball rules.

2. The batter may take only one step in kicking the ball. He may not "run up" on the ball. Warn children about this — if it persists, call the batter "out" for running up.

3. An umpire to call strikes and balls is almost a necessity.

4. Pitching distance should be shorter than for softball. Pitcher must roll the ball, not throw it.

5. Arrange for the fielding team to rotate positions so that all pupils eventually get to play every position. It is helpful to keep a written record of playing positions and/or batting order.

6. If there is a softball backstop, have the members of the batting team line up *behind* the backstop while they are waiting for turn to bat. Batters should not interfere with the catcher.

7. After the pupils have a general understanding of the game, encourage the following strategy:

   a. Baserunners should run to the base even though it appears they will be out.

   b. Basemen — first, second and third — When a runner is approaching their base and the baseman is waiting to catch the ball, the baseman should stand toward the *inside* corner of his base. This permits him to catch the ball without interference from the runner. Catcher should do likewise.

8. Usually there is not time, in one class period, to play a long enough game so that it is satisfying. Continue game for 2 or 3 days, or for a certain number of innings, three or five.

9. A variation of the game may be played as follows:

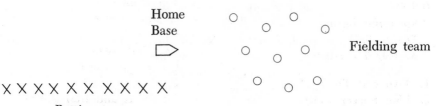

Home
Base
⊳                                                    Fielding team

X X X X X X X X X
Batting team

Note above line-up.

The first player on the batting team throws (or kicks) the ball into the fielding area and then runs around his own team as many times as possible before being put out.

The member of the fielding team who fields the ball, *stands in place* and his teammates quickly line up behind him. He passes the ball back over the heads of all. When the last player in line gets the ball, he runs up to the head of the line and holds the ball up over his head.

A score is made by the batter each time he runs around his team before the opposing team gets the ball back up to the head of the line.

A caught fly ball is an immediate out.

When all members of the batting team have had a turn to bat, teams change places.

Comment: The maturity of the group and the size of the group will probably determine whether or not this version of the game is played.

**At Bat in Kick Ball**

# FOURTH GRADE GAMES

*Review* —

   *Steal the Bacon*
   *Dodge Ball*
   *Kick Ball — (spring)*

1. Two and Three Deep
2. Line Soccer (fall)
3. Tag Games
4. Stealing Sticks
5. Octopus
6. End Ball (winter)
7. Guard the Castle
8. Prison Dodge Ball
9. Throw It and Run (spring)

## 1. Two or Three Deep

Play area — Circle 25′ to 30′ in diameter, indoors or outdoors.

Equipment — None.

Formation — Players form a single circle, all facing center. A runner and a chaser are chosen.

The chaser tries to catch and tag the runner who may run around or through the circle. The runner is safe when he stands in front of a player in the circle, and that player then becomes the runner. When the runner is tagged, he becomes the chaser and the game continues.

TEACHING SUGGESTIONS

1. Variations of this game include the following:
   a. Players may form a circle in partners, one standing behind the other; the game then becomes Three Deep.
   b. In Three Deep, when the runner steps in front of a pair, the last person, instead of becoming the runner, becomes the *Chaser*. Thus the first chaser has to change quickly to being the runner.
2. Children should play the game wtih frequent changes, i.e., the runner should not run too long before he stops in front of someone. If the runner runs too long, the teacher can blow a whistle — or use some other signal — signifying that the runner must get in front of someone.
3. This game may be combined in a lesson with some other game such as Dodge Ball or with several relays. Children lose interest if this game is played too long. Play long enough, however, so that all get a turn to run.

## 2. Line Soccer

Play area — Rectangular field on playground 60′ long and 40′ to 50′ wide. Side lines, center line and end zones should be marked.

Equipment — one soccer ball.

Formation — Two teams with eight to twelve players on a team. Each
  team lines up in their own end zone. Two players, one from
  each team, play in the center area.

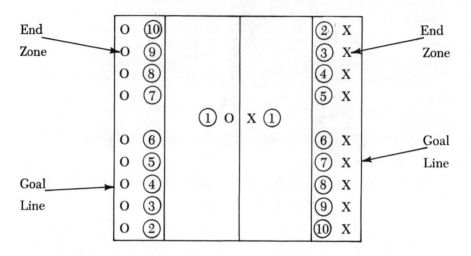

The ball is placed on the ground in the center of the field. At a
signal (whistle) the center players attempt to kick the ball across the
opponent's goal line, shoulder level or lower. Other players attempt to
prevent a score being made over their goal line, by blocking the ball.
When a score has been made (or after a certain period of time) center
players go back to the line, the line moves up to the right, and the next
two players (No. 2's) come out to play in the center.

RULES

1. Center players may go anywhere on the field except in the end zones.
   Line players must stay in their end zone.

2. No player may touch the ball with his hands. Folded arms may
   be used to block the ball in front of the body, but players may
   not 'advance' the ball with their arms.

3. A score is made when the ball crosses the goal line shoulder height
   or lower, regardless of who kicked it last.

4. Balls that go out of bounds on the side lines or over the heads of
   the goal line players are put in play as follows: the player on the
   end line nearest the ball gets it, and puts it back in play by tossing
   it in with a two handed overhead throw.

5. Penalties are incurred for the following:
   a. Touching ball with the hands.

Two handed overhead throw

   b. Unnecessary roughness, pushing, holding, shoving.
   c. Going out of playing zone — center players must stay in center
      area; end players must stay in end zone.

   The penalty is a free kick for the other team. The ball is placed
on the center line and the player kicks it. The opposing center player
must stand at least 5 yards away until the ball has been kicked. Only
line players may attempt to block the kick.

TEACHING SUGGESTIONS

Skills. (See ball skills under 4th grade self-testing activities.)

1. Kicking the ball.
   a. Use full leg swing for long kick.
   b. Contact ball with instep, not toe.
   c. Dribbling — short kicks with either or both feet. Keep ball close.
2. Two ways of blocking — or stopping — the ball with the feet.
   a. Put ball of foot on top of ball, 'trap' the ball.
   b. Feet and legs together, get in front of approaching ball. Bend
      knees as ball hits legs, trapping it between the legs and the
      ground. Line players should block, or trap, the ball before
      kicking it.
3. Body blocks — teach children to protect head, face and body by
   folding arms and letting ball hit arms. This is legal if the ball is not
   'advanced' or pushed forward with the arms.

TEACHING SUGGESTIONS — General

1. Play outdoors if possible. If necessary to play indoors, use a partially deflated ball.
2. Line Soccer is a lead-up game to Soccer. It is necessary to spend some time on the game before children learn the skills and strategy sufficiently well to enjoy the game. The game should be played in the fall, and with most classes, 12 to 15 lessons on Line Soccer is not too much.
3. After the players understand the game, two, three or four players from each team may play in the center area. In that case, they should develop some team work between them. Each player should be responsible for a certain area of the field.

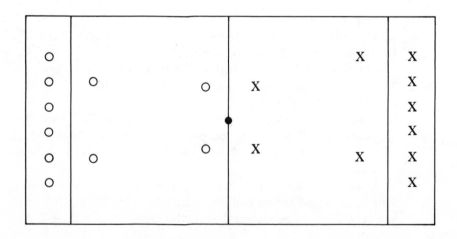

4. Have squads or teams which remain the same for two or three weeks.
5. Games may be played to a certain number of points, i.e. 11 points; or a period of time, i.e. two 10 minute halves.

Line Soccer

## 3. Tag Games

Play area — Any area inside or outside.

Equipment — None.

Formation — Pupils scattered at random about the play area.

Partner Tag — Children form partners, hooking inside elbows and with outside arm on hip, forming a loop. Select a runner and a chaser.

The runner is safe if he can hook on to a couple. The person on the other end of the pair then becomes the runner. (This is the same idea as Three Deep except that the formation is different.)

Chinese Tag — Player tagged must keep one hand on the spot on the body where he was tagged, shoulder, hip, knee, etc. Other rules are the same as for simple tag.

TEACHING SUGGESTIONS

1. See third grade tag games.
2. All will enjoy the game more if there are frequent changes.
3. Limit the area so that the runner and chaser do not wander too far from the group while the others wait.
4. Tag games are good to use at the end of a class period when there are just a few minutes left.
5. Small groups are preferable. Sometimes boys and girls like to play tag in separate groups.

## 4. Stealing Sticks

Play area — Gym floor or equivalent. May be played outdoors also.

Equipment — Twelve to twenty sticks, each about 15″ long. Dowling makes good sticks.

Formation — Each team is spread out in its own half of the floor.

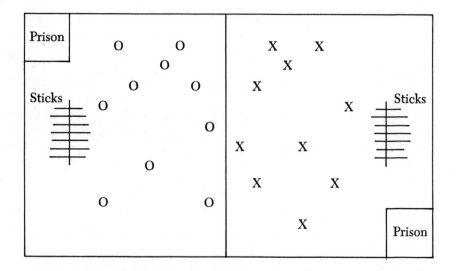

The object of the game is to secure all of the other team's sticks. This is done by getting through the opponent's field without being tagged. As soon as a player steps over the center line, into the other team's territory, he can be tagged. If a player reaches the opponent's sticks without being tagged, he may return with a stick in safety and place it with his own team's sticks. If he is tagged, he must go to the other team's prison and stay there until he is rescued.

To rescue a prisoner, a player must reach the other team's prison without being tagged. He may then bring a prisoner (one of his team-mates) back to his side of the floor in safety.

Players may not slide into the sticks. They must be on their feet. Only one player may guard the sticks, that is, stand close to them or over them. Sticks must remain spread out.

The game is won by the team which first gets all of its opponent's sticks.

TEACHING SUGGESTIONS

1. If played on a basketball court, sticks may be placed on a free throw line. The prison can be outlined with chalk.
2. It is helpful to have the team members identified by some means such as a piece of crepe paper or cloth tied around the wrist or upper arm.

## 5. Octopus

Play area — One gym floor or equivalent.

Equipment — One rubber ball or volleyball.

Formation — All pupils line up along one end of the gym. IT has the ball and stands in the center of the floor.

IT calls "Come, Fish, Come!" and everyone must run to the opposite end of the gym while IT tries to hit them with the ball waist level or below. If hit, they must stand at the spot on the floor where they were hit. They may pivot around but may move only one foot. These players then become helpers to IT and may tag anyone who gets close enough to them to be touched.

The game continues until all have been hit.

TEACHING SUGGESTIONS

1. After the pupils have learned the game two balls may be used, with IT having an assistant to throw the other ball.
2. IT should try to hit as many people as he can each time they run.
3. This is a good game with lots of action. It is good for variety as it is not a team game like most fourth grade games.

## 6. End Ball

Play area — One basketball court or equivalent. The playing area
should be divided by a center line and end zones should be
marked on each end of the court. The same markings can be
used as those for Prison Dodge Ball.

Equipment — One volleyball, soccer ball or junior sized basketball.

Formation — Two teams, each with 10 to 15 members. Four players from
each team start the game in their team's end zone. Players
should be numbered from one to however many there are on
a team.

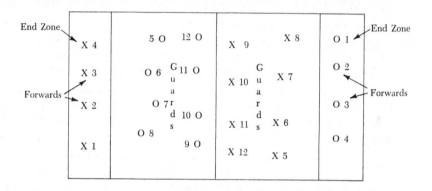

The game is started by the referee who tosses the ball upward
between two opposing guards standing in the center of the court. Each
of the guards may stand in the opponent's territory until after the ball
is hit when he shall immediately return to his own side of the court.
Each of the guards attempts to hit or tap the ball toward his team.

The object is for the guards to throw the ball over the heads of
the other team to their forwards in the end zone. Each time a successful
throw is made and caught, it counts one point for the team. The forward
should immediately throw the ball back to his guards for another throw.
The other team, in the meantime, tries to intercept the ball and throw
it to their own forwards.

Scores are made each time a forward successfully catches a ball
thrown by one of his guards. After each score the teams rotate, moving
in sequence according to the numbers on the diagram.

FOULS

1. Stepping over any line — center line, side line or end zone line.
2. Carrying the ball or travelling with the ball, i.e., taking more than
   one step while in possession of the ball. The ball must be thrown
   from the spot where it was caught.

3. Holding the ball more than three seconds.

4. Holding or pushing another player.

Penalty for fouls is loss of the ball. It is given to the other team. If the ball goes out of bounds, the player nearest the ball gets it and throws it in to a guard.

TEACHING SUGGESTIONS

1. End Ball is a lead-up game to Basketball. Throwing, catching and guarding are the main skills.

2. See Ball skills under self-testing activities.

3. Teach pupils to keep the ball moving, to throw quickly. Enforce the "three second" rule.

4. After the class has the idea of the game, dribbling the ball may be permitted. It is wise to limit the dribble to one bounce. The player may cover as much space as possible during the drbible.

5. The game can be varied the following way: after a score has been made, the forward player who caught the ball may attempt to shoot a basket from wherever he caught the ball. If he makes the basket, he scores an additional point for his team. If a basket is scored, the game is restarted with a toss-up at the center line.

6. Players must play their positions — that is, they cannot run all over the court — but they should not stand in one spot as though glued to the floor. Each player has an area for which he is responsible.

7. Players may pass the ball from one teammate to another in attempting to get it in the best position for a throw to the forwards.

## 7. Guard the Castle

Play area — Inside or outside.

Equipment — One rubber ball or volleyball and one Indian club for each group.

Formation — Groups of 8 to 10 children in circle formation. Place the Indian club in the center of the circle with one pupil guarding the Castle. There should be 2' to 3' between each player in the circle.

Circle players throw the ball and attempt to knock down the club as the Guard tries to prevent its being knocked down. He may stop the ball in any manner, blocking it with his body or legs, or catching it. Whoever throws the ball and knocks down the club becomes the next Guard. If the Guard accidently knocks down the club, the circle player who last threw the ball becomes the new Guard.

TEACHING SUGGESTIONS

1. If Indian clubs are not available, use a block of wood or a quart milk carton.

2. A circle drawn on the floor is very helpful. Circle players may not step into the circle.

3. Boys and girls may like to play this game separately.

## 8. Prison Dodge Ball

Play area — Gym floor or equivalent.
Equipment — Two or more rubber balls or volleyballs.

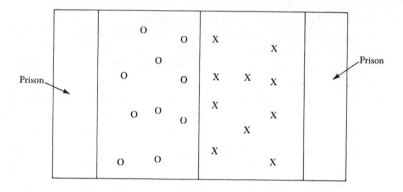

If played on a basketball court, free throw lines and extension thereof can be used for prison lines. Mark lines on floor with chalk, masking tape or some more permanent type of tape.

Formation — Two teams, one on each side of the center line.

The game starts with each team in possession of a ball. The object of the game is to hit the members of the opposing team with the ball, waist level or below, and thus force them to go to the prison behind one's own team. Prisoners can still participate in the game when the ball comes to them. The team which gets all of the opposing team in prison first is the winner of the game.

RULES

1. Catching a fly ball does not count as a hit.
2. If a player attempts to catch a ball and fumbles it, it counts as a hit.
3. Once a ball has hit the floor, it may be picked up and thrown. Contacting a ball on the floor, such as a rolling ball, does not count as a hit.
4. A prisoner may get out of prison in the following ways:
   a. Catch a fly ball thrown by one of his teammates not in prison. Prisoner may then give the ball to a teammate in prison.
   b. Get a ball and hit one of the opposing team members.

5. All players must stay in their own playing areas, i.e., players, before being hit, may not go into the prison area nor cross the center line. Prisoners must stay in the prison area until they work their way out by #4 a. or b. Penalty is to give the ball to the other team.

TEACHING SUGGESTIONS

1. The game may be played until either team is in prison or in two 10 minute halves, in which case the team having the *least* number in prison at the end of the game is the winner.
2. A player may run with the ball. If someone in the rear of the court catches a ball, he should pass to a teammate near the center line and let that person throw at the opponents. This is not a rule, just smart strategy.
3. Do not let more aggressive players monopolize the game. Players may not take the ball away from another player.
4. This game provides throwing practice as well as considerable action. It almost runs itself, the teacher needing only to observe and make decisions if necessary. Pupils must be honest and admit when they are hit. "Everyone is his own referee."
5. As skill and knowledge of the game improves, each team may start with two, or three, balls instead of one.

## 9. Throw It and Run

Play area — A softball diamond.

Equipment — If available, use a fleece ball or a soft softball. If not, use a regular softball. (Old balls are softer than new ones.)

Formation — Two teams with 8 to 10 players on a team, one team at bat, and the other in the field.

Before Starting Throw It and Run —

1. Review all rules for Kick Ball — see third grade.
2. Play Kick Ball for two, three or four lessons until all pupils understand rules and strategy of the game.

Throw It and Run, like Kick Ball, is a softball lead-up game. All softball rules (see fifth grade) apply except the following:

The pitcher tosses the ball to the batter who catches it and immediately throws it, anywhere within fair territory. In other words, instead of using a bat and batting the ball, the batter catches it and throws it.

It is important, even though pitching is not the important skill that it is in softball, that pupils get in the habit of pitching correctly. The pitching rules for softball are —

1. Preliminary to pitching, the pitcher shall come to a full stop, facing the batsman, ball held in both hands in front of the body, with both feet squarely on the ground, for not less than one second before starting the wind-up.
2. The pitch must be an underhand throw; the pitcher is allowed one step in delivering the ball, and this must be toward home plate.
3. The pitcher shall make no motion to pitch without immediately completing the delivery to the batter. Failure to observe these rules shall constitute an illegal pitch, causing a "ball" to be called in favor of the batter and allowing base runners to advance one base without being put out.

In Throw It and Run, the pitcher should not pitch the ball hard, but more or less toss it to the batter. Pitching distance should be shorter than for softball. A strike is called on the batter if the batter touches the ball but does not catch it, or if the ball is in such a position that the batter could have caught it but does not. The batter must throw the ball as soon as he catches it.

TEACHING SUGGESTIONS

1. See fourth grade ball skills for instructions for underhand and overhand throws.
2. See teaching suggestions for Kick Ball, third grade.
3. While it is desirable, as far as possible, to keep the class together, if there are any pupils whose throwing skills are especially poor, take them aside while the remainder of the class plays. Give these pupils extra practice in throwing and catching, helping them individually. There should be one ball for every two players. Be sure they use correct throwing stance.
4. Weaknesses in skills will appear. If, for example, pupils have difficulty in catching fly balls, use teacher and class formation and practice these skills. This can be done in the gymnasium as well as outside.
5. When playing in the field, players should play too far back — or out — rather than too close in. It is easier to run up on a ball than it is to have the ball go over one's head and have to turn around and chase it before throwing it in. Say, "Try not to let the ball get behind you."

6. In fielding grounders — those balls on the ground — players should keep feet and legs behind the ball, so that if they miss it with their hands it will not go through and behind them.

## FIFTH GRADE GAMES

*Review —*
*Two and Three Deep*
*Prison Dodge Ball*
*Octopus*

1. **Simplified Soccer** (fall)
2. **Tag Games**
3. Bombardment
4. **Net Ball**
5. Basketball Lead-up Games (winter)
6. **Streets and Alleys**
7. **V-B-B**
8. **Softball** (spring)

1. **Simplified Soccer**

Play area — Soccer field or football field. Playground area approximately 150' wide and 250' long. End zones, 5' wide and side lines should be marked.

Equipment — One soccer ball.

Formation — Two teams with from 10 to 20 on a team. Twelve or fourteen on a team is preferable. Teams take positions as on diagram.

The object of the game is to make a score by kicking the ball across the opponent's goal line. The ball must be advanced with the feet, legs or body. Use of hands or arms to advance the ball is not allowed. Arms may be used, however, to block the ball.

The ball is put in play by the center forward of one team. All other players must be at least 3 yards away at the time the ball is kicked. After a score, players rotate — forwards return to play in the end zone, halfbacks move up to forward positions and three more

|   |   | Half backs | For- wards | For- wards | Half- backs |   |   |
|---|---|---|---|---|---|---|---|
| O |   |   |   |   |   | X |   |
|   |   | O | O | X | X |   | ←—End Zone |
| O |   |   |   |   |   | X | ←—Goal Line |
| O |   |   |   |   |   | X |   |
|   |   | O | O | X | X |   |   |
| O |   |   |   |   |   | X |   |
| O |   |   |   |   |   | X |   |
|   |   | O | O | X | X |   |   |
| O |   |   |   |   |   | X |   |

End Zone→
Goal Line→

end zone players come out to play the halfback position. After a score, the team scored upon kicks off in the center of the field.

RULES (same as for Line Soccer — fourth grade)

1. End zone players must stay in the end zone. Center players legally may go anywhere in the center area. (See teaching suggestions.)
2. No player may touch the ball with his hands. Folded arms may be used to block the ball in front of the body, but players may not advance the ball with their arms.
3. To score, the ball must cross the goal line shoulder level or below.
4. Balls that go out of bounds on the side lines or over the heads of the goal line players are put in play as follows: The end zone player on the end of the line nearest the ball gets it and puts it back in play by tossing it in to one of his teammates with a two-handed overhead throw.
5. Pushing, holding, shoving and unnecessary roughness are fouls.
6. Going out of the playing zone is a foul.

PENALTY FOR FOULS

Free kick for the team that did not make the foul on the spot where the foul occurred. All other players must be at least 3 yards away.

TEACHING SUGGESTIONS

1. Play line soccer (fourth grade) before playing simplified soccer. It will readily be seen that this game is similar to line soccer, the main differences being that the playing area is larger and there are more players in the center area. All rules and skills used in Line Soccer apply in Simplified Soccer. If pupils have not played Line Soccer, use the fourth grade plan and suggestions.
2. Center players should play their own positions and play on their portion of the field. Forwards should be ahead of their halfbacks. Halfbacks play behind the forwards. Forwards usually make the scores. Halfbacks have a double purpose; defensive — to prevent the opponents from advancing to scoring position, and offensive — to move the ball ahead to their own forwards.

    Each player is responsible for a certain area of the field. When the ball comes into that area, it is that player's job to play it.

    Forwards should, as a rule, not go more than halfway back to their end zone. This is not a rule, just good strategy.
3. Players should develop teamwork, passing the ball between them and attempting to get as near the opponent's goal as possible before attempting a score.

4. If too long a time passes with no score, have players rotate.
5. To avoid injury, pupils should not wear street shoes. Gym shoes are preferred.
6. If pupils can play fairly well, put four forwards and four halfbacks in the center, with consequently fewer players in the end zone.
7. Play outdoors if possible. If necessary to play indoors, use partially deflated ball.
8. Teach pupils to protect their faces, heads and bodies by folded arms. The ball may bounce off the arms.
9. The game may be played in two 15 minute halves with teams changing goals at the half.
10. It is a good idea for teams to wear some identification such as a headband or a piece of colored cloth tied around wrist or upper arm.

The following may be used for practicing soccer skills. Use for 5 to 10 minutes before playing soccer.

1. Circle Kick Ball — Players form a circle with hands joined. With the feet, pass the ball around and across the circle. If the ball goes out of the circle, the two players — or one player — who let the ball go out, are eliminated. They drop out and start another game. Play until only five players are left in the original circle.
2. Three against Three — One ball to every six players. Mark a goal about 10' wide with sticks or some other object. Three players defend the goal while the other three attempt to score through the goal.

## 2. Tag Games

Play area — Any area, inside or outside.

Equipment — None.

Formation — Pupils scatter at random over playing area. Some boundaries should be agreed upon.

1. Ostrich tag — To avoid being tagged, player must put his right arm under his right knee and grasp his nose.
2. Chain tag — As soon as a runner is tagged, he joins the tagger. With inside hands joined, the two continue trying to tag with their free hands. Each person tagged joins the two by taking a place in the center of the line. Only the two outside members may tag others. If the line breaks, no one may be tagged until the line has re-formed. Runners may dodge under the arms of the players in the tagging line. If trapped, they may be detained until an end man can tag them.

1. See third and fourth grade tag games including Simple Tag, Stoop Tag, Partner Tag and Chinese Tag.
2. Tag games are good to use for a few minutes at the beginning or end of a class period.
3. If the groups are kept small, there is more action.
4. Boys and girls sometimes like to play tag separately.

## 3. Bombardment

Play area — Approximately half a basketball court. Game is best played crosswise a basketball court. Make a line with chalk or tape dividing the area in half.

Equipment — Ten to fifteen Indian clubs or tenpins for each team, one or two rubber balls, soccer balls or volleyballs for each team.

Formation — Two teams, each spread out on their half of the court.

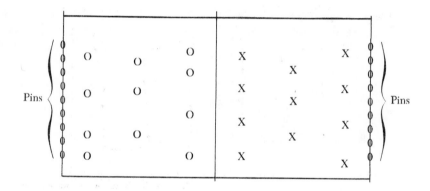

Each team tries to knock down the pins of the other team by throwing the balls. The team knocking down all of the other team's pins is the winner, or limit the time and see which team can knock down the most pins in that time.

Players may not cross the center line. If a pin is knocked down, it must stay down. This includes players' knocking over their own pins.

TEACHING SUGGESTIONS

1. Instruct the players to make underhand throws.
2. Pupils should throw the balls quickly to catch the other team off guard.
3. Each player should stay approximately in his own area so that one or two players do not dominate the game.

4. If a player catches a ball near the goal line, he should pass it to a teammate near the center line and allow him to throw at the opponent's pins.

5. In guarding the clubs, players may not stand over them.

6. Players may be numbered and rotate periodically at the teacher's signal so that all get to play in different positions.

**4. Net Ball** (sometimes called Newcomb)

Play area — volleyball court or equivalent. Area about 60' long and 30' wide, divided by a center line.

Equipment — One volleyball net. If net is not available, a rope can be used. Top of net or rope should be about 5' high. One volleyball.

Formation — Two teams of 8 to 12 players each. If there are more in the class, establish a waiting line alongside the court.

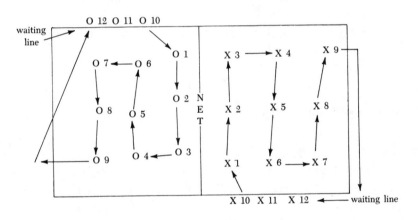

The object of the game is to throw the ball across the net so that the opposing team cannot return it. A score is made when the opposing team cannot return the ball or when they make a foul.

The umpire tosses the ball to one of the teams to start the game. Each team may pass the ball as many as three times among themselves before throwing it over the net.

After a score is made, teams rotate as indicated on the diagram. After a score, the team scored upon starts the game again.

Violations — a score is made by the team which did not make the violation.

1. Failure to return the ball.

2. Passing it among themselves for more than three times.

3. Dropping the ball to the floor.
4. Throwing the ball into the net. If the ball hits the net and then goes over, it is in play.
5. Player touching the net.
6. Player stepping over the center line.
7. One player holding the ball more than three seconds.
8. Throwing the ball out of bounds. A player may step out of bounds to catch a ball but the ball must cross the net in bounds.

TEACHING SUGGESTIONS

1. This is a lead-up game to volleyball. It is the first game in this curriculum which uses a net.
2. Teach players to play their position on the court and not run all over. Each player is responsible for an area on the court. Any ball that comes into that area is his responsibility.
3. The game can be varied by the teacher calling "Rotate!" while the play is going on.
4. Players should be coached to throw the ball to teammates nearest the net and they throw across the net.
5. The game may be played in two 10 or 15 minute halves, or to a certain number of points, 15 or 21.

5. **Basketball Lead-up Games**

Most fifth graders, boys especially, are ready and eager to play some basketball type games. The difficulty encountered is the limited number of players who can play at one time. In the game of basketball, 10 players use the entire floor. The following games use basketball skills, providing the players with practice in those skills and also having elements of the game. This satisfies most fifth graders.

Play area — Gymnasium with at least two basketball baskets, or black-topped area outside with basketball baskets. If possible, baskets should be 9 feet from the floor instead of the regulation 10 feet.

Equipment — Basketballs. Junior size basketballs, soccer balls or volley-balls can be used.

*Keep Away Games* (involve passing the ball, dribbling, guarding)

1. Two against Two — Divide the class into groups of four. Two of the players (A's), by passing and dribbling the ball, try to keep the ball away from the other two (B's). The B's in turn try to intercept the ball and then keep it away from the A's. Boundaries should be established. A quarter of a basketball court is adequate space.

2. Three against Three — Same as the foregoing except that there are three on a team.
3. Five against Five — Same as #1 except that there are five on a team.
4. Keep away with score — Five to eight players on a team. Play cross-wise the basketball court, using half a court. A player from each team stands behind the goal line (side line). The object is to pass the ball to the catcher. A score is made by making a completed pass to the catcher. Start the game with a toss-up in the center or by giving the ball to one team out of bounds. May try two catchers for each team.

TEACHING SUGGESTIONS

1. Use different passes, e.g., chest pass, bounce pass, overhead pass.
2. Limit dribbling to two or three bounces for each dribble.
3. Basketball rules apply where applicable.
4. When guarding, the primary principle is to try to stay between the opponent and the basket. Face the ball. The object is to get the ball.
5. When there are three or more players on a team, some identification is necessary. Use pinnies, if available, or colored cloth tied around the wrist or arm.
6. Most of the time have mixed teams. Boys will be better players than the girls, but girls learn from playing with the boys. From time to time, let boys play against boys and girls against girls.

Games involving shooting for the basket —

1. *Basketball Throw* — Divide the class according to the number of baskets available. Pupils line up at the free throw line. Each, in turn, gets three attempts to shoot a basket. Five points are earned if the first shot is made, three for the second shot, and one for the third shot. The first shot is taken from the free throw line; subsequent shots are taken from wherever the ball is recovered. If first or second shots are made, next attempt is taken from the free throw line.

   Do not have long lines of children waiting to shoot. If there are only two baskets and the class is large, have half the class play some other activity, such as Keep Away, while others are shooting. Weaker pupils will shoot underhand. Others should be encouraged to use chest shot or push shot.

   Individual scores can be added to compile a team score.

2. *One Basket Basketball* — Three to five on a team. Both teams shoot at the same basket. Start game by awarding ball to one of the teams out of bounds on the side line. By passing and dribbling, players move the ball near the basket. A score is made when a player shoots

a basket. If the basket is made, the other team starts the play again from out of bounds. If the basket is missed and the same team recovers, they may shoot again. If the basket is missed and the other team recovers, these players must pass the ball at least once before attempting a shot.

A free throw for the other team is awarded for a foul. Two points are scored for a basket and one point for a free throw.

3. *Basketball Twenty One* — Four to five players in a group, lined up at the free throw line. Start game by having one player attempt a goal from the free throw line. If he scores, he throws again from the free throw line and continues until he misses. If he misses, he goes to the end of the line and the next player attempts a goal from the point of recovery. If he scores, he then goes to the free throw line and attempts a goal. If successful, he continues until he misses. Continue until 21 points have been scored. Each basket counts 1 point. The first person to make 21 points is the winner.

4. *Twenty one* — Four or five players in a group. Each player, in turn, makes a shot from the free throw line. He takes a second shot, a follow-up shot — from wherever he recovers the ball. The first shot, if made, counts two points, the second shot counts one point. The object is to make 21 points. A one bounce dribble may be allowed to get in position for the second shot.

*Basketball Rules*

Violations — Infractions of the rules for which the other team is given the ball out of bounds on the side lines.

1. Traveling with the ball — Players may take only one step in any direction while in possession of the ball. Pivoting is legal if one foot remains in contact with the floor.
2. Stepping out of bounds, or hitting the ball out of bounds.
3. Kicking the ball.
4. Holding the ball more than three seconds. (Not an official rule, but good to use with beginners to get them to pass the ball.)
5. Dribbling — In boys' official rules, there is no limit on dribbling. However, with fifth graders it is well to limit the dribble to two or three bounces. A player may not dribble, then stop, then dribble again.
6. In boys' rules, a player may take the ball out of another player's hands. For fifth graders, in order to develop a better passing game and not have a series of tie balls, prohibit players from touching the ball while in the hands of another player or taking the ball out of another's hands.

Fouls — An infraction of the rule against another player for which the penalty is a free throw for the other player. If a player was fouled in the act of shooting, he is awarded two free throws.

1. Holding.
2. Pushing, shoving, hitting.
3. Charging — A player with the ball runs into a defensive player.
4. Unnecessary roughness.

Other rules —

1. A toss-up is held if two players get the ball at the same time (tie ball).
2. A toss-up is held if two players hit the ball out of bounds at the same time.
3. A toss-up is held if each team commits a violation at the same time.
4. Two points are awarded for a basket, one point for a successful free throw.

*Basketball Skills*

Passing — Ball should be held, so far as possible, with the fingers and not with the palm of the hand.
  a. Bounce pass — Ball is held with both hands chest or waist high. Aim ball to hit the floor about two-thirds of the way between passer and catcher.
  b. Chest pass — Standing with left foot slightly forward, ball is held with both hands about chest high. Elbows should be close to the body. (A comomn fault is elbows out to the side.) Pass the ball by pushing it forward. Aim at teammate's chest. Follow through with arms and hands going toward point of aim, and weight transferring to the left foot.
  c. Overhead pass — Ball is held overhead with both hands. Most of the passing impetus comes from the hands and wrists. Used when ball is received overhead, or to pass over a guard.
  d. When passing to a player who is on the run, aim the ball *ahead* of the runner.

Dribbling — See fourth grade ball skills.

Shooting — Ball may be aimed to fall into the basket from the top or to hit the backboard and rebound into the basket.
  a. Underhand shot — Ball is held in both hands, arms hanging relaxed in front of body. Lift arms and release ball at about shoulder height. Pupils will get more distance if they start with slightly bended knees and straighten them as the arms come up.

b. Chest shot — Ball is held at chest level with both hands. Push ball forward by extending arms and stepping forward on left foot. Knee extension helps this shot, too.

c. One hand push shot — Ball is held in both hands, in front of right shoulder, with right hand behind the ball (if right handed) and left hand in front to help balance the ball. Shot is made by pushing the ball forward with the right hand and arm. Follow through with right arm is important. Player should be in forward-backward stride position with weight transferring to left foot as the ball is released.

d. Teach pupils to aim the ball, not just throw it at the basket. They should aim to loop the ball through the top of the basket, or to hit the backboard.

Guarding — Feet should be in small stride position, so that player is able to move quickly in either direction. Arms are extended to the side. At this grade level, the guard should stand beside, or slightly in front of the player he is guarding. The main object is to get the ball. Emphasize, "Never let your opponent get between you and the basket."

6. **Streets and Alleys**

Play area — Inside or outside.

Equipment — None.

Formation — Players line up in parallel lines, arms distance apart, so that there are approximately the same number of players in each line as there are lines.

```
X   X   X   X   X

X   X   X   X   X

X   X   X   X   X

X   X   X   X   X

X   X   X   X   X
```

When the players in each line join hands and face the leader or the teacher, they form 'streets.' When they face to the right from this position and join hands with the players on either side of them, they form 'alleys.'

One player is chosen to be the Runner and another is IT. IT attempts to tag the Runner and the leader calls "Streets" or "Alleys." Upon this signal, the players quickly drop hands, face in the other direction and catch hands with the players on either side of them, thus changing the direction of the chase.

The Runner and IT may run through any aisle and on the outside of the group, but may not break through the clasped hands of the group, nor crawl under their arms.

When IT catches the Runner, a new IT and Runner are selected — or each chooses someone to take their place — and the game continues.

TEACHING SUGGESTIONS

1. If Runner and IT become fatigued, let them choose pupils to take their places.
2. Call "Streets" and "Alleys" unexpectedly and thus add to the interest of the game.

## 7. V-B-B

Play area — Gymnasium or equivalent with basketball basket. Mark out home plate and bases on the floor as for softball.

Equipment — 1 volleyball.

Formation — Two teams with 10 to 15 players on a team. Each team selects three (or four) basket shooters. One team scatters over the field with the shooters taking positions near the basket. The other team lines up as a team at bat.

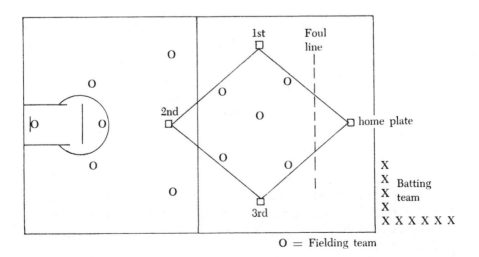

O = Fielding team

The object of the game is to hit the volleyball from home plate into fair territory, using a volleyball serve. Upon hitting the ball, the player runs around the bases, attempting to circle the bases without stopping and reach home plate before the members of the other team can retrieve the ball, make three passes to their respective teammates and pass the ball to their shooters who in turn try to score a basket. If the runner reaches home plate before the ball goes through the basket, the runner scores a point. If, on the other hand, the ball goes through the basket first, the runner is declared out. Three outs retire a side.

RULES

1. Shooters may stand anywhere they wish.
2. The three passes must be to three different players.
3. Fielders may not run or 'travel' with the ball.
4. Batter must hit the ball over the foul line. (Draw a line with chalk about 10 feet in front of home plate.)
5. Batters bat in order as in a softball type game.

TEACHING SUGGESTIONS

1. V-B-B is a combination of volleyball, basketball and baseball skills. It is a good game for boys and girls to play together.
2. The volleyball service: Stand with left side (if right handed) toward the target area. Hold ball on left hand. Swing right arm back and forward to hit the ball with the heel of the right hand. Hand may be open or closed. Serve should end with the right hand pointing in direction ball is to go, and weight on left foot.
3. Alternate boy and girl shooters — boys shooting one inning and girls the next.

## 8. Softball

Fifth graders have had, in this curriculum, considerable experience with softball type games. They should understand the major rules and strategy of the game. Some rules will be new to them including the rules pertaining to batting, foul tip, bunting, pitcher's balk, the third strike rule, etc. It is well to have several chalk sessions on rules before starting softball, and during the season as the need arises.

Play area — One or more softball diamonds.

Equipment — A minimum of four softballs. One ball for every two pupils is preferable.

Review Throw It and Run from the fourth grade. Fifth graders also occasionally like to play Kick Ball (3rd grade.)

*Softball Rules*

There are many variations and interpretations of softball rules throughout the country. The following rules have proved satisfactory for fifth and sixth graders. A second shortstop, to make ten players on a team, may be added to play between first and second base.

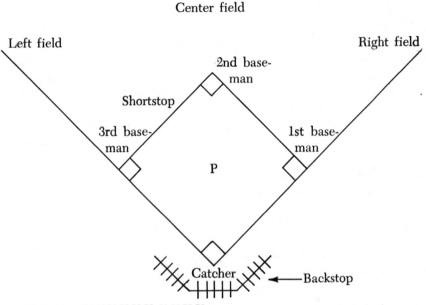

Center field

Left field                                              Right field

2nd base-
man

Shortstop

3rd base-                                          1st baseman                                                man

P

Catcher         ←———Backstop

Batters — X X X X X X  X X X X

1. *The Diamond*: 50 feet between bases; 37 feet pitching distance.
2. *Equipment*: Rubber home plates and bases should be used when available. When not available, substitutes should be provided. Top of bases and of home plate should be level with the ground so that pupils will not trip over the edges.

   Balls should be those provided by the school.

   Bats should be softball bats provided by the school.

   All catchers must wear masks when catching and should wear pads.

   Players may provide their own mitts or gloves:

   a. Mitts may be used only by the catcher and the first baseman.
   b. Gloves may be worn by any players. Lacing or webbing between the thumb and body of a glove or mitt worn by any fielder shall not be more than four inches in length.

No spikes on shoes should be allowed.

There should be a backstop, or 'cage,' behind the catcher. This is a protection and also saves time as it traps balls that the catcher misses.

3.  The team consists of nine players; Catcher, pitcher, first, second and third basemen, shortstop, left, center and right fielders.

4.  *The Game*: Five innings.

5.  *Pitching Rules*:

    a.  Preliminary to pitching, the pitcher shall come to a full stop, facing the batsman, ball held in both hands in front of the body, with both feet squarely on the ground and in contact with the pitcher's plate for NOT LESS THAN ONE SECOND before starting the wind-up.

    b.  The pitch must be an underhand throw; the pitcher is allowed one step, in delivering the ball, and this must be toward home plate.

    c.  The pitcher shall make no motion to pitch without immediately completing the delivery to the batter. Failure to observe these rules shall constitute an illegal pitch, causing a "ball" to be called in favor of the batter, and allowing base runners to advance one base without liability of being put out.

    NOTE: Strict compliance with the pitching rule is necessary. Umpires and teachers should check closely.

6.  *Batting Order*:

    The order in which the players of a team shall bat shall be determined before the game and strictly observed during its progress. In each new inning, the first batter shall be the player who follows the last player to bat in the preceding inning.

7.  *A Batter Shall Be Out If*:

    a.  Three strikes are called or made.

    b.  Any batted fair or foul fly ball is caught.

    c.  A foul tip occurs on the third strike.

    d.  Batter bunts foul after the second strike.

    e.  If he fails to take his correct turn at bat.

    f.  If he interferes with the catcher.

    NOTE: To correct those who may have a habit of throwing the bat after hitting, they may be called out if the bat is thrown.

8.  *Batter Becomes a Baserunner When*:

    a.  He makes a fair hit.

    b.  Four balls have been called on him.

    c.  He is struck by a pitched ball unless he makes no effort to get out of the way, in which case the umpire shall call a ball or a strike.

d. "Third Strike Rule" — "If first base is not occupied, regardless of the number of outs, the batsman becomes a baserunner on three strikes, and the third strike must be caught or he must be thrown out." Page 8, MacGregor Goldsmith, Official Rules. NOTE: Teachers may ignore the "Third Strike Rule" if they wish.

9. *The Baserunner Is Out If*:

a. After hitting a fair ball, he fails to reach first base before it is touched by a player of the opposing team who has possession of the ball.

b. If, when not touching the proper base while the ball is in play, he is touched by the ball in possession of a fielder.
NOTE: In running from home plate to first base, the baserunner may, if he reaches first safely, continue past the base without liability of being put out, provided he makes no attempt to go to second base. Turning toward second shall be considered an attempt to go to second base.

c. After a fly ball is caught, a fielder in possession of the ball touches the base occupied by the baserunner when the ball was pitched, or touches the baserunner with the ball before the baserunner retouches the base.
NOTE: Teach players not to run when batter hits a fly ball, but wait to see whether or not it is caught.

d. When he legally loses the right to the base by reason of the advance of another baserunner, a fielder touches the next base while in possession of the ball. This is known as a "force out."

e. He is struck by a fair hit ball not previously touched by a fielder.

f. He is not touching his base when a legally pitched ball leaves the pitcher's hands. He may not "lead off."

g. He 'slides' to a base or home plate. No sliding is allowed.

h. He does not touch each base as he advances around the diamond.

i. He does not stay within three feet of the base line except when running around a fielder playing the ball.

j. Passes a preceding runner in advancing around the bases. The runner doing the passing is out.

10. *Scoring*:

a. A score is made each time a baserunner legally completes the circuit of the bases and crosses home plate.

b. A run coming in to score on the third out does not count.

c. A runner may not "steal" home. He must be played on, hit in, or forced in.

11. *Terminology*:

a. *Strike*:

(1) A "strike" is called when a pitched ball passes over any part of home plate, before touching the ground, not lower

than the batter's knees and not higher than the batter's shoulders.

(2) The batter swings at the ball without touching it.

(3) The batter bats a foul ball that is not caught.

b. *Balls*: A "Ball" is called when a pitched ball:

(1) Does not pass over any part of the plate between the batter's knees and shoulders.

(2) Touches the ground before passing home plate, provided it is not struck at by the batter.

(3) Is an illegal pitch.

(4) The umpire may call a "Ball":

(a) When the pitcher balks, i.e., Makes any motion to pitch without immediately delivering the ball to the batter.

(b) Each time the pitcher delays the game by failing to deliver the ball to the batsman for a longer period than 20 seconds.

NOTE: At the beginning of each inning the pitcher is allowed to deliver 4 balls to his catcher as a 'warm-up.'

c. *Fair Ball*: Any legally batted ball that comes to rest on fair ground between home and first base, or between home and third base, or that first falls in fair territory beyond first or third base, or that touches the person of an umpire or player in fair territory is a fair hit ball.

d. *Foul Ball*: A foul hit is a legally batted ball that comes to rest in foul territory between home and first base or home and third base, or that rolls past first or third base in foul territory, or that falls in foul territory beyond first or third base, or that while on or over foul territory touches the person of an umpire or player.

e. *Foul Tip*: A foul tip is a foul ball that is caught and held by the catcher. A foul tip is a foul hit ball which does not rise higher than the batter's head, and which goes directly to the catcher's mitt.

f. *Walk*: (Or free bases) A walk shall be given to the batter if the pitcher delivers four pitches which are called 'balls' by the umpire. The batter may advance to first base without liability of being put out.

g. *Overthrow*: Any ball thrown from one fielder to another which goes into foul territory on a play at first, third, or home. Runner may advance one base without liability of being put out.

h. *Wild pitch*: A legally delivered ball so high, low or wide of the plate that the catcher cannot and does not stop and control it with ordinary effort.

"Ball" called on batter. Runners may advance with liability of being put out.

*Softball Skills*

Pupils will need practice on throwing and catching skills. Even major league ball players continue to practice skills. Use squad formations to practice skills, having at least one ball and one bat for each squad.

1. Underhand throw — See 4th grade ball skills.
2. Overhand throw — See 4th grade ball skills.
3. Catching — See 4th grade ball skills.

POINTS TO EMPHASIZE

a. Correct stance. This is essential to a good throw, either underhand or overhand.
b. Grip ball with fingers — do not palm it.
c. Follow through in direction of target.
d. In catching, keep the eyes on the ball, follow the ball into one's hands. 'Give' with the ball at the instant of contact. The fingers must be relaxed to avoid injury. When possible, use two hands to catch the ball.

4. Pitching — Note pitching rule, page 210.
   Pitching, in softball, is an underhand throw.

POINTS TO EMPHASIZE

a. Pitcher must start with feet even and together.
b. Aim at the catcher's mitt.
c. Once the pitcher has started the pitching movement, he must continue and pitch the ball. However, there is no rule limiting the type of wind-up used.
d. As soon as the ball is released, the pitcher should get ready to field any ball that comes toward him.

5. Batting — In this curriculum, batting has not been taught up to this point. It is the only softball skill with which the pupils have had no experience.
   Use a softball bat, not a hard ball bat.
   The right handed batter stands facing home plate with his left side toward the pitcher. He should be in a comfortable stride position, weight slightly on the rear or right foot and far enough away from home plate so that when he swings the bat, the hitting part of the bat will pass over home plate.
   Grasp the bat two to three inches from the end of the bat with the right hand above the left hand. Trademark on the bat should be up. Bat is over right shoulder but not resting on the shoulder, and elbows should be away from the body.
   As the pitcher pitches the ball, the batter swings the bat forward and meets the ball. At first, pupils should not attempt to hit the

ball hard, merely contact it. As the ball is hit, the right elbow
straightens. Follow through with the bat swinging around the left
side as the weight transfers to the left foot.

The bat, during the swing, hit and follow through, should make
a line more or less parallel to the ground.

※      ※      ※

TEACHING SUGGESTIONS

1. The main fault with beginners is that they tend to face the pitcher
   instead of having their side toward the pitcher. It is impossible to
   bat correctly or well unless the side is toward the pitcher.
2. Many have a tendency to stand too close to home plate — to 'crowd'
   the plate. Toes should be 10 to 15 inches away from home plate.
3. Batting requires good hand-eye coordination. If a pupil has trouble
   batting right handed, let him try batting left handed.

Good Batting Stance                    Awaiting the Pitch

6. Fielding Grounders (balls on the ground)
   a. Players should run up on the ball — run up to meet it.
   b. Hands should be together, with fingers pointing to the ground.
      To keep ball from going through, player should turn slightly to

his right and bend the left knee so that the left leg is nearly parallel with the ground. Left knee will be near right foot. Thus, if the hands miss the ball, it will hit the leg.

❊          ❊          ❊

*Skill practice*

Safety procedures should be observed at all times. Keep class spread out on the playground. Pupils must be alert and watch the ball. No bats should ever be thrown or tossed.

1. Use teacher and class formation to practice throwing and catching.

| #7 throws to each person in the line, then takes #6s, place and #1 takes #7's place. | X 1 | X 2 | X 3 | X 4 | X 5 | X 6 |
| --- | --- | --- | --- | --- | --- | --- |
| | | | | X7 | | |

2. Circle formation, 8 to 10 players in a large circle. One pupil in the center. Center player throws the ball hard on the ground or rolls it, toward a circle player. Circle player fields the ball and tosses it back to the center.

    Rotate center players. Circle players may walk around the circle counterclockwise. Keep the circle big.
3. Running Bases — Groups of eight players, four runners and four basemen. Runners, one at a time, run around the bases while catcher and basemen throw the ball from home to first, to second, to third, to home. Runner tries to beat the ball around the base. Throwers must be careful not to hit runner with the ball.
4. Batting practice — In squads. One or two players at bat, one pitcher and the remainder are fielders. Pitcher should be able to get the ball over the home plate to avoid wasting time. Give each pupil ten times to bat. Rotate players.

    Batting tees can be purchased and are good to use for concentrated batting practice.

*One Old Cat* — 5 to 10 players.

One or two players are batters, a pitcher, a catcher, a first baseman and the remainder are fielders. Batter hits the ball and runs to first base and to home again. This may be varied by allowing runner to stop on first base until another runner approaches. Outs are made the same way as in softball, and fielders move up as outs are made. When batter makes five scores, without being put out, rotate.

*Work-Up* — 8 to 12 players.

Three batters, pitcher, catcher, first, second and third basemen, and the remainder in the field.

When an out is made, all fielders move up as follows:
Left field to center field;
center field to right field;
right field to third base;
third base to shortstop;
shortstop to second base;
second base to first base;
first base to pitcher;
pitcher to catcher;
catcher to batter.

Batter, when out, goes to left field. Batter stays up until he makes an out.

The game may be played that when a fielder catches a fly ball, he changes places with the batter, and the other fielders do not move up.

Outs are made the same way as in Softball. If no umpire is available, do not count 'balls.' Count only hits, foul balls and strikes where the batter swings and misses the ball.

GENERAL TEACHING SUGGESTIONS

1. Give pupils experience in umpiring.
2. Razzing of the umpire and opposing players — a part of the adult game of baseball — has no place with elementary age children.
3. Since softball is a fairly inactive game for most of the players, the warm-up of running and calisthenics should be vigorous.
4. A typical lesson would include the following:
   a. Warm-up — 5 to 8 minutes
   b. Skill practice — 8 to 10 minutes
   c. Play game — 15 to 20 minutes

## SIXTH GRADE GAMES

*Review* —
*Tag Games*
*Prison Dodge Ball*
*Bombardment*
*V-B-B*
1. Soccer (fall)
2. Flag Football (fall)

3. **Beater Goes Round**
4. **Volleyball (winter)**
5. **Corner Dodge Ball**
6. **Basketball Lead-up Games (winter)**
7. **Last Couple Out**
8. **Softball (spring)**

1. **Soccer**

Play area — Soccer field — from 240' to 300' long and 150' to 180' wide. Football field may be used. Goalkeeper's area should be marked.

Equipment — Soccer ball.

Formation — Two teams of 11 players each.

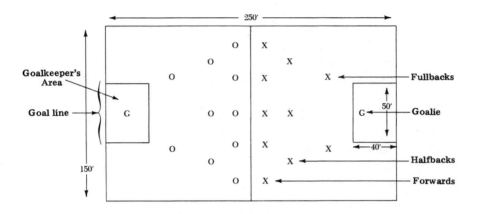

Review Soccer unit from the fifth grade. If pupils have played no soccer, go back to Line Soccer, fourth grade.

The object of the game is to make a score by kicking the ball through the opponent's goal. The ball must be advanced by the feet, legs and body. Use of hands or arms to advance the ball is a foul.

RULES

1. Game started by — Place kick on the center line.
   Rules for kick-off:
   a. All opponents must be six yards away.
   b. No player may cross the center line until the ball has been kicked.
   c. Kicker may not play the ball again until it has been touched by someone else.
   d. Ball must go forward.
2. Out of Bounds play
   a. Player on team opposite to the one which kicked the ball out of bounds throws it in with a two handed overhead throw.
   b. Ball is thrown in at the spot where it crossed the side line.
   c. All players must be at least 6 yards away from the ball.
   d. All players must be 'on side' at the time the ball is thrown.

3. After a score
   a. The ball is put in play by a center kick by the team that was scored upon.
   b. Kick-off rules apply.
4. Free Kicks — are awarded for
   a. Pushing another player.
   b. Holding, tripping.
   c. Using hands or arms to advance the ball.
   d. Off side.
   e. Unnecessary roughness.
   Rules for free kicks are the same as for kick-off except that the ball may be kicked in any direction.
   Free kicks are taken on the spot where the foul occurred.
5. Goalkeeper
   a. Goalkeeper may use his hands in the goal area.
   b. He may pass, kick or throw the ball, but may not take more than two steps with the ball.
   c. He may play out of the goal area but may not use his hands out of the goal area.

   Offside Rule — A player must be on line with, or behind the ball on free kicks, out of bounds plays and the kick-off. Behind the ball means on the side closest to his own goal.

Teaching Suggestions

1. The main difference between fifth and sixth grade soccer is that in the sixth grade all players, except the goalkeeper, play in the center area. The goalkeeper may pass or throw the ball, use a place kick, drop kick or punt.
2. Teams should wear some identification. Use pinnies, football flags or strips of cloth tied around the wrist, arm or waist.
3. Gym shoes should be worn, not street shoes.
4. Players should learn to play their positions and not run all over the field. Players should aim to stay in approximate positions, in relation to teammates, as on the diagram. Forwards are considered the offensive players, halfbacks play both offense and defense. Fullbacks and the goalkeeper are defensive players.
5. Soccer (sometimes called soccer football, or just football) is played by more people in the world than any other game. It is especially popular in Europe and South America where the professional players are comparable to our major league baseball players in prestige and salary. It is a vigorous game, requiring skill, endurance and intelligence.

## 2. Flag Football

Play area — Playground area 240′ to 300′ long and 150′ to 180′ wide. Football goals, if available, should be 18 feet wide and the cross bar should be 10′ above the ground.

Equipment — Footballs. Junior size balls are preferable. Football flags. These may be made of cloth 3″ wide and 20″ to 24″ long. Football flags, made of plastic material, can be purchased from sports stores. Each player wears two flags, one on each side, tucked under the belt, or one in front and one in the back. At least half of the flag must be visible.

Formation — Two teams of 11 players on a team.

The object of the game is to get the ball across the oppoent's goal line by carrying it across or by making a completed pass across the goal line. Each team has four consecutive tries — called 'downs' — to score. If no score is made, the opposing team gets the ball on the spot where the previous play ended and it then attempts to score. If a score is made, the team which made the score kicks off to the 'receiving team' and the receiving team then attempts to make a score.

Play begins with the kick-off. On subsequent plays, the center bends over the ball, his halfbacks are behind him and the remainder of the players are on the scrimmage line even with the ball. The center passes the ball between his legs to a back who tries to advance the ball toward the opponent's goal by running with it or by passing it to a teammate, or by kicking the ball. When the ball is kicked, it

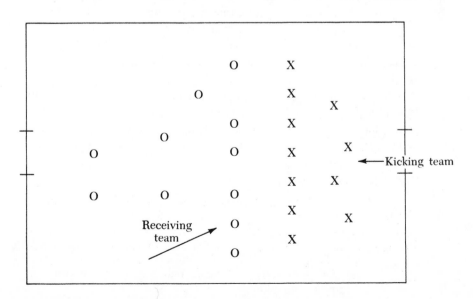

automatically goes over to the other team at the spot where the ball hit the ground. Thus, if no score has been made on the first, second or third downs, it is wise to kick the ball so that it will be as far away from one's goal as possible.

A player is stopped when an opponent grabs his flag (there is no tackling). The succeeding play starts on the spot where the runner was 'tackled.'

RULES

1. The kick-off. The ball is put in play at the beginning of each half and after a score has been made by a kick-off from a point 25 yards from the kicking team's goal. Players on the kicking team may not be ahead of the ball. The restraining line for the receiving team is a line 10 yards in advance of the ball. All players must stay back of their restraining line until the ball is kicked. If the ball does not travel 10 yards on the kick-off, it is brought back and kicked over.

   If the ball goes over the goal line on a punt or the kick-off, it is brought out to the receiving team's 20 yard line.

   The receiver of the kick-off may advance the ball by running or throwing a lateral pass (pass thrown toward his own goal line.)

2. Play. Each play is started by the center of the offensive team who throws the ball (through his legs) to a back. As soon as the ball is thrown, all players may move.

   On plays from scrimmage, the ball may be advanced by forward or lateral passes and by running. Forward passes may be thrown from any point behind the line of scrimmage.

   If a forward pass is not caught, it counts as a down and the ball is put in play again at the same spot.

   All plays must originate by the center passing the ball to a backfield player. When a team punts, regardless of the down, it loses the ball.

   A team which desires to kick from scrimmage must signify its intentions by calling, 'punt formation.'

   A player is down and the ball is dead when the opponent captures the flag of the ball carrier, or when the ball carrier's knee touches the ground.

The ball is also dead when:

   It goes out of bounds or the player carrying it steps out of bounds.
   It strikes the goal posts.
   A forward pass is incomplete.

   The first player to touch a fumbled ball is given the ball at the spot of the fumble (no pile-up).

3. Scoring. Carrying the ball over the goal line or completing a pass over the goal line constitutes a touchdown and counts six points.

4. Fouls and Penalties. For penalties which occur within 10 yards of a team's goal line the ball is not placed closer to the goal line than 1/2 the distance between the scrimmage line and the goal line.

   a. Offside on scrimmage line — 5 yards.
   b. Stiff arming — 15 yards.
   c. Blocking shall be done by the use of the arms and body without the use of the hands. Both feet must remain on the ground when blocking. Screen and bear blocks are permitted; (screen is a standing block; bear is a side block with both feet on the ground.) Penalty for illegal block — 15 yards.
   d. Penalty for grabbing the flag before the player gets the ball — 15 yards.
   e. Penalty for tackling — 15 yards.
   f. Penalty for unnecessary roughness — 15 yards.
   g. Receiver of punt or kick-off shall not throw forward pass — 15 yards.
   h. Backfield shall not move toward line of scrimmage before the ball is passed by the center — 5 yards.
   i. Punts shall not be blocked by opposing team — 10 yards.
   j. Fouls include tripping, holding, tackling, pushing, striking, kneeing —15 yards.
   k. Penalty for interference with pass receiver — offensive team gets ball, first down. (A defensive player must not interfere with an opponent endeavoring to receive a pass except in an honest attempt to get the ball.)
   l. Using hands to hold, pull or in any way handicap an opponent — 15 yards.
   m. Taking more than 30 seconds in the huddle or delaying the game for any other reason — 5 yards.
   n. Unsportsmanlike conduct — 15 yards.
   o. Illegal pass, illegal receiver, (legal receivers are ends and backfield players), illegal lifting ball off the ground — Penalty is loss of down.
   p. Piling up on fumble — 15 yards.
   q. Player may not use his hands to prevent an opponent from grabbing his flag — 15 yards.

TEACHING SUGGESTIONS

1. If the sixth grade teacher is completely unfamiliar with the game of football, it would be advisable to omit this game and concentrate on soccer. There are several good reasons for this —

a. There is the possibility of injury to pupils if they are permitted to play flag football without strict observance of the rules.

b. Unless the teacher has some basic knowledge of the game, the pupils' achievement will be insignificant, and they may even develop incorrect habits and concepts.

c. Soccer is an excellent game for fitness and can be challenging and interesting to the pupils. There is every justification for considering it the major fall activity in the 6th grade.

2. Gym shoes should be worn; no street shoes or cleated shoes are allowed.

3. To officiate, stay as even with the ball as possible. Blow the whistle immediately when a player's flag is pulled to stop the play, thus preventing piling on and rough play.

4. Girls should be allowed to play flag football too. Their enjoyment of the game as spectators will be greatly enhanced if they have had some opportunity to play. If rules are strictly enforced, there should be little danger of injuries.

5. Rotate team positions so that the same players do not always get the choice positions.

6. For skill practice, divide class into groups of 4 to 6 pupils with each group having a ball.

*Football Skills*

1. Throwing — Throwing a football is, because of the shape of the ball, a different skill than throwing a round ball. The throw is basically an overhand throw. The ball is held slightly behind it's center, resting on the palm of the throwing hand, fingers spread and gripping the ball. The other hand may be used on top of the ball to help balance it. Left foot is forward for a right handed thrower, and the body turned so that the left side is toward the target. Bring ball back to the right ear, throw it forward with a full arm movement, weight transferring to the left foot. Follow through with arm pointing in direction ball is to go.

2. Carrying the ball — Carry the ball against the body in the notch formed by the arm and the elbow. Fingers should be over the end of the ball to hold it securely.

3. Punting — Hold the ball along its sides with both hands in front of the body about waist high. Feet slightly apart. Step forward on left foot as the ball is dropped and kicked with the right foot. Contact should be made on the top of the foot. Follow through with kicking leg.

*Skill Practice*

1. Punt Back. Four to six on a team. The object of the game is to punt the ball over the opponent's goal line. Each time the ball is kicked over the line, one point is scored. Teams kick alternately.

    Team A, standing on their own goal line, kick the ball. Team B recovers the ball at the spot where it hit the ground, or a player may catch the ball on the fly. If a player catches the ball, he may punt back immediately. If the ball hits the ground, players on the kicking team must line up even with the ball before the kick is made. No one may interfere with a player attempting to catch the ball. Penalty is that the ball is moved back toward the player's goal five yards.

2. Keep Away — Play with Football. See fifth grade basketball unit.

3. Newcomb — Play with football. See fifth grade game, Net ball.

Carrying the Football

## 3. Beater Goes Round

Play area — Inside or outside.

Equipment — A rolled up newspaper.

Formation — Players stand in a circle, facing the center with their hands grasped behind their backs. One person is IT and carries the newspaper.

IT goes around the outside of the circle and places the beater in the hands of one of the players. This person immediately begins striking the player next to him (on his right) and the player so hit runs once around the circle and back to place, attempting to outrun his pursuer and so avoid being hit. The player with the Beater follows the runner, striking him as often as he can.

Beater is then placed in the hands of another player and the game continues as before.

TEACHING SUGGESTIONS

1. Don't allow pupils to 'beat' too hard.
2. By the time that pupils are sixth graders, they should be able to see that everyone gets a turn.
3. Ten to twelve in a circle is a good number. If the class is large, have two games going simultaneously.

## 4. Volleyball

Play area — Volleyball court, inside or outside. 60' long and 30' wide, divided by a center line.

Equipment — A volleyball net. If a net is not available, a rope may be used. Top of the net, or rope, should be about 6 feet from the floor. Strips of cloth may be tied to the rope to make it more visible. Volleyballs.

Formation — Two teams with eight to ten players on a team.

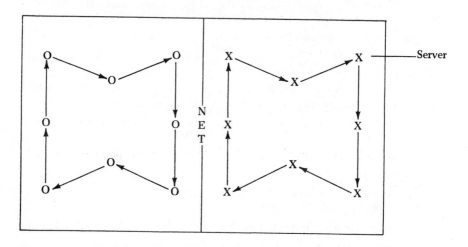

The object of the game is to hit the ball across the net in such a a way that the opposing team cannot return it.

RULES

1. Scoring — Scores are made only by the serving team. A point is made each time the receiving team fails to legally return the ball.

    If the serving team fails to make a legal return, the other team gets the ball for service. This is called 'side out' and neither team make a score. Games may be played for two 15 minute halves or to a certain number of points, i.e. 15 or 21 points.

2. Serving — The player in the right back corner of the court is the server. Players rotate when their team gets the ball for service, as indicated on the diagram.

    The server stands behind the baseline and serves the ball by hitting it with one hand. The hit may be overhand, or underhand, with open or closed hand. The server, on the first serve, has two chances to make a good serve. An assisted serve may be used in which one player, besides the server, may hit the ball once.

3. Playing rules —
   a. The ball must be hit, not caught or held on the hands.
   b. A player may hit the ball twice in succession, but no more until the ball has been hit by another player.
   c. Only three players on a team may hit the ball before it must be returned to the other side.
   d. The ball may be hit with one or both hands, with open or closed fist.
   e. The ball must be hit with the hands or forearms and may not touch any other part of the body.
   f. A player may not touch the net, nor step under it nor reach over it to hit the ball.

4. Penalties —
   a. If the serving team commits a foul, they lose the ball and the other team wins the serve. No points are scored.
   b. If the receiving team commits a foul, the serving team wins a point.
   c. If both teams foul, it is a double foul and the point is replayed.

5. Out of Bounds —
   a. Any ball which hits the ground outside of the boundary lines is out of bounds.
   b. A player may step out of bounds to hit the ball, but the ball must cross the net in bounds.
   c. A ball falling on the boundary line is considered good.
   d. A ball which hits the ceiling is out of bounds.

*Volleyball Skills*

1. Service — (Sixth grade pupils may stand inside the baseline if they have difficulty getting the ball across the net.)

   The server stands in forward-backward stride position with the left food forward (right handed pupil) and weight on both feet. The ball rests on his left hand. Look at the ball. Swing the right arm forward, elbow almost straight and hit the ball with the 'heel' of the right hand. The hand may be open or the fingers may be tucked under. Follow through with the arm pointing in the direction of the target as the weight transfers to the left foot.

2. Overhand hit — The hands are nearly together with the thumbs to center, palms facing forward and fingers relaxed. The player needs to be under the ball. Hit the ball upward and forward using the fingers to control the direction. Whenever possible, use two hands on the ball.

3. Underhand hit — When balls are received waist level or lower the underhand return is used. This is similar to an overhand hit except that the fingers point toward the floor with the little fingers together. Always use two hands on the ball.

Volleyball Serve

*Volleyball Skill Practice*

1. Bounce Ball — The rules are the same as for volleyball, except that the ball is allowed to hit the floor once and bounce before it must be returned to the other side.

2. Keep It Up — With half of each team on opposite sides of the net, volley the ball back and forth across the net. See how many consecutive hits can be made without a miss. Count each hit as one. Teams may compete with each other to see who can make the highest number of hits.

   The same game can be played in circle formation without a net.

3. The ball may be volleyed against the wall. Divide the class into as many groups as there are balls. Line up in file formation. The player volleys the ball against the wall as many times as he can without a miss. When he misses, the next person takes his return.

TEACHING SUGGESTIONS

1. Whether or not sixth graders can successfully play volleyball depends upon their level of skill and their maturity. If the class does not play well enough to enjoy this game, play Net Ball (5th grade) or Bounce Volley. It might be well to start the volleyball unit with one of these games before progressing to volleyball.

2. The game is more interesting if there are no more than ten on a team. If the class is large, establish a waiting line (see 5th grade Net Ball) or have two games going simultaneously.

3. Volleyball is a good game to use with boy and girl mixed teams. Girls usually do as well as boys. There are some differences between boys' and girls' rules. At this grade level, it is probably wise to use girls' rules for all players.

4. Players must play their positions and not run all over the court. Each player is responsible for balls that come into his 'area' on the floor.

5. Pupils should attempt to hit balls to their teammates who are playing near the net and they, in turn hit them across to the other team.

6. A referee is necessary. He should position himself at one end of the net.

7. In recent years there have been changes in volleyball rules and skills. "Power Volleyball" is played in some junior high schools and most senior high schools. The main changes are (1) the use of the closed hand or fist instead of the open palm, and (2) only one hit per player (instead of two) and three hits by a team before returning the ball. If sixth graders are strong and skilled enough to play the official game, the teacher may want to use these rules.

   (Secure rule books from the American Association for Health, Physical Education and Recreation, 1201 Sixteenth Street, N. W., Washington, D. C. 20036, or college bookstores.)

## 5. Corner Dodge Ball

Play area — Gymnasium or equivalent. Mark bases, approximately 6′ x 8′ with chalk, on the floor in each corner, inside of the basketball court boundaries.

Equipment — Two rubber balls, soccer balls or volley balls.

Formation — The class is divided into four groups, with each group on one of the bases. Two players, called Captains, are in the center of the floor, each with a ball.

The leader, or teacher, calls a number, e.g. "5." The pupils must run counterclockwise through five bases while the Captains try to hit them with the ball as in Dodge Ball. When the groups reach their fifth base, they stop. All who are hit are eliminated and the winner is the last one to be hit.

The leader may call any number from one to twenty. All hits must be waist level or lower, and must be on a direct throw from the Captain.

Captains must stay in the center of the floor except to retrieve a ball, after which they must go back to the center before throwing again.

If a runner steps out of a base, he cannot go back. Runners are allowed ten seconds to get out of a base after the leader has called a number.

TEACHING SUGGESTIONS

1. Children must watch where they are running in order to avoid collisions.
2. This is a vigorous game with considerable activity of a running nature.

## 6. Basketball Lead-up Games

Play area — Gymnasium with at least two basketball baskets, or black-topped area outside with basketball baskets.

Equipment — Basketballs. Some means of identifying players such as pinnies, T shirts, or strips of cloth tied around wrist, waist or arm.

See fifth grade unit on Basketball for basketball rules, skills and practice games. Review all. A higher level of skill and comprehension should be expected from sixth graders.

*Additional Skill Drills*

1. Dribble, pivot and pass — Five to eight players line up in a single file. The first pupil dribbles the ball to a designated mark, 15′ to 20′ ahead of the line, stops, pivots around to face the second player

in line, passes ball back to him and goes to the end of the line. Specify type of pass to be used. Do not race. Concentrate on doing the skills correctly and smoothly.

2. Single line. Dribble around a mark or object such as a chair, and pass back to the next person in line.

3. Players line up in a single file about as far away from the basket as the free throw line. First person dribbles the ball one bounce, shoots, recovers the ball, passes it back to the next person and goes to the end of the line. Vary this with different positions around the basket, i.e. right side, center and left side.

*Practice Games*

1. Line basketball — Players arranged as in diagram. Each team has three or four players in the center area who play as in regular basketball. The remainder of the players position themselves on the sidelines, with approximately equal space between each player.

    Center players may pass to a lineman at any time and should be encouraged to do so frequently in order to make the game more interesting. Linemen must stay on or behind the sidelines. Out of bounds ball are tossed into a center player by a linesman nearest the ball.

    Penalty for violations is to give the ball to a linesman on the opposite team for him to pass in to one of his center players.

    After a score has been made, or after three minutes of playing time, players rotate according to number. Numbers 5, 6, 7, and 8 go into the center and others move up. Numbers 1, 2, 3, and 4 go on to the line in numbers 12, 11, 10 and 9 positions.

2. In and Out Basketball — Organize class into teams with 5 or 6 players on a team. Two teams play while the others observe. At

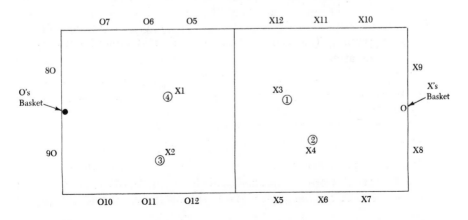

three minutes intervals, rotate teams. The scores of teams may be combined and this adds to the interest. For example, the Reds and the Blues may play against the Greens and the Whites. First, Reds play the Greens. After three minutes, the Blues plays the Whites, and so on. Combine scores of Reds and Blues and those of the Greens and the Whites.

TEACHING SUGGESTIONS

1. If further clarification of rules is needed, secure a copy of the current issue of the Official Basketball Rulebook, available at sports stores.
2. It is desirable, at this grade level, to have girls play with girls and boys with boys. In a game such as Line Basketball, the groups could be so arranged that either boys, or girls, are in the center area at the same time.
3. Basketball should not be considered a major activity at the sixth grade level. The teacher's objective should be to give the pupils an opportunity to practice skills and to give them some idea of the game.

## 7. Last Couple Out

Play area — Inside or Outside.

Equipment — None.

Formation — Pupils line up in partners, in one line all facing the same direction. A single player stands in front of the line with his back to them. He must not turn his head around, but must look straight ahead. He is IT.

IT calls, "Last Couple Out." The pair at the end of the line run forward and try to join hands with each other somewhere in front of IT without being tagged by IT. When a runner comes within vision of the caller, IT may chase him. If IT fails to tag either runner, he remains IT. If he tags a runner, he takes that player's partner and they go to the head of the line. The person caught becomes the new IT.

TEACHING SUGGESTIONS

1. If there are more than six or eight couples in the line, have two games going simultaneously.
2. Set boundaries. Do not let pupils run too far away from the group.
3. Boys and girls like to play this game together.

## 8. Softball

Review all softball rules and skills from fifth grade unit on softball. Work on fielding and batting skills. Help individuals whose skills are poor. For batting, check these items:

1. Check position at plate; side should be toward pitcher.
2. Emphasize *meeting* the ball with the bat. Do not try to hit hard.
3. Be sure grip on bat is correct. Grip a few inches from the end of the bat.
4. Let pupil try batting from either side of the plate.

In throwing — check these items:

1. Be sure starting position, or stance, is correct.
2. Ball should be gripped with fingers and thumb.
3. Follow through should be smooth and continuous; in direction of the throw.

Fielding problems — May be done orally, on blackboard or in action on the playing field.

1. Runner on first base; batter hits to third baseman.
   (Throw to second base, then to first.)
2. Ball hit to second baseman.
   (Throw to first.)
3. Runner on first and third, batter hits to shortstop.
   (Throw to home to keep run from scoring.)
4. Runner on third base, ball hit to right fielder.
   (Throw to home if chance to get the runner; otherwise, to first.)
   (Runner must stay on third until ball is caught.)
5. Bases loaded, ball hit to pitcher.
   (Throw to home, then to first base.)
6. Runner on second base, ball hit to first.
   (First baseman step on first base, then throw to third.)
7. Ball hit over the head of the center fielder.
   (Center fielder chase the ball, second baseman go out to 'relay' the ball in, shortstop cover second base. Throw ball in to base *ahead* of the runner.)
8. Runners on first and second base. Fly foul ball hit behind the catcher.
   (Catcher gets the ball, throws to third base. Runners hold base.)
9. Runner on first base. Ball hit to second baseman.
   (Second baseman step on second base, throw to first.)
10. Runner on third base. Ball hit to first baseman.
    (First baseman step on first, throw to home. If not in position to step on first base, throw immediately to home.)

Pupils may think of other possible plays. Catcher should remember to step up on the inside of home plate whenever the ball is hit.

TEACHING SUGGESTIONS

1. Play Work-up and One Old Cat fairly frequently as these games give the players more practice than the regular game of Softball.
2. Play a game which continues consecutively from day to day for a total of five or seven innings.

3. Give pupils experience in umpiring, but be there to observe and make decisions if necessary.
4. Be sure that all pupils are given opportunities to play different positions.
5. Enforce safety provisions at all times.

## CLASSROOM GAMES

There are times during the school year when, because of special events, conflicts or inclement weather, it is necessary to have physical education in the classroom. Activities which create a lot of noise, which might cause something in the room to be broken or which would be dangerous to children moving in a limited space cannot be done in the classroom. It is possible to do some calisthenics in the room whether desks and chairs are movable or not. Certain 'quiet' games can be played in the classroom. This type of game, while not providing the opportunity for exercise and skill development, provides a break in the classroom routine and is relaxing and enjoyable to children.

1. **Huckle Buckle Beanstalk** (primary grades)

    All children, but one, put their heads down on their desks and cover their eyes. IT hides some selected object (a beanbag, a thimble, a rolled up paper, etc.) somewhere in the room. The object must be visible when one is close to it. When IT is ready, children raise their heads and walk around the room looking for the object. When they see it, they return to their seats and say "Huckle Buckle Beanstalk." They should not let others know where the object is. The game continues until most — or all — of the class has found the object. The one who first spotted it, becomes IT for the next game.

2. **Seven Up** (all grades)

    All pupils in the class, except seven, fold their arms on their desks and put their heads down on their arms. One of their thumbs is sticking up. The 'seven up' go around the room, each child touching one person's thumb. The leader says "Seven Up" and those who have been touched stand up. In turn, each tries to guess who touched them. Each gets only one guess. If he guesses correctly, he takes that person's place among the seven. If he does not guess correctly, players remain in their same positions.

3. **Little Mouse** (primary grades)

    One child is selected to be IT. He sits in a chair at the front of the room with his back to the class and eyes closed. Others (teacher indicates who) tiptoe noiselessly around him and one child touches the chair when they are close enough. When IT is sure that he heard someone touch his chair, he calls, "Stand" and all must stop where they are.

It says, "Little mouse, little mouse
What are you after?"

The little mouse squeals 'cheese' and IT tries to guess who the mouse is. If he guesses correctly, he retains his position. If not, another child takes his place.

4. **Buzz** (Fourth grade and up)

A number between two and nine is selected to be the 'buzz' number. "Seven" is most often used. The group starts counting around the room consecutively. When that number, a number containing it, or a multiple of it is called, the word 'buzz' is said instead. If a player says the number where he should say 'buzz,' a point is scored against him, or he may pay a forfeit. If 7 were used, 71 would be 'buzz one.' Seventy-seven would be 'buzz, buzz.' Start over when 100 is reached. The lowest score wins.

'Fizz — Buzz' is when two numbers are used, one to be the 'fizz' number and one the 'buzz' number.

5. **Indian Running** (primary grades)

Five or six players are chosen to leave the room. These players arrange themselves in any order, return to the room, run once around it and leave again. When they return, the class tries to name the correct order of their line-up. The child who is successful may choose five other pupils to leave with him and the game is repeated.

6. **Cities** (Third grade and up)

The first player names a city, and the next player must name one beginning with the last letter of the city just given. For example, the first player calls 'Washington,' the second 'New Orleans,' the third 'Syracuse,' the fourth 'Elmira,' and so forth. Each player must name the city before a count of ten. Those who fail to name a city are eliminated. The one who stays in the longest is the winner.

The same game can be played with other categories such as rivers, foods, states.

7. **Arithmetic Spin the Platter** (Third grade and up)

Players number off consecutively around a circle with numbers above 10. There is one player in the center. He spins the platter and identifies the one who is to catch it by calling an arithmetical device to indicate the player's number. Player 15 might be indicated, for instance, as number 5 x 3, or number 25 — 10. Any one number process, or all four may be used. If the player catches the platter, he is IT for the next time.

The platter may be a paper plate, lid, pie pan or anything that will spin. The game may be played with a balloon in which case the player must catch it before it touches the floor.

8. **I Say Stoop** (primary grades)

The teacher or leader stands in front of the players and gives the command, "I say STOOP" or "I say STAND." The players follow her commands, not her actions. She may stoop when she says stand, or stand when she says stoop. Anyone not following her commands becomes IT (or may be eliminated from the game) and takes the place of the leader.

9. **Simon Says** (all grades)

One player who is the leader stands in front of the room. Other pupils stand and face the leader. The leader gives commands some of which are prefaced with "Simon Says," and some of which are not. The group is to do everything which 'Simon Says' but must not obey any commands without 'Simon Says.' Any child who follows the wrong command, must sit down. When the leader has so caught three pupils, he joins the class and another leader is chosen. The three players may get into the game again as the new leader begins, or players may be eliminated from the game when they are caught.

The game may be played with "O'Grady Says" instead of "Simon." Typical commands might be — hands on hips; touch your knee; right face, left face, about face; stoop, jump, etc.

10. **Find the Leader** (all grades)

Children stand in a circle around the room. A player is sent out of the room. One player in the room is selected to be the leader. He starts any motions he chooses with his feet, legs, arms, heads, etc. The other children follow his motions. The child who left the room is called back. He watches the children change activities and tries to locate the leader who changes the activity.

11. **Memory Run** (all grades)

One child runs quickly and touches any object in the room, naming it as he touches it and returns to his seat. A second child touches the same object the first child did, then touches and names another object. A third child touches and names in order the objects that the first two children touched. And so on. Continue until a mistake is made. Select different children for the next game.

12. **Busy Bee** (primary and Fourth grade)

Couples are in scattered formation; there is one extra player who is the 'caller.' The caller gives directions, i.e. 'Face to Face' or 'Back to Back' or 'Face the Windows' or Stoop,' etc. When he calls, "Busy Bee," all players must change partners, and the caller tries to get a partner for himself. The extra child becomes the caller. Children should not have the same partner twice.

13. **I'm Very Very Tall** (primary grades)

Children stand in a circle. One player is in the center with his hands over his eyes. Players in the circle recite the verse,

"I'm very very tall,
I'm very very small,
Sometimes tall, sometimes small,
Guess which I am now."

When the verse tells the players to be tall, they stand on tip-toe and raise their arms; when they are told to be small, they stoop down as low as possible. On the last line, they are tall or small as the teacher directs with her hand. The child in the center tries to guess whether they are tall or small. The child in the center chooses another player to take his place.

14. **Chase the Animal Around the Circle** (all grades)

An object — beanbag, book, chalk or anything else easily available in the room — is given the name of an animal and passed around the circle. The second time around, another object — with the name of another animal — is introduced to chase the first animal around the circle. The game becomes progressively more difficult by increasing the number of objects — each with an animal's name — around the circle.

15. **Object Passing Relays** (Third grade and up)

Some relays can be done in the classroom without too much commotion, particularly those that involve passing something from one child to the next. If the room is arranged in rows, each row may be a team.

a. Pass a beanbag or any other suitable object to the person behind, to the back of the row and to the front again. The team which completes the passing first, is the winner.
b. Vary the relay by passing different objects — or several objects.
c. Children may stand facing the front of the room, stand sideways or sit at their desks while playing these object passing relays.

# RECREATIONAL GAMES

There are some recreational games which are enjoyed by children of most ages in the elementary school. These are good to have available for noon hour, recess and other supervised play periods.

## RECREATIONAL GAMES

1. Four Square
2. Tether Ball
3. Hopscotch

4. Croquet
5. Table Tennis
6. Sidewalk Tennis

## 1. Four Square

Play area — Hard topped surface, 16' x 16' divided into four squares.

Equipment — One rubber ball.

Formation — One player in each square.

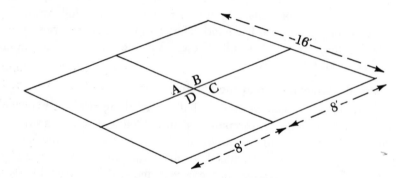

The object of the game is to advance to "A" square and remain there as long as possible.

The player in "A" Square starts the game by letting the ball bounce in his own square and then hitting it underhanded so that it bounces in any of the other squares. If it goes into square "C," the player in that square must hit it underhanded, on the first bounce, into some other square. The player in that square tries to hit it into some other square. Play continues until someone misses, hits the ball wrong or hits it out of bounds. When that happens, he goes to square "D" and the others move up one.

Fouls

1. Failure to return the ball to another square.
2. Striking the ball with the fist.

3. Causing the ball to land on any inside line. (If the ball hits on an outside line, it is considered good.)

4. Allowing the ball to touch any part of the body except the hand or hands.

TEACHING SUGGESTIONS

1. If other players wish to play, a line is formed and when a player misses, instead of going to square "D," this player goes to the end of the line and the first player in the line moves into square "D,"

2. 'Two Square' may be played with two players, with one line between them. Outside boundaries are helpful, but not necessary. Players should agree on where 'outside' is.

3. It is desirable to have the lines painted on the playing area. The court may be outlined in chalk, however.

## 2. Tether Ball

Play area — Inside or Outside. Hard surface area is preferable.

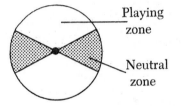

Playing zone

Neutral zone

Circle 20' in diameter. Anywhere on this circle locate two points 17' 4" apart. From these two points draw two lines through the center of the circle.

Equipment — A pole 10' high. Tether ball attached to a rope which is attached to the top of the pole. Ball should be 3' from the ground. A 'foul mark' should be marked on the pole 5' from the ground.

Formation — Two players, one on each side of the pole.

The player who serves first is chosen by lot. After the first game, the winner serves first. One player stands in each court. The server starts the game by tossing the ball into the air and striking it with his hand or fist in the direction he chooses. His opponent may not strike the ball until it passes him on its second swing around the pole. As the ball travels, each player tries to hit it in an effort to wind the rope completely around the pole. The player who winds the rope completely around the pole above the foul line and in the direction of his play, wins the game. The opponent must hit the ball at least once. During the play each player must remain in his own playing zone. The ball may be hit more than once consecutively by the same player. The ball may be hit with one or both hands, open or closed. Players may not wear gloves.

FOULS

1. Hitting the ball with any part of the body other than the hands or forearms.
2. Catching or holding the ball.
3. Touching the pole or base with any part of the body.
4. Hitting the rope.
5. Playing the ball while standing outside of the playing zone.
6. Stepping on the neutral zone lines, or on or over the dividing line.
7. Throwing the ball.
8. Winding ball around pole below the foul mark.

SCORING

The game is won by the player who first winds the rope completely around the pole or by forfeit because of a foul committed by his opponent. A set consists winning of four games out of seven.

PENALTY

A player who commits any of the fouls listed above forfeits the game to his opponent. Play stops immediately after a foul has been committed.

TEACHING SUGGESTIONS

1. If there are no court marks, draw a line dividing the playing area in half.
2. Poles are best when they are installed in cement permanently. If it is desirable to be able to move the poles, they may be set in cement in old tires.
3. This is a good game for 'releasing tensions.'

3. **Hopscotch**

Play area — Level hard surface area. May be sidewalk, blacktop, etc.

Equipment — Each player needs a 'puck.' This may consist of a scrap of wood or a small stone.

Formation — One to six persons may play at one time.

Procedure —

1. Player stands outside of space #1. He throws the puck inside space #1, hops into #1 on one foot, picks up puck and hops out.

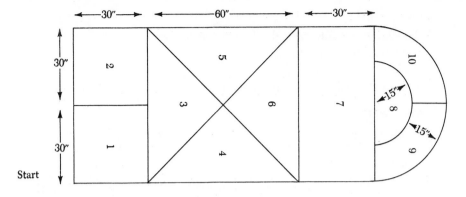

2. Throws the puck into space #2. Hops into# 1, #2, picks up puck, hops to #1 and out. All hops are on one foot.

3. Throws the puck into space #3. Stands on one foot, leaps into squares landing with right foot in #1, left foot in #2, hops on either foot into #3, picks up puck, jumps on both feet — right in #2, left in #1 — and out.

4. Throws puck into #4. Advances as in stunt 3, retrieves puck and returns.

5. Throws puck into #5 space. Advances as in #4, retrieves puck and returns.

6. Throws puck into space #6. Advances as in Stunt 3 up to space #3, leaps and lands with right foot in space 4 and left foot in space 5; one foot in space 6, retrieves puck, lands with left foot in space 4, right foot in space 5 and out.

7. Throws puck into space 7. Adance as in stunt #6, land on both feet in space 7. Proceed as before.

8. Throw puck into space 8. Proceed as in Stunt #7, hopping on one foot in space 8.

9. Throw puck into space 9. Advance as in #8, retrieve puck and return.

10. Throw puck into space 10. Advance, retrieve puck and return.

11. Without throwing puck, proceed as before to space 8, land with left foot in space 10 and right in space 9; about face and reverse position of feet; continue out as before.

The first player to complete all stunts wins the game. No more than six persons should play at any one time. A player's turn continues until he makes a mistake. On his next turn, he starts where he left off.

FOULS

1. Touching any line with the foot, puck or hand.
2. Touching the hand to the ground.
3. Failing to throw the puck into the proper space.
4. Losing the balance and putting the other foot down when hopping.

TEACHING SUGGESTIONS

Children may devise other hopscotch 'mazes' and rules.

4. **Croquet**

Play area — Level ground area approximately 100′ long and 50′ wide.
Equipment — Croquet set with mallets, balls and wickets.
Formation — Four or eight players.

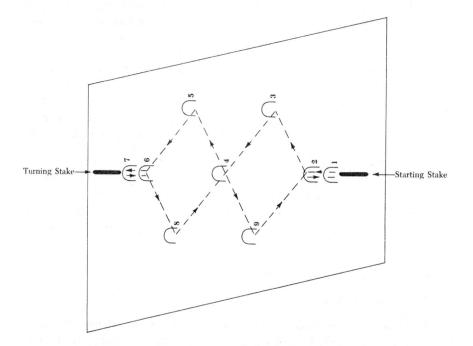

Approximately mallet handle length from starting stake to Wicket #1; same from Wicket #1 to #2; Mallet handle length from Turning stake to Wicket #7; same from Wicket #7 to #6. Adjustments may be made according to the space available. Put Wicket #4 in the center and arrange side wickets in proportion.

The object of the game is to complete the tour through the wickets before the opponents do. See diagram for proper order.

Order of play is determined by the order of colors on the starting stake. Each player, in turn, gets one stroke. This must be hit, not a push, and each stroke counts even though the ball moves only slightly.

Play starts a mallet head's length from the starting stake. If a ball goes through an arch, the player is entitled to one extra hit. An extra hit is also gained when the player hits the halfway stake. When a player hits the starting stake with his ball, after completing the tour through the wickets (or arches) he has finished his game.

When a player's ball hits another ball, he may

1. Take two extra strokes, after laying his ball a mallet head's length away from the ball he hit

OR

2. He may 'croquet' another ball and take one extra stroke. 'Croquet' means to place one's own ball next to the other ball and place one's foot on one's own ball and hit the other ball in any direction.

A player, after he has completed the tour through the wickets but before he has hit the starting stake, may elect to be a 'Rover.' A Rover may go anywhere on the court (in turn) his object being to hit other balls. He has not won the game, however, until he hits the starting stake. This is used usually when players are playing in partners and the Rover helps his partner by hitting opponents' balls.

TEACHING SUGGESTIONS

Croquet is usually played one person to one mallet, either individually or in partners. It may, to accommodate more children, be played in partners with two children using one mallet, rotating in hitting the ball.

5. **Table Tennis** (sometimes called Ping Pong)

Play area — Indoors.

Equipment — The table should be 5' x 9' and 30 inches from the floor. It should be painted dark green with a 3/4 inch white strip painted down the center (lengthwise) and around the edge of the table top. The net should extend across the width of the table, and the top edge of the net should be 6 and 3/4 inches from the table.
Table Tennis paddles and ball.

Formation — Opponents stand at opposite ends of the table and may play a singles or a doubles game.

Rules

1. Serving — The server, standing behind the end of the table, must keep his ball and racket behind the end line of the court (table) and between the sidelines as if they were extended. The ball is dropped or tossed by the server and is then struck so that it will hit the table on the side of the server before bouncing over the net. Each server serves the ball five times consecutively.

2. Receiving — Taking the ball following the first bounce (on his side of the table) the receiver endeavors to return the ball to the server's side in such a way that the latter cannot return it. The ball is never hit on the fly. Play continues until one side or the other misses the ball.

   In singles, the ball may be hit anywhere on the opposite half of the table.

   In doubles, the ball must be served to the diagonally opposite court but following the service it may be hit anywhere and doubles partners must alternate in hitting the ball.

3. Order of Service in Doubles — If A and B are playing No. 1 and 2, A may serve first, No. 1 serves second, B serves third and No. 2 serves fourth.

   Each server serves five times consecutively. The server becomes the first receiver on his side, and the receivers then alternate in receiving the serve.

4. Let Ball — A 'let' ball is a ball which strikes the top of the net as it goes over on a serve. A let serve is served again. To qualify as a 'let,' the serve must hit into the proper court on the receiver's side after hitting the net. A let return is a legal return and is not replayed.

5. Scoring — A player makes points each time an opponent makes an error, whether he is the server or the receiver. Points are made when

   a. A player fails to make a good service.
   b. A player fails to make a good return.
   c. A player permits the free hand to touch the surface of the court when the ball is in play.
   d. A player permits clothing or racket to contact an opponent's ball before it crosses the net.

   A score of 21 points wins the game. If the score is tied at 20 points, service changes after each point and the side wins which first gets two consecutive points. A match is two out of three games.

TEACHING SUGGESTIONS

A table tennis table can be made out of a sheet of plywood which is placed on saw horses or something similar so that it is at the correct height.

## 6. Sidewalk Tennis

Play area — Four squares of a sidewalk, each three feet square. Line B divides the court and constitutes an imaginary net. Lines A and C are foul lines behind which the server stands.

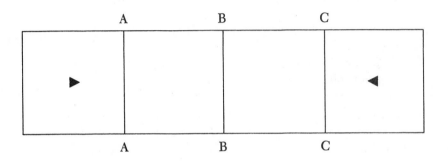

Equipment — A tennis ball or any similar small rubber ball.

Formation — Two or four players.

RULES

1. The players stand as indicated. The server must not step over the foul line in serving. He tosses the ball and bats it with the palm of his hand so that it falls in the court over line B. Only one attempt at service is allowed.

2. A served ball must bounce once before being played. Thereafter it may be volleyed or played on the first bounce. The hand must be kept open and the ball 'palmed.'

3. Scoring — Only the server scores. He continues to serve as long as he wins. He scores one point each time the opponent fails to return the ball legally. He loses the serve when he

   a. Fails to serve into the opposing court.
   b. Steps over the foul line in serving.
   c. Fails to return the ball legally into the opposing court.

The game consists of eleven points, except when the score is tied at ten points. In this case, the server must win two consecutive points to win.

TEACHING SUGGESTIONS

Chalk lines or painted lines on a blacktop area may substitute for sidewalk squares.

# The Curriculum

# Rhythms

# 7

# Rhythms

Rhythmic activities are an important part of every well balanced physical education curriculum in the elementary schools. This type of activity includes creative and free rhythms, singing games, folk dancing and marching.

These activities contribute to the achievement of all of the objectives of physical education. In addition, traditional, national and popular singing games and folk dances are a part of every child's heritage as are literary, artistic and musical classics. In this curriculum, 30 per cent of the total time for physical education in the primary grades (equal to 54 lessons) and 25 per cent of the total time in the 4th, 5th and 6th grades (equal to 45 lessons) is designated for rhythmic type activities.

All rhythms in this book are planned to be done to music on records. Some teachers are fortunate enough to be able to play the piano well enough to accompany their classes. However, the teacher cannot be two places at once — at the piano and on the floor teaching the activity or helping a pupil. Therefore, the writer believes that all teachers will find it advantageous to use records.

The record player should have amplifiers so that the music can be heard clearly. It should also have a speed regulator in order that records may be played slowly when the pupils are learning a step or a dance, and can then be played at normal speed when the activity has been learned. A microphone is most helpful when the teacher wishes to count, or give cues while the record is playing.

The school should provide all records necessary for physical education classes. Records are best kept in some type of a case or file and should be indexed so that they can be quickly and easily located. The acquisition of records can sometimes be a frustrating experience. Record companies come and go, records change from 78 rpms to 45's to 33's and what was available a year, or even six months ago, may no longer be on the market. A good music store may be a help in securing what the teacher needs. Send for catalogs and get on mailing lists. The following is a list of some companies which manufacture and distribute educational and folk dance records. Most have catalogs or brochures available.

1.  Bowmar Records, 10515 Burbank Blvd., North Hollywood, California.
2.  Children's Music Center, Inc., 5373 West Pico, Los Angeles, Calif.
3.  Columbia Records, Education Department, 799 Seventh Ave., New York, N. Y.
4.  Educational Record Sales, 157 Chambers Street, New York, N. Y. 10007.
5.  Educational Recordings of America, Inc., P. O. Box 6062, Bridgeport, Conn. 06606.
6.  Folk Dancer, Box 201, Flushing, Long Island, New York, N. Y.
7.  Folkraft Records, 1159 Broad Street, Newark, New Jersey.
8.  Honor Your Partner Records, Square Dance Associates, Freeport, N. Y. 14464.
9.  Imperial Records, 137 N. Western Ave., Los Angeles, California.
10. Kimbo Educational Records, P. O. Box 55, Deal, New Jersey 07723.
11. MacGregor Records, 729 South Western Ave., Hollywood, California.
12. Methodist Publishing House, 150 Fifth Ave., New York, N. Y.
13. RCA Victor Education Dept. J., 155 East 24th Street, New York, N. Y.
14. Russell Records, P. O. Box 3318, Ventura, California 93003.
15. Shaw, Lloyd, Record Company, Box 203, Colorado Springs, Colorado.
16. Square Dance Records, Teaching Aids Service, 31 Union Square W., New York, N. Y. 10003.
17. Windsor Records, 5530 N. Rosemead Blvd., Temple City, California.

## COMPLETE RECORD LIST FOR THIS CURRICULUM

Records listed here are known, by experience, to be good for the purposes suggested.

### Primary Grades

Bowmar Marches — Album, Records #1569, 1570, 1571—all grades
Bowmar Album I — Singing Games for Primary Grades

Bowmar Album II — Singing Games for Primary Grades
Bowman Album III — Singing Games and Folk Dances
Phoebe James Records #1, #2, #5
Children's Record Guild —
    #1012 — Nothing To do
    #1017 — A Visit to My Little Friend
RCA Victor Records
    45-5066 — Paw Paw Patch
    45-6180 — Pop Goes the Weasel
    45-6179 — Children's Polka
    45-6177 — Come Let Us Be Joyful
    45-6182 — Csebogar
Audio Education, Inc., 13108, Decca Records
Total-— 4 albums, 11 single records

## Intermediate Grades

RCA Victor Records
    45-6169 — Ace of Diamonds — 5th grade
             Bleking — 4th grade
    45-6170 — Gustaf's Skoal — 4th grade
    45-6172 — Bingo — 5th grade
             Seven Jumps — 4th grade
    45-6178 — Oh Susanna — 5th grade
             Irish Reel — 4th grade
    45-6180 — Virginia Reel — 5th grade
             Pop Goes the Weasel — 3rd grade
Imperial Records
    1007 — Wooden Shoes — 4th grade
    1022 — Korobushka — 6th grade
    1044 — Glowworm — 4th grade
    1045 — Cotton Eyed Joe — 5th grade
    1046 — California Schottische — 6th grade
    1085 — LaRaspa — 6th grade
    1099 — Oh Johnny — 5th grade
Lloyd Shaw #3-121 — Five Foot Two — 6th grade
Four Star #1365 — Little Brown Jug — 4th grade
Columbia #20117 — Starlight Schottische — 4th grade
Folk Dancer #1055 — Swedish Schottische — 5th
Windsor — #7S4 — All American Promenade — 6th grade
                    Sicilian Circle — 4th grade
MacGregor 649 — Alice Blue Gown — 4th and 5th grades
                    Tennessee Waltz
MacGregor 608 — Chiapanecas — 5th grade
MacGregor 309 — Blackhawk Waltz — 6th grade
Broadcast #416 — Lili Marlene — 6th grade
Decca — Ed Gilmore Grand Square Quadrille — 6th grade
Total — 22 single records
Total cost — between $80.00 and $90.00

Teachers may wish to use modern, current and contemporary records which have a good rhythm and good beat, especially for free rhythms, movement exploration, marching and other locomotor skills.

Most teachers prefer to spend an entire lesson on rhythms rather than combining rhythms with some other type of activity in one lesson. If only rhythms are taught in a lesson, the teacher need not be concerned with getting supplies or equipment ready other than the record player and the records. Of course, the warm-up run and conditioning exercises should be included in every lesson at the beginning of the class period. Before starting the rhythms unit, it will be helpful to the teacher to know what the pupils should have learned in the preceding grade, their level of accomplishment in rhythms, and she should start by reviewing some of the rhythms from the preceding grade level.

Some communities and some religions object to the teaching of dancing in the public schools. These instances are becoming fewer all the time but may create a problem for the teacher. It has been found that if the activity is called "rhythms" or "folk games" the objection often fades away. If the community objects to rhythms, regardless of what they are called, the teacher can still provide some rhythmic experiences for the pupils by doing such activities as marching, running, skipping and galloping to music. Conditioning exercises can also be done to music.

If any children bring legitimate notes from their parents indicating that their religion forbids dancing, the teacher has no choice but to excuse these pupils. In this event, the pupil can do the warm-up and conditioning exercises with the class and then be permitted to observe or, if he is not permitted to observe, he can be excused to do some classroom activity.

Even an experienced teacher cannot teach rhythms 'off the top of her head.' Some preparation, before class, is necessary. The teacher should know what she is going to do and to be sure that all necessary records are available.

With adequate space, a good record player and the records ready, with the lesson plan in mind, if not on paper, the teacher may be assured of a successful and enjoyable lesson for both the class and herself.

Rhythms are a good activity to use for programs or demonstrations. Another class or parents may be invited to observe. It is a worthwhile experience for children to do things occasionally in front of an audience as this aids in the development of poise and self confidence. In planning a program, the following should be kept in mind:

1. Every child should participate.
2. Vary the program, including different types of rhythms, different formations.
3. Have all records ready.
4. The program should be planned ahead of time and everyone should know what he is going to do.
5. Do not have the program too long. Twenty to twenty five minutes is long enough for both the children and the audience.

## RHYTHMS IN THE PRIMARY GRADES

The specific objectives of teaching rhythms in the primary grades are:

1. to help the pupils learn to move freely in time to music. This is the fundamental and most important goal because without this, more advanced rhythms cannot be learned, and without this, moving to music is no fun. Moving in time to a rhythmic pattern or to music is a pleasureful sensation for all children (boys, too!) and in fact, for all people. Some children have difficulty in doing this; others are born with 'a sense of rhythm.' Everyone can be taught to move to music, though with some individuals, it is a long process. To move in time to music involves listening to music — at first consciously and then sub-consciously.
2. to learn fundamental steps such as walking, skipping, galloping in different tempos or rhythms.
3. to improvise, or create, movement patterns to music, individually and in groups.
4. to learn folk dance formations and patterns such as circles, lines, partners, and to learn folk dance terminology.
5. to become aware of our cultural heritage in singing games and folk dances. Most of these are traditional dances. Many of the tunes will be familiar.

The primary teacher, while meeting the immediate needs of primary age children and working toward her goals in physical education, is building a foundation upon which more advanced and possibly more enjoyable rhythms and dances can be done in the higher grades and in adult life.

It is wise to start the rhythm curriculum wth 'free' rhythms. This means a scattered formation on the floor — no formal formation, but all moving in a general, counter-clockwise direction and the pupils expressing the music in some appropriate action. Many good records for 'free' or creative rhythms are now available, including the following:

1. Bowmar Records — 10515 Burbank Blvd., North Hollywood, Calif.
2. Children's Record Guild — 27 Thompson Street, New York, N. Y.
3. Evans, Ruth. Childhood Rhythms Series. Chartwell House, Inc. 280 Madison Ave., New York 16, N.Y.
4. James, Phoebe, Educational Series AED #1 to #12. Whitney's. 150 Powell Street, San Francisco, Calif.
5. RCA Victor Records — Folk Dance Series. RCA Victor Record Division, 155 E. 24th Street, New York 10, N. Y.
6. Estamae and Osborne Records — Album No. 1 and Album No. 4. Grace O. Rhonemus, Box 1213, Grand Forks, North Dakota.
7. Young Peoples Record Club, Inc. 40 W. 46th Street, New York 19, N. Y.

Suggestions and help from the teacher may be needed until the children have experienced a 'repertoire' of movements. A possible progression is as follows:

1. Use records on which there are words or directions which tell the pupils what to do such as

   Children's Record Guild — Nothing To Do
                                                A Visit to My Little Friend
   Phoebe James Record — Five Ponies

2. Records without words, but with a distinct pattern of time and accent such as Phoebe James Record #2, "Free Rhythms" and Phoebe James Record, #5 "Fundamental Rhythms." These include music for walk, run, skip, gallop, hop, etc. Also waltz music for some stationary movements such as bending, stretching, twisting, swaying.

3. Teacher Suggestion — with or without music. "Can you" or "Who can?"

   Hop —                                    Strike —
     like a bird                     driving a nail
     like a hail stone               like chopping wood
     with sore feet                  like beating drums

   Skip —                                   Leap —
     for fun                          over a brook
     like a clown                     over a mud puddle
     high, like a bird                over a fence

Run —
   to get out of the rain
   like a baby
   like an old lady
   slowly, as if tired

Slide —
   very slowly like a giant
   lightly like a fairy
   lazily

Gallop —
   like ponies
   like cowboys' horses
   like farm horses

Swing —
   like flowers in the breeze
   like a playground swing
   like trees in a storm

Walk —
   like elves
   like lions
   using baby steps
   on tiptoes like fairies
   like mother
   as if you were late
   as if you were tired
   up hill
   one leg in a splint

Jump —
   like rabbits
   like grasshoppers
   like birds that jump
   like bouncing balls
   like jack-in-the-box

4. Let the children develop a feeling for form and pattern by suggesting directions, groupings, and sequences. For example, slide to the center of the floor eight slides, bounce in place for eight counts; gallop with a partner for eight gallops followed by eight slides in the same direction; do four skips, then four jumps in place, etc.

5. Pupils may then wish to make up a rhythm pattern — individually or in groups.

The teacher should be alert to good responses from the children and point them out to the other pupils. Do not force children to participate. The few strays will gradually enter in.

When pupils have achieved a sense of rhythm and a few basic skills, simple singing games and folk dances can be introduced. These may be combined with 'free' rhythms in a lesson as follows:

1. Warm-up run and conditioning exercises.
2. Phoebe James record 'Fundamental Rhythms.'
   a. Individually
   b. In groups
3. Singing game, "Round and Round the Village."

A few suggestions about choosing partners may be helpful. At the primary level, the teacher will often need to place the pupils in partners. There are several ways to do this that are objective and take little time.

1. Boys make a circle. Girls make a circle outside of the boys' circle. Girls walk around circle, counter-clockwise, until the teacher says, "Stop." Boy nearest the girl is her partner.
2. Boys line up on one side of the room, girls on the other. As in marching formation, "down the center by two's" to form partners Leaders lead around to form a circle or whatever formation is desired.
3. Occasionally have boys' choice or ladies' choice, in which case the boy — or the lady — chooses his own partner.

It is not necessary to have boy-girl partners all of the time. Vary this with partners of the same sex from time to time. It is often desirable for the teacher to participate in the rhythms with the children. Sometimes there is an odd number in a class. If a partner is needed, the teacher can fill in, rather than having a child stay out of the activity because he has no partner. Most teachers will enjoy this, and of course, class members enjoy having the teacher participate with them.

## RHYTHMS IN THE INTERMEDIATE GRADES
### (4th, 5th and 6th Grades)

Rhythms, including folk dancing and marching, are a part of every well-balanced physical education curriculum in the intermediate grades. There are a number of reasons for this:

1. Rhythmical activities help to meet the physical education objective of fitness. They are vigorous and stimulating.
2. Rhythmical activities require a certain analysis of skill which is not true of all activities in the curriculum. They require the pupil to *think* as he moves.
3. Rhythmical activities contribute to the development of coordination, and smooth, efficient — call it graceful — movement.
4. Rhythmical activities provide a situation where wholesome boy-girl relationships can be practiced and where boys and girls can learn the right thing to do (etiquette) in many social situations.
5. Moving to music is a pleasant activity which all humans enjoy and which can lead to a desirable leisure time activity in adolescence and adult life. Rhythmic movement provides a means of release from tensions.

6. Folk dances are a part of the culture and history of our nation. The colonists danced, as did the pioneers, early settlers and citizens of the late 1800's. Some folk dances are readily correlated with the history or social studies taught in the classroom, making both subjects more meaningful.

A satisfactory rhythms curriculum can be taught by every teacher, including men. If a teacher's background and experience in dancing is meager, it may be necessary to spend more time in preparation. A certain amount of preparation is necessary to teach any subject, and the teacher should expect to give physical education its due time also. If a teacher is completely incapable of teaching a rhythm, perhaps some one else on the staff — or in the upper grades, a pupil — may be able to give assistance. Many phonograph records are now available which give instructions for a dance so that the teacher can learn along with the class. The teacher should not deny her pupils the benefits of rhythmical activities because she feels inadequate or lacks confidence. It is safe to say that if a teacher sincerely tries to teach rhythms, some measure of success will be achieved.

What can be taught in the fourth grade, or any succeeding grade, will depend to a large extent on the quality of the rhythms program in the primary grades. If the progression outlined herein has been observed, fourth graders will have no difficulty with the curriculum outlined for them. In fact, they will approach rhythms in the fourth grade with anticipation, eagerness and confidence. If a class has an inadequate background, it may be necessary to teach a few of the third grade rhythms before proceeding to the fourth grade curriculum. If this is necessary, Jump Jim Jo and Paw Paw Patch, at least, should be included. It will also be necessary to introduce the two-step.

Because pupils ten and eleven years of age are becoming aware of the opposite sex, they are, at this age, likely to be more self-conscious about standing beside each other or joining hands than they were earlier — or will be later! Some boys, in order to cover up their feelings of insecurity, will be reluctant to participate in rhythms. After all, no ten year old boy can admit that he 'likes to dance.' This is contrary to the mores of our culture. However, the teacher should — as far as possible — ignore this. Men have an important and leading role in dancing. By pointing out the importance and responsibility of the boy's or man's role in dancing, the teacher can convince boys that this is no 'sissy' activity, but rather one that shows manliness. Provide for frequent changes of partners as in mixer type dances. Point out the similarity of some rhythm steps to certain sport skills, such as the fact that the two-step is similar to the foot pattern in guarding in basketball. Some athletic coaches use dance patterns and movements and techniques as a part of the training procedure. For a change, some dances can be done in boy-boy partners.

Following are some suggestions and rules that will prove helpful:

1. Always move in a general counter-clockwise direction in folk and ballroom dancing. This is called "Line of Direction" or "LOD."
2. Boys should always have their partner on their right side. Thus, in a circle formation, facing counter-clockwise, boys are on the inside of the circle and girls on the outside. In a line formation, such as for the Irish Reel and the Virginia Reel, boys are in the line to the teacher's *right* – girls in the line to the teacher's *left*.
3. The boy, in partner dances, supports the lady's hand. The boy should hold his palm up. The lady places her hand on top of the boy's.

   a. When the instructions call for "Inside Hands Joined," the boy supports the lady's left hand on his right hand, at shoulder height.
   b. For 'both hands joined,' the lady places her hands on top of the boy's hands.
   c. 'Promenade' position means hands crossed in front of the body. This is sometimes called 'skater's position': left hand to left, and right hand to right hand.
   d. 'Varsouviene' position: standing side by side, the girl puts her right hand at her shoulder; boy puts his right arm around the back of the girl and grasps her right hand. Left hands are joined in front.

4. Walking steps should be smooth, feet staying close to the floor. This is also true for the two-step and the waltz, and to a lesser extent, for the schottische step. The Virginia Reel and square dances are done with a *walking* step, not a skip.
5. There are several ways of selecting partners. For the most part, these should be as objective as possible.

   a. Boys make a circle. Girls make a circle outside of the boys' circle. Girls walk around the circle, counterclockwise, until the teacher says "stop." The nearest boy is the girl's partner.

b. Boys line up on one side of the room, girls on the other. As in marching formation, "down the center by two's," partners are formed. Leaders then lead around to form a circle or whatever formation is desired.

c. Occasionally have boys' choice or ladies' choice in which case each chooses his own partner.

6. Have an occasional 'choice day' when pupils choose the dances they will do that day. Or a 'choice dance' may be selected to end the class period.

7. It is sometimes a motivating factor to work toward a special event. Rhythmic activities are a good activity to 'show.' The school principal and/or another class may be invited to observe the rhythms or to participate with the class. Parents may be invited to a rhythms program as a culminating activity for a rhythm unit.

## FIRST GRADE RHYTHMS

1. Looby Loo
2. Round and Round the Village
3. Mulberry Bush
4. Oats, Peas, Beans
5. Farmer in the Dell
6. Did You Ever See a Lassie
7. How D'Ye Do My Partner
8. The Swing
9. Brothers and Sisters
   *Creative Rhythms*
   *Marching*

1. **Looby Loo**

   Record — Bowmar 1514, Folkraft 1102, Audio Education, Inc. 13108

   Formation — Single circle, hands joined.

   Description —

   "Here we go Looby Loo,
   Here we go Looby Light,
   Here we go Looby Loo,
   All on a Saturday night."

   Children skip 16 skips around the circle in a counterclockwise direction.

   Circle stops, all drop hands and perform the following with the words,

   "I put my right hand in, I put my right hand out,
   I give my right hand a shake, shake, shake,
   And turn myself about."

Chorus repeats.

Continue with the following verses:
"I put my left hand in"
"I put my two hands in"
"I put my right foot in"
"I put my left foot in"
"I put my head way in"
"I put my whole self in."

TEACHING SUGGESTIONS

1. Encourage a good circle during the chorus. If children cannot maintain a good circle while skipping, they may drop hands and skip alone.
2. Different records have various sequences of movement, but all present the same general idea.

2. **Round and Round the Village**

Record — Bowmar 1512, Folkraft F1191.

Formation — Single circle, hands joined. One player is on the outside of the circle.

Description —
"Go round and round the village,
Go round and round the village,
Go round and round the village,
As we have done before."

The circle walks to the right. The player on the outside walks around the circle.

Circle stops and all raise arms, hands joined, forming 'windows.

"Go in and out the windows," etc.

Player on the outside of the circle goes in and out under the raised arms.

"Now stand and face your partner," etc.

Player in the center chooses a partner and stands in front of him.

"Now follow me to London," etc. (or any other city)

Player and partner skip around outside of the circle.

The sequence is repeated with the player and his partner each alone, on the outside of the circle. Continue until all players in the circle have been chosen.

1. If the group is large, start with two players on the outside instead of one.
2. Girls may choose boys for partners and vice versa.
3. The game may be played without a record, with children singing.
4. Some records have a different sequence of words.

## 3. Mulberry Bush

Record — Bowmar 1513, Audio-Education, Inc., 13108.

Formation — Single circle, hands joined.

Description —

"Here we go round the mulberry bush,
The mulberry bush, the mulberry bush,
Here we go round the mulberry bush,
So early in the morning."

The circle moves to the right walking or skipping to the music.

Circle stops and children dramatize the following actions:

"This is the way we wash our clothes
So early Monday morning."

"This is the way we iron our clothes
So early Tuesday morning."
"This is the way we scrub the floor
So early Wednesday morning."
"This is the way we mend our clothes
So early Thursday morning."
"This is the way we sweep the floor
So early Friday morning."
"Thus we play when work is done
So early Saturday morning."
"This is the way we go to church
So early Sunday morning."

1. Other movements may be substituted, such as: clap our hands, wash our hands, brush our hair, tie our shoes, or suggestions from the pupils may be used.
2. Do movements in time with the music.
3. This may be done without a record, with children singing the words.

**4. Oats, Peas, Beans and Barley Grow** (English)

Record — Bowmar 1512, Folkraft 1182.

Formation — Single circle, hands joined; one player, the farmer, is in
        the center.

Description —

    "Oats, peas, beans and barley grow,
    Oats, peas, beans and barley grow,
    Can you or I or anyone know
    How oats, peas, beans and barley grow?"

    The circle walks to the right.

    "Thus the farmer sows his seed,
    Thus he stands and takes his ease,
    He stamps his foot, claps his hands,
    And turns around to view the land."

    Circle stops, all face center and the children imitate the farmer who
    pantomimes the above actions.

    "Waiting for a partner,
    Waiting for a partner,
    Open the ring and choose one in
    While we all gaily dance and sing."

    Circle continues walking to the right as the farmer chooses a partner.

    "Tra, la la," etc. OR
    "Now you're married, you must obey,
    You must be true to all you say,
    You must be kind, you must be good
    And keep your wife in kindling wood."

    Circle continues to the right; farmer and his partner skip around
    to the left, inside the circle.

**5. Farmer in the Dell**

Record — Bomar 1511, Folkraft 1182, Audio Education, Inc., 13108.

Formation — Single circle, hands joined. One player in the center, the
        Farmer.

Description —
    "The farmer in the dell,
    The farmer in the dell,
    Heigh ho, the derry oh
    The farmer in the dell."

The circle moves to the right (counterclockwise) by walking in rhythm to the words.

"Farmer plants the seed." The Farmer chooses five to ten children to be 'seeds.' They stoop down in the center of the circle.

"The rain begins to fall." The 'rain' (a child selected by the Farmer) walks around shaking fingers to indicate rain — or any way the child wishes to indicate rain.

"The sun begins to shine." The 'sun' walks around in the center of the circle and 'shines.'

"The seeds begin to grow." 'Seeds' slowly stand up and stretch their arms overhead.

"Wind begins to blow." The 'wind' blows around the circle and the seeds sway in the breeze.

"Farmer cuts the grain." The 'seeds' let arms fall.

"Farmer binds the sheaves." The Farmer stands the seeds in groups of two or three.

"Now the harvest is done." All skip around the circle.

TEACHING SUGGESTIONS
1. It is wise to select the seeds, rain, sun and wind before the rhythm begins.
2. Emphasize doing movements in time with the music.
3. Discuss difference between the way this Farmer does things and the way modern farmers plant seed and harvest the crop,
4. This may be done without a record with children singing.
5. This version of Farmer in the Dell is preferred because there are more children in action and there is more action. Many records have the following words: "The farmer takes a wife, the wife takes a child, the child takes a nurse, etc." In this case, those chosen stand in the center of the circle.

6. **Did You Ever See a Lassie** (American)

Record — Bowmar 1511, Victor 45-5066, Folkraft 1183.
Formation — Single circle, hands joined; one player is in the center of the circle.
Description —
"Did you ever see a lassie, (or laddie if a boy is the player in the center) a lassie, a lassie,
Did you ever see a lassie do this way and that?"

The circle moves to the right by walking in rhythm to the words. On "this way and that," the player in the center performs some movement, stunt or exercise.

"Do this way and that way, do this way and that way,
Did you ever see a lassie do this way and that?"

All the players imitate the leader's movements.

The leader chooses someone to take her place and the rhythm continues.

TEACHING SUGGESTIONS

1. The leader should be encouraged to do large, vigorous movements and, of course, these should be done in time with the music.
2. Boys may choose girls and vice versa.
3. This may be done without a record, children providing the accompaniment by singing.
4. Other names may be used instead of Lassie, such as Cowboy, Spaceman, Puppet, etc.

## 7. How D'Ye Do My Partner (Swedish)

Record — Bowmar 1513 or Folkraft F1190.

Formation — Double circle. Partners facing each other with boys on the inside of the circle and girls on the outside.

Description —
"How do you do, my partner" — boys bow
"How do you do today" — Girls curtsy
"Will you dance in the circle?" Shake right hands
"I will show you the way." — Shake left hands

Chorus: All skip counterclockwise with partner, inside hands joined.

TEACHING SUGGESTIONS

1. Teach the correct way for boys to bow, and girls to curtsy.
2. In this folk dance, children may be taught how to change partners as in a mixer. At the end of the chorus, girls may move forward (counterclockwise) to the next boy. Repeat the dance with the new partner.

## 8. The Swing

Record — Bowmar 1518.

Formation — In three's. Two children face each other, join both hands and thus form the swing. The third child faces forward (counterclockwise) and puts his hands on the joined hands of the 'swing.'

Description — Number three child pushes the swing forward and backward in time with the music for 15 counts. On the 16th, number three gives a big push forward and goes under the swing to the next couple.

TEACHING SUGGESTIONS

1. The swing should move in time to the music. The 'pusher' should stand with one foot slightly forward and children will do this naturally if they feel the music.
2. To get into position, have children 'count off' by three's.
3. Rotate positions so that all have an opportunity to be a 'pusher.'

## 9. Brothers and Sisters

Record — Any march record.

Formation — Each child selects a partner. Child then leaves his partner and goes to the line other than the one his partner is in. Line up in random fashion.

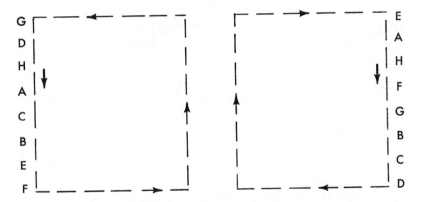

Description — When the music starts, children march (or walk or skip) as indicated on the sketch. When the music stops, each one runs to find his partner and sits down, back to back, wherever they find each other. Points may be awarded to the first couple down and back to back. All then return to their original line and the activity proceeds.

TEACHING SUGGESTIONS

1. Remind children of safety rules to avoid collisions when running to meet partner.

# SECOND GRADE RHYTHMS

1. Rig A Jig Jig
2. Yankee Doodle
3. Jolly is the Miller
4. Dance of Greeting
5. Chimes of Dunkirk

6. Seven Steps
7. A Hunting We Will Go
8. I See You
9. Marching
10. Creative Rhythms

## 1. Rig a Jig Jig

Record — Bowmar 1521.

Formation — Single circle with hands joined; one player in the center.

Description —

"As I was walking down the street, down the street, down the street,
As I was walking down the street, heigh o heigh o heigh o."

Circle walks around counterclockwise. Player in the center walks around inside the circle in the opposite direction.

"A pretty girl I chanced to meet, chanced to meet, chanced to meet,

A pretty girl I chanced to meet, heigh o heigh o heigo o."

Circle continues walking. Inside player chooses partner and takes her into the center of the circle.

"Rig a jig, jig and away we go, away we go, away we go,
Rig a jig, jig and away we go, heigh o heigh o heigh o."

Circle skips in counterclockwise direction. Player and partner skip around inside of circle in opposite direction, hands joined.

Repeat with the two center partners each choosing another player. Continue until all have been chosen.

### TEACHING SUGGESTIONS

1. Note the similarity between this and Round and Round the Village which was learned in the first grade.
2. As more children are chosen and the circle becomes smaller, the center pupils will have to go outside the circle.

## 2. Yankee Doodle (American)

Record — Bowmar 1522, RCA Victor 45-5064.

Formation — Single circle, all facing counterclockwise.

Description —

"Yankee Doodle went to town, riding on a pony"

All skip eight skips forward. (or gallop)

"He stuck a feather in his cap, and called it 'Macaroni.'"

All stop, face toward center of the circle, pretend to put feather in cap.

Bow, on 'Macaroni.'

"Yankee Doodle, ha, ha, ha, Yankee Doodle dandy,"

All join hands and take six slides to the right.
Stamp twice on word 'dandy.'

"Yankee Doodle, ha, ha, ha, buy the girls some candy."

Slide six times to the left, clap hands twice on word 'candy.'

TEACHING SUGGESTIONS
1. Point out the similarity between the slide and a gallop; the foot pattern is the same. On the gallop, one moves forward; on the slide, one moves sideward.
2. This rhythm contains some quick changes. Children must 'think ahead.'

## 3. Jolly Is the Miller (English)

Record — Bowmar 1521, RCA Victor 45-5067, Folkraft 1192.

Formation — Partners in double circle, inside hands joined and girls on the outside. All face counterclockwise.

Description —
"Jolly is the miller who lives by the mill,
The wheel goes around with a right good will,
One hand in the hopper and the other in the sack.
The right goes forward and the left goes back."

All walk forward (or skip) during the first three lines of this verse. On the last line, the girls move forward to the next boy as the boy moves backward to the next girl.

TEACHING SUGGESTIONS
1. This is a good rhythm in which to teach the proper way of changing partners. This what is called a 'mixer'—everyone get a new partner each time the dance is repeated.
2. After the class has learned the general pattern, let the children do it without words, listening to the music for the last phrase when it is time to change partners.
3. Use a walk step at first; later a skip may be used.

## 4. Dance of Greeting (Danish)

Record — Bowmar 1515, RCA Victor 45-6183.

Formation — In partners, single circle. Boy's partner is on his right, all face center.

Description — The movements are
clap, clap, bow
clap, clap, bow
stamp, stamp
turn yourself around

On the first line, the children bow to their partner,
On the second line, bow to one's neighbor.
Third and fourth lines, action is performed in place.
Chorus: All join hands, face counterclockwise, and run 15 steps
Repeat in opposite direction.

TEACHING SUGGESTIONS

1. For variation, change the bow to a curtsy; or have the boys bow while the girls curtsy.
2. This may be done with partners facing each other in a double circle. In that case, the chorus is done with only the partners joining hands.
3. Running steps should be small and light.
4. Make the dance a 'mixer' by having the girls move up to the next boy at the end of the chorus.

5. **Chimes of Dunkirk** (French)

Record — Bowmar 1516, RCA Victor 45-6176, Folkraft 1188.

Formation — Double circle, partners facing each other; boys on the inside, girls on the outside.

Description —
Stamp, stamp, stamp,

Clap, clap, clap.

Join hands with partner and run, with small steps, to the left in a small individual circle, returning to original place.

On last and fourth phrase, boys move up to the next girl.

TEACHING SUGGESTIONS

1. The clapping may be done with arms stretched overhead and bending from side to side to represent a bell pendulum.
2. This dance adds a new pattern, that of moving up to the next partner at the end of a turn.
3. Some records include a 'chorus' between each verse. In this case, pupils skip around the outside of the circle with inside hand joined with partner.

### 6. Seven Steps

Record — Bowmar 1515.

Formation — Double circle, boys on the inside, girls on the outside, inside hands joined. Face counterclockwise.

Description —

Walk forward seven steps

Walk backward seven steps. Face partner.

Walk backward, away from partner, three steps. (girls will be moving toward outside of circle, boys toward center of circle)

Walk forward to meet partner three steps,

Join both hands with partner and walk around in small circle for seven steps. Should end in original place.

Walk backward away from partner three steps,

Walk forward three steps toward new partner who is the one to the right of the previous partner.

Join hands with new partner and walk around for seven steps.

Repeat all with new partner.

TEACHING SUGGESTIONS

1. This presents a different pattern of changing partners.
2. Have children count steps out loud when learning the sequence of this rhythm.

### 7. A Hunting We Will Go (English)

Record — Bowmar 1515, Folkraft F1191, Audio Education, Inc. 13108.

Formation — Two parallel lines, boys in one line and girls in the other. All face center of the 'set.' Four to six couples in a 'set.'

Description —

"A hunting we will go,
A hunting we will go,
We'll catch a fox and put him in a box
And then we'll let him go."

On first two lines, the head couple join hands in the center of the set and do seven slides down the center of the set.

On the last two lines, the head couple do seven slides back up to the head of the set.

Girls  Boys

O  X ← Foot Couple
O  X
O  X
O  X ← Head Couple

☐◄ Caller or Teacher

Chorus: Head couple drops hands. Boy skips to his left, girl to her right, around the set. Head couple meets at the foot end of the set,

join hands to form an arch. Others follow the head couple and go
through the arch.

Head couple stays at the foot of the set, and the dance is repeated
with a new head couple.

TEACHING SUGGESTIONS

1. This is a new formation and there is new terminology. Teach correct
terms such as 'set,' 'head couple,' 'foot couple.'

2. The head couple should cover as much space as it can on the slides
down the center but partners should do the correct number of slides
and stay with the music.

3. The 'head couple' is usually defined as being the couple nearest
the music.

## 8. I See You (Swedish)

Record — Bowmar 1518, Folkraft 1197.

Formation — Four parallel lines, all facing center of the set.

Description —

"I see you, I see you, tra la, tra la, tra la, tra la,
I see you, I see you, tra la, tra la, tra la."

Boys, Girls    Girls, Boys

X O            O X

Boys place hands on girls' shoulders. Boys peek
over girl's shoulders, looking at opposite boy,
bending from right to left in time with the
music.

X O            O X

X O            O X

X O            O X

"You see me and I see you,
You take me and I take you."

face ⟶ ⟵ face

Boys skip to the center of the set, join hands with opposite boy and
skip around, to the left, once.

"You see me and I see you,
You take me and I take you."

Boys skip back to partner, join hands and skip around with partner.
Change places, so that girls are now behind boys. Repeat rhythm
with girls performing the action.

TEACHING SUGGESTIONS

1. The space between the two lines should be about 10 feet.

2. This may be done with boy-boy partners and girl-girl partners instead of boy-girl partners.

## 9. Marching

Record — Bowmar album of Marches, #1569, 1570, 1571.

Marching is an activity which children enjoy and it should be considered a part of the rhythms unit for all grades. Marching should be done with a free and rhythmical step, heads up, chins in and with a natural arm swing. Some pupils seem to think of marching as a high stepping stamp; this probably results from watching baton twirlers and marching bands. This is not marching as used in the class situation. Marching is a good way to start a class, and a good way to get into formation for rhythms or calisthenics.

### Progression

1. Have the class walk around the gymnasium or room in time to the music. It is important to select a good leader. Emphasize walking in time to the music, proper spacing and alignment. Do not worry about right foot or left foot.
2. When the class can do #1, think about spacing between the pupils in the line. There should be a little more than arm's distance "between you and the person ahead of you."
3. Formations
   a. Single file around the room — one person behind another in a single line.
   b. Single file down the center — leader leads the line down the center of the floor. Put a chalk or tape mark on the floor where the line is to turn.
   c. Down the center by two's — start boys on one side of the gymnasium and girls on the other (or any other division). Walk to center of one end of the floor, meet the person coming from the opposite direction, turn and go down the center of the floor in two's or partners.
   d. Right and left by twos — When first couple reaches the end of the floor (B) the first couple goes to the right, second couple to the left, etc. and around the room again.
   e. May go down the center by twos again, or down the center by fours, couples meeting at (A) to form fours.

4. Along with learning the above formations, pupils should learn the following commands:
   a. "Fall in" or "Line Up." Select leader, or leaders and get into place in a line.
   b. "Attention." Stand at attention in good posture, but not stiffly, and with proper spacing.
   c. "At ease." Place left foot slightly to the side, clasp hands easily behind the back.
   d. "Mark time." Step in place, keeping time with the music or the count. Keep feet close to the floor.
   e. "Forward March." (Pause between the two words.) Pupils step forward on the word "march."
   f. "Class halt, one, two." By Count two, all should stop, feet together, maintaining spacing.
   g. "Sa-lute." Raise right hand until tip of the forefinger touches the lower part of the forehead and slightly to the right of the right eye. The upper arm should be horizontal. Forearm and hands are straight, fingers together. This command is usually given when the pupils are at 'attention.' "At ease" may be the following command.

### THIRD GRADE RHYTHMS

1. Jump Jim Jo
2. Children's Polka
3. Paw Paw Patch
4. Pease Porridge Hot
5. Pop Goes the Weasel
6. Skip to my Lou
7. Cshebogar
8. Come Let Us Be Joyful
   Marching — Review Grade 2
9. Introduce two-step

### 1. Jump Jim Jo (American)

Record — Bowmar 1521, Folkraft 1180.

Formation — Double circle, partners facing each other. Boys on the inside of the circle, girls on the outside.

Description —

"Jump, jump, jump Jim Jo"

All do two slow jumps in place, then three fast jumps.

"Take a little turn and away we go"

Join hands with partner and make one complete turn to the left back to place; walk, or light running steps.

"Slide, slide and stamp just so"

Hands still joined, take two slides counterclockwise, and three stamps in place.

"Then you take another partner and Jump Jim Jo."

Girls move up to the next boy. Three jumps in place.

TEACHING SUGGESTIONS

On the jumps, count "one, two and one, two, three." The rhythm is slow, slow, fast, fast, fast.

2. **Children's Polka** (Kinderpolka) (German)

Record — Bowmar 1519, RCA Victor 45-6179, Folkraft 1187.

Formation — Partners face each other, boys with left side to the center of the circle, girls with right side toward the center of the circle. Hands joined.

Description —

Part I. Two slow slides, moving toward the center of the circle. Stamp in place three times.
Repeat, moving toward outside of the circle.

Repeat all.

Part II. Each child claps own thighs once.
Each child claps own hands once.
Each child claps partner's hands three times.
Repeat.

Shake right finger three times at partner, resting right elbow in left hand.
Shake left finger three times at partner, resting left elbow in right hand.

Each child turns around in place, clapping hands over head or snapping fingers.

TEACHING SUGGESTIONS

1. To help children get the rhythm, count "slow, slow, fast, fast, fast;" or "one, two, one, two, three."
2. Girls, or boys, may move up to the next partner after the turn.
3. Vary by having children, in Part I, hold arms straight out to the side with partner, and bend toward the center of the circle when moving in, and bend toward the outside of the circle when moving out.

**3. Paw Paw Patch** (American)

Record — RCA Victor 45-5066, Folkraft 1181.

Formation — Partners in two parallel lines; boys in one line, girls in the other. Girls should be on the boys' right. All face forward toward the head of the set.

```
Girls   Boys
  O       X  all face
  O       X  |
  O       X  ↓
  O       X
          head
          couple
```

Description —

First verse — "Where oh where is dear little ............?
Where oh where is dear little ............?
Where or where is dear little ............?
Way down yonder in the Paw Paw Patch."

The head lady skips around the set, starting to her right. All others stand still and sing or clap to the music. The first name of the head lady is used.

Second verse — "Come on boys, lets go find her,
Come on boys, lets go find her,
Come on boys, lets go find her,
Way down yonder in the Paw Paw Patch."

The head lady again skips around the set, followed by all the boys, until all are back in their original places.

Third verse — "Picking up paw paws, put 'em in a basket,
Picking up paw paws, put 'em in a basket,
Picking up paw paws, put 'em in a basket,
Way down yonder in the Paw Paw Patch."

The head lady turns to her right, head man turns to his left. They skip to the end of the set, followed by all others. Head couple meets at end of the set, forms an arch with their joined hands and all others go under the arch.

Repeat with new head couple.

TEACHING SUGGESTIONS

1. This follows, in the progression, "A Hunting We Will Go" from the second grade. If children have not learned "A Hunting," teach that before Paw Paw Patch.
2. Children should use all of the music when skipping around the set, and not get back to their positions until the end of the music.

**4. Pease Porridge Hot** (sometimes called "Bean Porridge Hot")

Record — Bowmar 1519.

Formation — Double circle, partners facing; boys on the inside of the circle, girls on the outside.

Description —
"Pease Porridge Hot"

All clap own thighs, all clap own hands,
Clap partner's hands.

"Pease Porridge Cold"

All clap own thighs, all clap own hands,
All clap partner's hands.
"Pease Porridge in the pot nine days old."
Clap own thighs, clap own hands,
Clap partner's right hand with right hand,
Clap own hands,
Clap partner's left hand with left hand,
Clap own hands,
Clap both hands with partner.

Repeat all

On chorus, join inside hands with partner and skip sixteen skips counterclockwise around the circle. Girls move up to the next partner.

TEACHING SUGGESTIONS

1. Some records repeat the chorus. In that case, pupils skip 32 skips around the circle instead of sixteen.
2. Some children have trouble with the clapping coordination. Help them by standing behind them and holding their wrists, and then guiding them through the motions. Or let them practice with another child who does it well.
3. The clapping sequence can be learned in the classroom or in other limited space.

**5. Pop Goes the Weasel** (American)

Record — RCA Victor 45-5066, RCA Victor 45-6180, Folk Dancer MH 1501.

Formation — Groups of three. Join hands to form a small circle. The trios stand so so as to form a large circle.

Description —
The groups of three skip to their left around in a small circle for 12 skips. On the words, "Pop Goes the Weasel," Number One is popped under the arms of the other two and moves up counterclockwise to the next group.

Continue.

TEACHING SUGGESTIONS

1. Pupils should be numbered one, two and three. Rotate positions so that numbers two and three have an opportunity to be 'popped.'
2. The trios will probably skip around their small circles twice before the 'pop.' They must end in position so that Number One can move ahead to the next group.

## 6. Skip to My Lou

Record — Bowmar 1522, Folkraft 1192.

Formation — Double circle, boys on the inside, girls on the outside, all facing counterclockwise. Several extra boys (or girls) are in the center of the circle.

Description —

Verse — "Fly in the buttermilk, shoo fly shoo,
Fly in the buttermilk, shoo fly shoo,
Fly in the buttermilk, shoo fly shoo,
Skip to my Lou my darling."

The outside circle walks or skips counterclockwise. The center players each choose a couple from the outside circle by tapping the boy on the shoulder. On the chorus, the three form a small circle inside the big circle and skip around. The boy who did the choosing becomes the girl's new partner and they go back into the big circle. The other boy stays in the center, chooses a new couple on the next verse and the game continues.

Chorus — "Lou, Lou, skip to my Lou
Lou, Lou, skip to my Lou
Lou, Lou, skip to my Lou
Skip to my Lou my darling."

Verse 2 — "Going to Texas, two by two"
Verse 3 — "Lost my partner, what'll I do?"
Verse 4 — "I'll get another, prettier than you"
Verse 5 — "Chickens in the haystack, two by two"
Verse 6 — "Pigs in the fence and can't get through"

TEACHING SUGGESTIONS

1. Pupils may make up words to other verses.
2. This is a typical American folk dance of the Pioneer era.

## 7. Cshebogar (Pronounced shay-bo-gar) (Hungarian)

Record — RCA Victor 45-6182, Bowmar 1520.

Formation — Partners in a single circle facing the center of the circle. Boy has his partner on his right side. All hands joined.

Description —

Part I.   All do seven slides to the right, stop on count eight.
All do seven slides to the left, stop on count eight.
Four skips forward toward the center of the circle.
Four skips backward to place.

Hook right arms with partner. Raise left arm above head.
Skip around with partner for eight skips.

Part II.   Face partner. Boy's left side should be toward the center of the circle, and girl's right side. Boy's hands on girl's waist; girl's hands on boy's shoulders.
Four draw steps (or slow slides) toward the center of the circle.

Four draw steps away from the center of the circle.
Two draw steps in,
Two draw steps out.

Repeat turn as above, finishing with a shout.

TEACHING SUGGESTIONS

1. This is a typical Hungarian rhythm, contrasting slow and fast rhythms.
2. Partners should lean back away from each other on the turn.
3. On the skips toward the center of the circle, lean forward. On skips backward from center, raise joined hands over head.

## 8. Come Let Us Be Joyful (German)

Record — RCA Victor 45-6177.

Formation — Two girls and a boy form a line of three with the boy in the center, hands joined with each girl. Trio A faces Trio B and so on around the circle in sets of six. There should be approximately four steps between the trios facing each other.

Description —

Part  I.   Walk forward three steps, boys bow, girls curtsy.
Walk backward three steps bringing feet together on fourth count.
Repeat.

Part II.　Boy hooks right elbows with girl on his right and skips
around with her for four skips while the other girl skips
in place. Boy hooks left elbow with girl on his left and
skips around with her for four skips while the other
girl skips in place.
Repeat.

Part III.　Repeat Part I, i.e.
Walk forward three steps. Walk backward three steps.
Walk forward eight steps, passing through opposite trio
and on to meet the next trio. Repeat all with the next trio.

TEACHING SUGGESTIONS

1. This is a new formation and a new pattern, and 'leads up' to more
difficult dances in the fourth and fifth grades.
2. Depending upon the number of boys and the number of girls in
the class, the center person does not necessarily have to be a boy.
3. When trios 'pass through', pass the opposite person right shoulder
to right shoulder.
4. Children may walk on the turn instead of skipping.
5. For variation, only boys may 'pass through' to the next group.

## 9. The Two-step

Record — Any rather slow two or four beat music. May use records for
fourth grade rhythms, i.e. Glowworm or Oklahoma Mixer.

Formation — In one or two lines, all facing the same direction.

Description —

| | |
|---|---|
| Step forward (or diagonally forward) | Cues |
| left. Bring right foot up to left and | "one and two" |
| step on right. Step forward again left. | or "Left right left" |
| Repeat, starting with right foot. | or "Step close step" |

TEACHING SUGGESTIONS

1. If third graders do quite well in rhythms and complete the foregoing
dances, they may be ready to learn the two-step.
2. The teacher, or a pupil, may do the two-step in front of the class
as the rest of the pupils perform the step in lines.
3. Children should learn the step alone, by themselves, and then with
a partner.
4. Sometimes it helps a child to get the feel of the step if you stand
beside him, take his hand and do it with him. Or a pupil, who has
mastered the step, may do it with him.

5. After pupils have learned the two-step forward, try it backward, then in combinations such as eight steps forward, eight steps backward; four steps forward, four steps backward, etc.

6. The final formation involves performing the two-step in partners, standing side by side with inside hands joined.

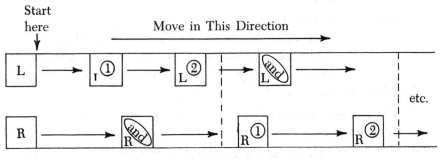

(Symbols Encircled Are Counts)

## FOURTH GRADE RHYTHMS

1. Seven Jumps
2. Glowworm Mixer
3. Gustaf's Skoal (square)
4. Bleking
5. Patty Cake Polka
6. Irish Reel
7. Wooden Shoes
8. Oklahoma Mixer

9. Sicilian Circle
   *Continue two-step*
10. Introduce waltz step
11. Marching
    (If this is too much material for a particular class, omit Seven Jumps and/or Wooden Shoes.)

1. **Seven Jumps** (Danish)

   Record — RCA Victor 45-6172.

   Formation — Single Circle, all hands joined.

   Description —

   Chorus:  Seven step-hops (or slow skips) to the right. Jump once in place. Repeat in opposite direction.

   Figure 1:  Release hands, place hands on hips.
   Raise right knee and hold until second note.
   Stand on third note.
   Repeat chorus.

   Figure 2:  Repeat Figure 1, add identical figure with left knee.
   Repeat chorus.

Figure 3: Repeat Figures 1, 2 — add kneel on right knee.
Repeat chorus.
Figure 4: Repeat Figures 1, 2 and 3 — add kneel on left knee.
Repeat chorus.
Figure 5: Repeat Figures 1, 2, 3 and 4 — place right elbow on floor.
Repeat chorus.
Figure 6: Repeat Figures 1, 2, 3, 4 and 5 — place left elbow on floor.
Repeat chorus.
Figure 7: Repeat Figures 1, 2, 3, 4, 5 and 6 — place forehead on floor.
Repeat chorus.

TEACHING SUGGESTIONS

1. There may be a leader, or a small group in the center of the circle.
2. This dance may be done by boys alone and/or girls alone, or with mixed groups.

2. **Glowworm Mixer** (American)

Record — Imperial 1044, or Windsor 7613 or Four Star 1365.

Formation — Double circle, boys on the inside, girls on the outside. Couples join inside hands, facing counterclockwise.

Description —

Walk four steps forward.

Face partner and walk four steps backward. (Boys backing up toward center of circle; girls toward outside of circle.)

Four steps diagonally forward to the right to meet new partner.

Join hands with new partner and walk four steps around turning with new partner.

Cues

"Walk, 2, 3, 4"

"Back, 2, 3, 4"

"New partner"

"Turn, 2, 3, 4"

TEACHING SUGGESTIONS

1. This is a well liked, simple and effective mixer.
2. After pupils have learned the basic pattern, teach them to hold hands at shoulder level. Boys put the outside hand on hip, while girls hold their skirts.
3. Boys should 'lead' the new partner into position for starting a repeat of the dance.
4. Glowworm may be done to any contemporary 2/4 or 4/4 music that has a steady rhythm and a strong beat such as Butterball,

Peanuts and Green Pepper on Herb Alpert's A & M Record SP 4110.

3. **Gustaf's Skoal** (Swedish)

Record — RCA Victor 45-6170 or Windsor A7S2 or Folkraft F1175.

Formation — In sets, or squares of four couples, all facing center, two head couples and two side couples. Boy has his partner on his right, inside hands joined at shoulder height.

Description —

Part I. Head couples walk forward three steps. On count 4, bow to opposite couple.

Head couples walk backward three steps to 'home' position and bow to each other.

Side couples perform same action.

Repeat all.

Part II. Side couples hold up joined hands to form arch. Head couples skip out to the center of the set, turn, and each person goes through the nearest arch; then back to home position. Join both hands with partner and skip around in place turning once.

Side couples repeat action as head couples form an arch.

Square Dance
Formation

O X

X                         O

O                         X

X O

X = Boys
O = Girls

Head Couple

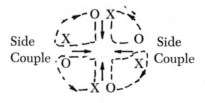

Side Couple          Side Couple

Head Couple

TEACHING SUGGESTIONS

1. This, while not a typical square dance, is done in square dance formation. It is an easy dance through which to introduce children to the square dance.

2. Square dance terminology —
   a. Square — dance formation for four couples, each couple forming one side of the square.
   b. Head Couple — usually considered the couple nearest the music. In this dance, there are two head couples, standing opposite each other.
   c. Side Couple — couples who stand on the sides of the square.
   d. A square is sometimes referred to as a 'set.'
   e. 'Home' is the place where the couple starts the dance.
3. In Part I, be sure pupils take *three* steps before the bow.
4. In Part 1, for variation, pupils may raise hands and say 'hi' or 'skoal' instead of bowing.
5. Other variations — in Part II — Clap hands once just before starting the skipping part.
6. If there are extra couples or individuals, they may 'cut in.' Whenever a couple or an individual is gone from his 'Home' position, (as on the skipping part) someone else may take his place.

4. **Bleking** (Swedish)

Record — RCA Victor 45-6169

Formation — Circle with partners facing each other and hands joined. Boys on the inside, girls on the outside.

Description —

Part I. Bleking Step.                                    Cues

Hop on left while placing right foot forward —                                  "Slow or "1

Hop on right while placing left foot forward —                                  slow       2

Hop on left while placing right foot forward —                                  fast       1

Hop on right while placing left foot forward —                                  fast       2

Hop on left while placing right foot forward —                                  fast"      3"

Repeat three times.

Part II. Arms out to the side, elbows straight, partners facing and hands joined.

Boy does step-hop on left foot, swinging the other leg out to the side. Girl does step-hop on right foot, swinging the other leg out to the side.

Repeat on opposite feet and continue for 16 times in all.

Teaching Suggestions

1. Teach the foot pattern first; then add arm movements as follows:
   Part  I.  As the right heel goes forward, the right arm goes for-
             ward, elbow straight; the left arm is brought back, elbow
             bent. Arms change as the feet change.
   Part II.  Outstretched arms go up and down, arm going up on the
             same side on which the leg is swung out.
2. After the foot and arm movements have been learned, couples may
   turn around while doing part II.
3. The Bleking step may be taught with pupils in a single line, all
   facing in the same direction, first by themselves and then with a
   partner.
4. Select several couples who do the dance well to demonstrate for the
   class.
5. This is a vigorous dance and may appeal to boys more than some
   of the other folk dances. It may be done in boy-boy couples or
   girl-girl couples.

5. **Patty Cake Polka** (American)

Record — Four Star 1365 "Little Brown Jug," Columbia 52007, Folk
    Dancer MH1501 "Buffalo Gal."

Formation — Double circle, partners facing each other. Boys on the
    inside, girls on the outside, both hands joined.

Description —

| | | Cues |
|---|---|---|
| Part  I. | Heel-toe. Boy places left heel to the side, then left toe back of right foot. | |
| | At the same time, girl places right heel to side, then right toe in back of left foot. | "Heel, toe heel, toe slide, 2, 3, 4" |

Repeat.

Four slides counterclockwise (to boy's left).

Repeat all with opposite feet, moving in opposite direction.

| | | |
|---|---|---|
| Part II. | Clap both hands together | "Together |
| | Clap partner's right hand with right hand | right |
| | Clap own hands together | together |
| | Clap partner's left hand with left hand | left |
| | Clap own hands together | together |
| | Clap both of partner's hands | both |
| | Clap own hands together | together |
| | Clap own knees | down" |

Hook right elbows with partner and walk    "Turn"
around 8 counts, 8 steps, boys moving
ahead to the next girl.

TEACHING SUGGESTIONS

1. On the heel-toe emphasize that both partners' feet should go out
on the same *side* — boy's left and girl's right.
2. Walk, do not skip on the turn.

**6. Irish Reel** (Irish)

Record — RCA Victor 45-6178.

Formation — Two parallel lines (a longways set) of four couples
facing each other with hands on hip. Boy stands opposite
partner, his partner on his right if they were facing forward.

Description —

Part    I.    Hop on right foot four times, tapping    Cues
left toe in front.                                "Hop

Hop on left foot four times, tapping
right toe in front.

Hop on right foot four times, tapping
left toe in front.

Hop on left foot four times, tapping
right toe in front.              16 counts

Part   II.   Head couple and second couple step    Star
out to the center of the set, touch right
hands up in center forming a 'right
hand star.' Skip around, clockwise, 8
skips. Reverse, making a left hand star
and skip around 8 skips. Pupils should
end in original position.

At the same time, the two foot couples
are doing the same figure.

16 counts

Part III.   The head couple joins hands in the    Slide
center of the set and does 8 slides down
the center of the set and 8 slides back
to home. At the same time, the foot
couple does 8 slides (boy behind boys'
line and girl behind girls' line) up to
head of set and 8 slides back to home.

Two center couples stand in place and
clap.                              16 counts

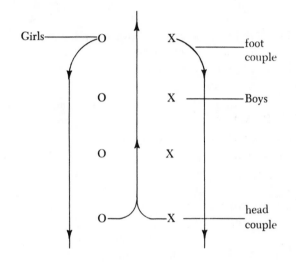

Part IV.    The head couple leads the group   Around"
            around the set, (girl turning to her
            right, leads the girls' line; boy turning
            to his left, leads boys' line) they form
            an arch and all others pass under the
            arch.                              16 counts

            Repeat all with new head couple.

TEACHING SUGGESTIONS

1. This is a fast moving folk dance that requires quick thinking. Tell
   the pupils that while they are doing one part, they should be
   thinking of what comes next.
2. On Part III, let couples cover as much space as they can while
   doing the 8 slides.
3. New terminology includes longways set, right and left hand star.

7. **Wooden Shoes** (Lithuanian)

Record — Imperial 1007.

Formation — Double circle, facing counterclockwise. Boys on the
            inside, girls on the outside. Inside hands joined at shoulder
            height, outside hands on hips.

Description —                                                       Cues
    Part    I.  Walk forward 8 steps (8 counts)     "Walk
              Reverse by turning in toward partner
              and walk forward 8 steps in opposite
              direction. Join right hands, or hook    Turn
              right elbows and walk around partner
              for 8 steps. Reverse, join left hands or
              hook left elbows, walk around partner
              8 counts.

    Part  II.  Face partner (boy's back to center of   Face partner
              circle)
              In time with the music
              Stamp 3 times
              Clap 3 times
              Shake right finger at partner 3 times.
              Shake left finger at partner 3 times.
              Turn around in place.
              Repeat clapping sequence

    Part  III.  With inside hands joined at shoulder   two step"
              height and moving counterclockwise,
              do 16 two-steps around the circle, girl
              moving up to new partner on the last
              few steps.

TEACHING SUGGESTIONS

1. This is a brisk, simple routine with appealing music.
2. Pupils may skip on the last part (Part III) until they have learned the rather fast two-step used here.

## 8. Oklahoma Mixer (American)

Record — Columbia 20117 "Starlight Schottische" (or any slow schottische).

Formation — Double circle facing counterclockwise. Boys on the inside, girls on the outside in varsouvienne position. Boy, with his right hand, holds girl's right hand at her right shoulder. Boy holds girl's left hand, with his left hand, in front.

Description —                                                       Cues
    Part I.  Both starting left foot        "Two step left
           Two step left (toward center of circle)
           Two step right (toward outside of
           circle)                    Two step out
           Step (walk) left, right, left, right.    Walk 2, 3, 4

Part II. Heel-toe. Left heel forward, then left     Heel toe
toe behind right foot. Step left, right,
left. During these three steps, drop right
hands. Girl moves across in front of boy    Turn the lady
ending up on his left side, facing the        back
next boy in the circle. Left hands are
still joined at shoulder height. Boy does
three steps in place.

Heel-toe. Right heel forward, then right     Heel toe
toe behind left foot. Step right, left, Back she goes."
right as girl moves back to next boy.
Repeat with new partner.

TEACHING SUGGESTIONS

1. This is the first time the two-step has been used in a dance. It is
   done slowly and all in the same direction. If certain chlidren have
   trouble with it, give them extra practice on the two-step, or let
   some child who does it well help them. Doing the step with the
   child is often very helpful. (See Grade 3 for instructions for two step.)
2. In order for the turn to be successful (Part II) the girl must, with
   her right hand, reach for the next boy, and he, in turn, must reach
   for her with his right hand and 'lead' her to turn around in order
   to be in proper position to repeat the dance.
   The girl should *not* turn under the boy's arm.

9. **Sicilian Circle** (American)

   Record — Windsor A-7S4, Methodist 104, Folkraft 1115, Folkraft 1242
         (with calls).

   Formation — Double circle. Boy's partner on his right, inside hands
              joined, boy supporting girl's hand on his, at shoulder height.
              Every other couple faces clockwise, to form sets of four.

   Description —
   1. "Circle to the left" — all four join hands and walk 8 steps to
      the left, returning to original position.
   2. "Swing partner" — Each boy hooks right elbows wtih his part-
      ner and walks around 8 steps, returning to original position.
   3. "Right and Left Through" — The two couples pass through
      each other passing right shoulders. Each gentleman may take
      the right hand of the opposite lady as he passes her. He takes
      his partner's left in his left, when they have passed through,
      and places his right hand at her waist. He makes a left pivot,
      leading his lady around with him and they face the opposite
      couple again. (4 steps to pass through, 4 steps to turn)

4. "Right and Left Back" — Repeat above, returning to home position. (4 steps to pass through, 4 steps to turn)
5. "Ladies Chain" — The two ladies advance, join right hands and pass each other. Each lady gives her left hand to the opposite gentleman and he turns her by putting his right hand on the small of her back. (4 steps for lady to cross over, 4 steps for turn)
6. "Chain them back home" — Repeat above, returning to home position.
7. "Forward and back" — Each couple walks four steps forward, toward other couple, and four steps backward to home position.
8. "Forward and pass through" — Four steps forward, passing through opposite couple (Ladies should go in the center) and four steps to advance to meet the next couple.
   Repeat with new couple.

TEACHING SUGGESTIONS

1. This may look complicated, but it really is simple. The turn seems to give the most difficulty. Be sure boys understand how they are to turn the ladies. Emphasize their reaching for the girl with their right hand.
2. Use above 'calls' (in quotes) as cues when learning the dance. After pupils know the dance, no calls are necessary.
3. If a pupil is capable, he may give the cues or calls.

10. **The waltz step**

Record — Use any rather slow waltz record such as MacGregor 649 "Alice Blue Gown," and "Tennessee Waltz."

Formation — In one, or two, lines facing same direction.

Description—

If fourth graders complete the list of folk dances, they may be introduced to the waltz rhythm and waltz step. The waltz is a three beat rhythm with a strong accent on Count 1. It has a very different 'feel' from any other step.

Step forward left
Step to the side right
Bring left foot to right and step on it
Repeat, starting right.

Cues and count —

"open, open, close."
"forward, side, together"
"*one*, two, three"

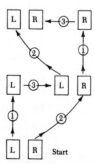

TEACHING SUGGESTIONS

1. Have children sit and listen to waltz music, clapping on count 1.
2. Walk in time to the music, stamping or accenting count 1. "*Down,* up, up." Do this in a circle, or line formation with hands joined.
3. Have pupils try it by themselves, in line formation. The teacher, or a pupil, may do the waltz step in front of, and with the class.
4. Keep the feet close to the floor.
5. If a student has trouble, the teacher — or a pupil who has mastered the step — can take his hand, stand beside him, and do the step with him.
6. When pupils can do a waltz step forward, try it backward and in different combinations such as 8 forward and 8 backward; 4 forward and 4 backward, etc.
7. Tell children they must 'think.' Their feet will not do the step correctly unless their brains tell the feet what to do.

## 11. Marching

Record — Bowmar Album of Marches — Records 1569, 1570, 1571, or any other march record.

Review all marching commands and formations from primary grades. See Grade 2.

Progression —

1. When pupils can march in time to music and keep good spacing, add marching in step. Always start by stepping forward on the left foot, "left, right, left, right," etc. Count 1, 2, 3, 4, emphasizing count on left foot.
2. Combine commands such as
   "Class, attention"
   "Mark time"
   "Forward — march"
   "Mark time"
   "Forward — march"
   "Mark time"
   "Class halt, one, two"
   "At ease."
3. Add Commands — While standing at "Attention" —
   "Right Face, one, two" — On Count one, lift right toe and left heel; pivot to the right. On Count two, bring left foot up beside right.
   "Left Face, one two" — On Count one, lift left toe, and right heel; pivot to the left. On count two, bring right foot up beside left.

"About Face, one two" — (to the right) On Count one, place the ball of the right foot slightly to the rear of the left foot. On Count two, pivot around on balls of feet, bring left foot up even with right.

4. Add formations —
   a. "Down the Center by Fours" — Couples meet at center of end of floor and march down the center in lines of four. Guide by individual at the left end of the line.
   b. "Down the Center by Eights" — same as a.
   c. "Down the Center by Fours," then two's, then single line.
   d. Other formations may be devised by the pupils, or the teacher, to make interesting patterns, such as
      (1) Single lines turn at corners and march diagonally across the room, crossing in order, at the center of the room. Makes "X" formation.
      (2) Sharp turn to opposite direction. (May use command, "To the Rear, March")

```
        O                   X
            O           X
    |   O       O  ↑ X       X   |
    |   O       O  | X       X   |
    ↓   O       O  | X       X   ↓
        O                   X
        O_ _ _ _ _ _ _ _ _ _X
```

## FIFTH GRADE RHYTHMS

*Review from 4th grade*
   *Gustaf's Skoal*
   *Oklahoma Mixer*
   *Sicilian Circle*
1. Mexican Clap Dance
2. Oh Susanna
3. Ace of Diamonds
4. Bingo

5. Virginia Reel
6. Cotton Eyed Joe
7. Schottische Step
8. Schottische Dance
9. Square Dance
10. Oh Johnny
   *Waltz step — continue*
   *Marching — continue*

1. Mexican Clap Dance (Mexican)

Record — MacGregor 608, "Chiapanecas."

Formation — Double circle, boys on the inside, girls on the outside. Partners facing, both hands joined.

Description —

Part A.  Boy — Step left, swing right leg across left leg.
Step right, swing left leg across right leg.
Step left, swing right leg across left leg.
Hold right leg there, while clapping own hands twice.
Girl does the same, starting with right foot. (On the *same side* as the boy's left foot.)
Repeat, starting opposite.

Part B.  Balance, keeping hands joined.
Step back away from partner, step toward partner, step back away from partner.
Clap twice.
Step toward partner, step away from partner, step toward partner.
Clap twice, the man reaching around his partner's waist, to clap, and the girl clapping her hands behind her partner's head.

Part C.  Face counterclockwise, inside hands joined. Moving counterclockwise, in time with the music.
Walk, walk, girl turns under boy's arm (towards him)
Walk, walk, boy turns under girl's arm (towards her)
Walk, walk, both turn (toward each other)
Walk, walk, girl moves up to the next boy.
Clap twice.

TEACHING SUGGESTIONS

1. The balance is a sort of rocking motion, one foot staying behind the other.
2. If the clapping behind the girl's waist and boy's head is just *too* much, they may clap as before.
3. If pupils can do the waltz step, Part C may be 16 waltz steps, performed side by side, or in social dance position.

2. **Oh Susanna** (American)

Record — RCA 45-6178.

Formation — Partners in single circle, all facing center. Boy's partner on his right.

Description —

Part A.  "Ladies to the Center"
Girls take three steps to the center of the circle; quick curtsy.
Girls take three steps backward to place.

"Gents to the Center"
Boys take three steps to the center; quick bow.
Boys take three steps backward to place.
Repeat all.

Part B. "Grand Right and Left"
Partners face each other. (Girls will be facing clockwise, boys counterclockwise). Give right hand to partner, walk past partner, passing right shoulders.
Give left hand to next person, passing left        Count 1
shoulders. Continue to #7. This person is new              2
partner.                                                   3, etc.

Part C. "Promenade"
Boys put new partners on their right side. Join inside hands at shoulder height and walk around the circle till the end of the music. (16 steps)

TEACHING SUGGESTIONS

1. · This is a good mixer and teaches square dance calls, including the grand right and left. Go through this slowly without music, at first. The important thing to remember is to give your right hand to your partner *first*. Then continue in the direction you are facing.
2. The boy should lead his new partner into position in the circle when the dance starts over.
3. Boys may stamp, when they go into the center, instead of bowing.

3. **Ace of Diamonds** (Scandinavian)

Record — RCA Victor 45-6169.

Formation — Double circle, partners facing. Boy's back toward the center of the circle.

Description —

Part A. Clap own hands once, then stamp left foot once. Hook left elbows with partner and with eight small running steps, make a complete turn returning to own position. Repeat, hooking right elbows.

Part B. With arms folded and held shoulder high, do four slow step-hops toward center of circle, boy moving backward and girl moving forward.
Repeat, girl moving backward and boy forward, moving back to original position.

Part C. Join inside hands, eight 'in and out' two-steps around the circle. Boy starts left foot, girl on right foot. On the first two-step, turn towards each other; on the second, turn away from each other, etc.

TEACHING SUGGESTIONS

1. Be sure the clap and stamp are clear and in rhythm.
2. If a pupil has trouble with the 'in and out' two-step, give him extra help or have another pupil take him aside and help him. Sometimes it helps a pupil to get the 'feel' of the step if someone, who does it well, can perform it with him.
3. On Part B, arms should be held high, away from the body.

4. **Bingo** (American)

Record — RCA Victor 45-6172.

Formation — Double circle, boy on the inside, girl on the outside, all facing counterclockwise. Promenade position (hands crossed in front, right hand to right, left hand to left hand.)

Description —

"A big black dog at on the back porch and Bingo was his name,
A big black dog sat on the pack porch and Bingo was his name."

Promenade around the circle for 16 steps.

"B i n g o, B i n g o, B i n g o and Bingo was his name."

Boy leads partner to position in front of him. All join hands to form a single circle. Continue walking around the circle for 16 steps.

" B I N G O,"

Grand right and left. Face partner and starting with partner on "B," move to another person on each letter; fifth person "O" is new partner. Be sure to count partner as 'one.' (See grand right and left description in "Oh Susanna.")

TEACHING SUGGESTIONS

1. This is a good mixer to do for variety. It sometimes appeals to boys more than some of the other dances.
2. Be sure that pupils start the grand right and left by giving the right hand to their partner, and continue moving around the circle in that direction.

5. **Virginia Reel** (American)

Record RCA Victor 45-6180.

Formation — Longways set with four to six couples in a set. Ladies on the gents' right.

Description —                                              Cues or Calls

Part A.  Forward and back: lines walk for-    "Forward and Back
         ward toward partner, three steps,
         quick bow. Walk three steps back to
         place. Repeat (16 counts)

         Right hand around: walk toward       Right hand around
         partner, grasp right hands, walk
O X      around partner and back to place.
         Repeat with left hand. (16 counts)
O X
         Both hands around: Walk toward       Both hands around
O X      partner, join both hands, turn around
         partner to left and return to place.
O X      Repeat, turning to right. (16 counts)

Ladies   Do Si Do: arms folded on chest, part-   Do si do"
         ners walk toward each other, pass
   Men   left shoulders and back up to place.
         Repeat, passing right shoulders. (16
         counts)

Part B.  Head couple steps out to the center  "Head couple down
         of the set and with both hands joined,  the center"
         does eight slides down the center of
         the set, and eight slides back up
         again. (16 counts)

         Reel — Head couple hook right el-     "Reel"
         bows and turn once and a half around
         (in the center of the set) until girl
         faces boys' line and boy faces girls'
         line. Leave partner, hook left elbow
         with next girl (or boy) and walk
         around that person and back to part-
         ner. Hook partner's right elbow, turn
         and go to second girl, etc. until all
         have been 'reeled.' Partners then join
         hands and slide up to the head of
         the set.

         Only the head couple is in action.
         Others stand and clap, or tap foot, in
         time to the music.

Part C.  March — Head lady turns to her       "March"
         right, head man to his left, each
         making a "U" turn, and all in the set

follow the head couple. At the foot
of the set, head couple forms an arch
by joining both hands. All couples
pass through the arch.

Head couple is now the foot couple
and the dance continues with a new
head couple.

TEACHING SUGGESTIONS

1. There are many versions of the Virginia Reel. This is one version,
   and fits with the suggested record.
2. The teacher, or a caller, should call out the sequence.
3. The walking step should be used throughout, except for the slides.
   Do not skip.
4. Four to six couples in a set are desirable.
5. Demonstrate the 'reel' with one set and one couple while the
   remainder of the class observes.
6. Pupils should have no difficulty with this formation. The only
   new technique is the 'reel.'

6. **Cotton Eyed Joe** (American)

Record — Imperial 1045 or MacGregor 604.

Formation — Double circle with partners facing. Boy's back is toward
center of circle.

Description —                                                     Cues

Part A. Heel toe, two-step, boy starting left, girl starting
right. Touch left heel diagonally forward, touch        "Heel, toe
left toe diagonally backward; step left to the
side, close with right, step left.)
Repeat, boy starting right, girl starting left and
both moving back toward starting position.

Part B. Circle away from partner, boy to left, girl to          Circle
right, doing four two-steps, and returning to
original position.

Part C. Both do three push steps to boy's left, girl start-     Push
ing right. Stamp twice. (Step left, push off with
ball of right foot.)
Repeat, starting right (girl left) moving back
to original position.

Part D. Inside hands joined. Four two-steps in line of          Two step"
direction, i.e. counterclockwise. Boy starting
with left foot, girl with right.

TEACHING SUGGESTIONS

1. This is a fast dance with quick changes. A 'catchy' tune makes it fun and stimulating to do.
2. Hand positions—
   Part A. Both hands joined.
   Part B. Girl holds her skirt; boy clasps hands behind back, or places thumbs under belt buckle. Strut.
   Part C. Hands on hips.
   Part D. Inside hands joined.
   Teach the hand positions after the step pattern has been learned.
3. In Part D partners turn toward each other on the first two-step, away on the second, etc. This is called an 'in and out' two-step.
4. This dance can be done as a mixer by having the girl move up to the next boy on the last two two-steps.

## 7. The Schottische Step

Record — Any schottische record. Folk Dancer 1055 preferred. Also Decca 25062 "Military Schottische" and Linden 29 "Balen Karlstad."

Formation — In one or two lines all facing same direction. See instructions for two-step (third grade) or waltz step (fourth grade).

Description —
Step left diagonally forward. Count 1
Bring right foot up to left and step on it. Count 2
Step left diagonally forward. Count 3
Hop on left. Count 4

Repeat all, starting right.

The schottische step is usually combined with four step-hops as follows:

Schottische left
Schottische right.
Step hop, left, right, left, right.

TEACHING SUGGESTIONS

1. The schottische step becomes more of a light running step than a walk.

   Cues — "run, run, run, hop" or
   "one, two, three, hop" or
   "left, right, left, hop."

2. Keep the feet close to the floor. The step should be smooth.
3. After pupils can do the schottische step, add the step-hops.
4. Pupils should practice and learn the step alone, then combine to form partners.

## 8. A Schottische Dance

Record — Folk Dancer 1055, "Swedish Schottische." Or RCA Victor 45-6177, "Bummel Schottische" or Linden 804 "Millpond Schottische."

Formation — Double circle, all facing counterclockwise. Inside hands joined at shoulder height.

Description —

The step pattern throughout is two schottische steps and four step hops.

Schottische step left, schottische step right. Four step-hops left, right, left, right, moving slightly ahead.

Schottische left, schottische right. Four step-hops. Boy does step-hops in place as girl turns to her right, under the joined hands.

Schottische left, schottische right. Four step-hops left, right, left, right. Girl does step-hops in place as boy turns under joined hands.

Schottische left, schottische right. Four step-hops as both boy and girl turn.

Repeat all.

TEACHING SUGGESTIONS

1. Other patterns, for the step-hops, may be devised by the pupils.
2. Vary by getting in sets of four, one couple standing in front of the other, all facing counterclockwise. Join inside hands with partner. With the other hand, the front boy joins hand with the boy behind him, and the front girl with the girl behind her.

   Schottische left, schottische right. On step-hops (four) the front couple drops hands and, turning to the outside (boy to his left, girl to her right), goes back to become the second couple. The second couple then moves ahead to become the front couple.

## 9. Square Dance

The following are square dance terminology, patterns and formations which fifth graders should know if the rhythms progression in this book has been followed:

1. Couples
2. Squares (Gustaf's Skoal, fourth grade)

3. Promenade (Oh Susanna and Bingo — fifth grade)
4. Grand Right and Left (Oh Susanna and Bingo, fifth grade)
5. Head and foot couples (Gustaf's Skoal, fourth grade; Virginia Reel, fifth grade)
6. Do Si Do (Virginia Reel, fifth grade)
7. Right and left hand star (Irish Reel, fourth grade)
8. Right and Left Through (Sicilian Circle, fourth grade)
9. Ladies Chain (Sicilian Circle, fourth grade)
10. Right and Left Around (Virginia Reel, 5th grade)

TEACHING SUGGESTIONS

1. If fifth graders have not learned Sicilian Circle (fourth grade), include it here.
2. Teachers may prefer to use records with calls on them. The following are suggested; they are listed in order of approximate difficulty:

   a. RCA Victor Album E3000 "Let's Square Dance" Album No. 1. Includes simple squares with calls —

      Shoo Fly
      Duck for the Oyster
      Red River Valley
      Girls to the Center
      Take a Little Peek
      Hinkey Dinkey Parlez-vous
      Divide the Ring
      Noble Duke of York
      Little Brown Jug (no calls)

   b. Bowmar Records for intermediate and upper grades. 10515 Burbank Blvd., North Hollywood, Calif.
   c. Decca Records, Ed Gilmore Square Dances. (Good)
   d. Square Dance Associates Records. Square Dance Associates, Freeport, Long Island, New York.

## 10. Oh Johnny

Record — Imperial 1099 "Oh Johnny" (no calls) or MacGregor 003-4 (calls), Folkraft 1037.

Formation — Squares of four couples. Boy has partner on his right side.
Description —
1. "All join hands and circle the ring."
   Join hands and walk eight steps to the right.
2. "Stop where you are, give your partner a swing."
   Hook right elbows and walk around once (eight steps) with partner.

3. "Swing that girl behind you."
   Each boy hooks left elbows with girl behind him (on his left, or
   'corner' maid) and walks around with her for eight steps.
4. "Go back home and swing your own."
   Swing partner as above, 8 steps.
5. "Allemande left with your corner girl."
   Boy gives left hand to corner girl (or girl on his left) and walks
   around her once, 8 steps.
6. "Do si do your own."
   Arms folded, shoulder height; walk around partner and back up to
   place. 8 steps.
7. "Then you all promenade with the sweet corner maid."
   Promenade with corner girl (girl on boy's left).
8. "Singing 'Oh Johnny, Oh Johnny, Oh.'"
   Continue promenade.

TEACHING SUGGESTIONS

1. This dance may be done in one circle instead of in squares.
2. Be sure that boys understand who their 'corner maid' is.
3. Pupils may need extra practice on the 'allemande left.'
4. The Buzz step may be used on the 'swings.' To do this, stand on
   one foot and push with the other as if riding a scooter.

## SIXTH GRADE RHYTHMS

*Review from fifth grade*
   *Oh Susanna*
   *Cotton Eyed Joe*
   *Schottische*

1. La Raspa
2. California Schottische

3. Lili Marlene
4. Blackhawk Waltz
5. All American Promenade
6. Grand Square Quadrille
7. Five Foot Two
8. Korobushka
9. Marching

1. **La Raspa** (Mexican)

Record — Imperial 1084, Folkraft F1119A.

Formation — Double circle, partners facing each other.

Description —
Part A. Bleking step. All hop left, put right foot forward, hop right,
        putting left foot forward, hop left, putting right foot forward,
        hold.
        Repeat, starting with left foot.
        Do a total of eight times.

Part B. Hook right elbows, left hands held high, turn in eight quick steps, ending in original position. Clap on 8th count. Hook left elbows, right hands held high, turn in eight quick steps, ending in original position. Clap on 8th count.
Repeat turns.

TEACHING SUGGESTIONS

1. For Part A, hands may be joined, or the boy may hold his clasped hands behind his back while the girl holds her skirt.
2. Couples may do a buzz-step on the turn instead of a running step. Lean away from partner.
3. After pupils know the step in Part A, they may turn around while doing it, or they may place the feet to alternate sides instead of in front.

2. **California Schottische**

Record — Imperial 1046, London 302 "Mistletoe Kiss" or any slow schottische music.

Formation — Double circle, facing counterclockwise. Varsouvienna position.

Description —

Part A. Both start with left foot. Point left toe forward, point left toe to the side; step left in back of right, step to the side right, bring left foot up to right foot.
Repeat, starting with right foot.

Repeat all

Part B. Walk forward two slow steps, left, right. Each do half turn to the right while taking three quick steps, left, right, left. Retain hand position. Girl is now on boy's left.

Repeat, walking backward right, left. Do half turn to left while taking three quick steps, right, left, right, returning to original position.

TEACHING SUGGESTIONS

1. The rhythm is "slow, slow, fast, fast, fast" or "one, two, one, two, three."
2. The boy should turn the girl or 'lead' her to turn. The hand position remains the same throughout the dance.
3. All should be able to do this dance as the rhythm is slow and there are no difficult steps.

## 3. Lili Marlene

Record — Imperial 1145, Broadcast 416.

Formation — Double circle, facing counterclockwise. Inside hands joined.

Description —

Part A. Walk forward four steps, starting with outside foot (boy's left, girl's right). Four quick slides in line of direction.
Repeat, moving clockwise (in opposite direction). Girl starts with left foot, boy with right.

Part B. Facing each other with both hands joined. Boy steps on left foot, girl on right. Kick other leg across. Do four times.

Part C. In original position, walk forward three quick steps. On count four, kick opposite leg. (Boy starts left, girl on right.) Repeat, in opposite direction, coming back to original position.

Part D. Do in-and-out two-step eight times. Starting on outside foot, on first two-step face toward each other, on second face away from each other, etc.

TEACHING SUGGESTIONS

1. To make this a mixer, have the girl move up to the next boy on the last four two-steps.
2. It is important that pupils start on their outside foot. Use the terms 'outside' and 'inside' rather than right and left.
3. The boy should 'lead' the girl with his arm, on in and out two-steps.

## 4. Blackhawk Waltz

Record — Imperial 1006 or MacGregor 309.

Formation — Double circle, partners facing each other. Both hands joined.

Description —

| Part A. Balance and Waltz | Cues |
|---|---|
| Boy steps forward on left foot, brings right foot up to left, but does not step on it. Girl steps back on right foot, brings left foot to right, but does not step on it. | "Balance |
| Repeat in opposite direction, boy stepping back right, girl stepping forward left. | Balance |
| Two box waltz steps (see waltz step, Grade 4) Boy steps forward left, to the side right, close with left. Girl steps back right, to the side left, | Waltz<br>Waltz |

close with right. Repeat in reverse, boy stepping back right, girl forward left.

Do four times in all.

Part B. Grapevine. Directions are for boys; girls do reverse, both moving in same direction.

| | |
|---|---|
| Cross left leg over right and step on left foot, pivoting hips. Cross right foot over left. Cross left foot over right. | Cross<br>Cross<br>Cross |
| Step to the side right, step with left back of right, point right toe to the side. | Step, step<br>Point" |

Do four times in all.

TEACHING SUGGESTIONS

1. 'Cross step' should be done with a pivot on the ball of the supporting foot, turning hips also.
2. It may be wise to teach the steps of this dance with the class in a line formation, facing the teacher or a pupil demonstrator.
3. Keep the feet close to the floor on the balance and waltz steps. The steps should be smooth.

## 5. All American Promenade

Record — Windsor A-7S4.

Formation — Double circle, facing counterclockwise. Inside hands joined.

Description —

Starting with outside foot, walk four steps counterclockwise. Turn in toward partner, changing hands, walk backward four steps.

Repeat, in opposite direction, starting with inside foot.

Standing beside partner with inside hands joined —
  two-step away from partner
  two-step together

Four walking steps while girl crosses over in front of boy and turns so as to end facing forward. Boy does four steps in place. (It is necessary to change hands)

Two-step toward each other, two-step away.
Girl moves across in front of boy and back to next boy in circle with four walking steps, while boy does four walking steps in place.

Teaching Suggestions

1. The boy should give the girl a strong 'lead' as she crosses over in front of him.
2. This record has good, peppy music, speeding up towards the end of the record.

## 6. Grand Square Quadrille

Record — Decca 40233, Ed Gilmore, caller.
Formation — Square dance, four couples in a square.
Description — Instructions and calls are on record.

Teaching Suggestions

1. This is a simple yet interesting and challenging square dance.
2. Pupils should be familiar with these patterns except for the "Grand Square" which is described on the record jacket.

## 7. Five Foot Two Mixer

Record — Lloyd Shaw 3-122, Honor Your Partner Album, Ed Durlacher, Album Series 111, Record 301.

Formation — Double circle, facing counterclockwise. Partners in varsouvienne position.

Description —
All start with left foot and move forward.
Two-step left, two-step right
Walk four steps forward (left, right, left, right.)
Repeat.

On 3rd walking step (Count 3) man releases lady's left hand and lady turns outward to join hands with man behind her. This makes a single circle, men facing out, ladies facing in.
Two-step forward (left foot) (in direction person is facing)
Two-step back
Man releases partner's right hand; left hand is joined with next lady.
Man walks forward four steps, holding left hands, turning the next lady to face out as he turns to face center of circle.
Two-step forward (left foot) Two-step back.
Man takes lady whose right hand he holds as his new partner.

Teaching Suggestions

1. The man actually passes one lady before he gets a new partner.
2. This is a good mixer with an interesting pattern.

8. **Korobushka** (Russian)

Record — Imperial 1022 or Folk Dancer MH 1059.

Formation — Double circle, partners facing each other with hands joined.

| Description — | Cues |
|---|---|
| Part A. Boy starting with left foot, girl with right. | |
| Schottische step away from center of circle. | |
| (See Grade 5 for schottische step) | "Schottische |
| Schottische step toward center of circle. | Schottische |
| Schottische step away from center of circle. | |
| Three Jumps in place — | Schottische |
|    1. Stride position | |
|    2. Feet crossed | Jump |
|    3. Feet together, hold Count 4 | |
| Part B. Drop hands and fold arms at shoulder height. | |
| Each person moves to the right in three steps, making a complete turn. Clap hands on count 4. | Walk, 2, 3, 4 |
| Repeat, turning to the left. | Walk, 2, 3, 4 |
| Join right hands and balance toward each other by stepping forward on right foot. | Balance |
| Balance away from each other. | |
| Four walking steps to exchange positions. (Girl now has her back to the center of the circle.) | Walk |
| Repeat all of Part B, girl moving to the outside of the circle and to the boy behind her on the last four walking steps. | Balance New partner" |

TEACHING SUGGESTIONS

1. Review the schottische step (grade 5) before starting this dance.
2. This is a good tune and an interesting dance.

# The Curriculum

## Relays

# 8

# Relays

Relays are a type of team activity where the object is to complete a pattern of activity before the other teams complete the same pattern. Some relays are recreational in nature and are done for exercise and for fun. Others incorporate skills and provide a method of practicing game skills that is more interesting to the elementary age youngster than 'just practicing.' Relays contribute to the achievement of all of the objectives of physical education. They provide opportunity for exercise and for skill development, for the practice of sportsmanship and cooperation, and are fun to play.

Relays are performed in squads or teams, usually in a line formation though some may be done in circles or square formations. Each person on the team performs the same pattern of activity. Teams should be selected before class, although teams can be quickly established in class by 'counting off.' In no circumstances, should teams be selected by having captains choose their players while standing in front of the class and calling out the names of the persons they want on their team. This is an unforgivably poor procedure as some children are always the last to be chosen, with consequent real damage to their egos. A relay team should consist of no more than eight players. Six on a team is better. If the class is large, have more teams rather than more players on a team. Never be caught with two teams with 12 to 15 children on a team, the long line standing and waiting while two children are performing. This is a waste of valuable time in the physical education class. Teams must have the same number of players. If the teams are uneven, have one child on the team do the activity twice to make up for the lack of one person. Do not ask a child to not participate because his team has an 'extra player.' Each team should have a captain or leader who heads the line and helps to 'manage' the team.

No relays are included in the first and second grades in this curriculum. In the third grade, when children begin to understand the team concept, 5 per cent of the total physical education time — equivalent to about nine lessons — is spent on relays. In the fourth, fifth and sixth grades, 5 per cent of the total time — equal to nine lessons — is to be used for relays. Thus it is apparent that, compared to other types of activities — games and sports, rhythms and self testing — little time is designated for relays.

Rarely, however, would an entire lesson be planned for relays alone. Usually they are combined, in the lesson with another activity, for example:

1. Warm-up run and calisthenics.
2. Two relays. Each relay may be done three times. See which team can win the most number of relays.
3. Game.

In the fourth, fifth and sixth grades, skills used in the games for those grades may be included in the relay. Thus, relays become a method of practicing skills. However, relays should not include skills until the pupils have learned the skills fairly well. A relay involves speed, and sometimes the speed element does more harm than good to a newly acquired skill.

Teaching Suggestions for Relays

1. Explain the relay carefully and demonstrate it with a few pupils if demonstration is necessary.
2. The start and finish of the relay should be definite and clearly understood by all. The starting signal may be, "Ready, Go!"
3. Be sure that children understand which hand they are to hold out to be 'touched off' by the preceeding player. Have teams go to the right or left — agree on this — when they return to the line.
4. Be sure that all players observe the starting line and do the activity correctly. Sloppy observance of the rules spoils the fun for those who try to do the relay correctly, and leads to arguments and dissatisfaction.

5. Be sure to watch and choose the winner carefully since pupils are greatly interested in the outcome of the contest. Announce first, second and third place finishers.
6. Teams should indicate when they have finished by a prearranged signal such as stooping, sitting, raising hands overhead, or raising both arms overhead when the relay is completed.
7. Other relays may be devised by the teacher or by the pupils.
8. The best position for the teacher is at one end of the starting line where she can observe the starting line and also the activity of each pupil.

1. **Third Grade Relays**

   *1. Running and stunt relays.*

     a. Children line up in file formation, one behind the other with the first person behind the starting line. There should be the same number on each team. Each player must start from behind the starting line.

       Run to a designated mark or line 20' to 30' ahead of the starting line. Run back, touch off the next person, and go to the end of the line. The next person should be ready to go and have one hand stretched out to be 'touched off.'

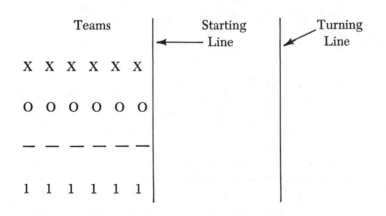

     b. Skip to turning line and run back (or hop or gallop).
     c. Walk to turning line and run back. (Heels must touch floor first.)
     d. Bear walk to turning line, get up and run back.

2. *Relays using beanbags.* Each team has a beanbag.
   a. Place beanbag on head, walk to mark; take beanbag off head and run back. If beanbag falls off head, pupil must replace it before proceeding.
   b. Stoop and stretch relay — First person holds beanbag in both hands. At the starting signal, he lifts it over his head and drops it to the floor behind him. The second person picks it up and repeats the action. When the last person in the line gets the beanbag, he runs up to the leader and hands him the beanbag.
   c. Throw the beanbag. Teams line up 20′ to 30′ from a wall. Throw the beanbag. It must hit the wall. Retrieve the beanbag and run back, handing it to the next person in line. If the beanbag does not hit the wall, pick it up and touch it to the wall before running back to the line.
3. *Relays using balls.* Each team has a ball.
   a. Carrying the ball, run to the turning mark, run back and hand the ball to the next person. If the ball drops, it must be recovered before the player advances.
   b. Teams line up about 25′ away from a wall. Roll the ball. It must touch the wall. If it does not touch the wall, pick it up and touch it to the wall. Carry the ball back to the next person in line.
   c. Place a ball for each team on a line, or in a circle, about 25′ ahead of the line. Player runs to the line, picks up the ball, and bounces it three times. Runs back to touch off the next player.
   d. Same as Relay c. for beanbags. Use a small ball rather than a large one.
   e. Stride ball relay. Players stand in stride position, one closely behind the other. Roll the ball between the legs. It must go through everyone's legs. Last person in the line picks up the ball and runs with it to the head of the line. He starts the ball through the line again by passing it first through his own legs. He stays at the head of the line. When the relay is finished, each player will be back in his original position.
   f. Circle Passing Relay. Players stand in a circle four to six feet apart. One player is designated the leader and he holds a ball. At the starting signal, he passes the ball to the player next to him. When the ball has been passed around the circle once, the captain (or leader) calls "One!" as he receives it. Each time the ball goes around the circle, the leader calls the number of times it has been around until the ball has been passed around the circle five times. The first team to reach the number 'five' is the winner.

**2. Fourth Grade Relays** (May review third grade relays)

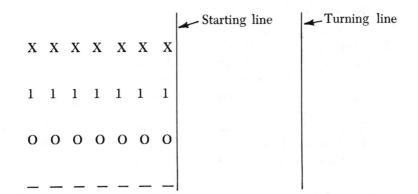

1 *Running or stunt relays*
   a. Run to a designated line or mark, do a coffee grinder in a complete circle (see self testing activities) run back, touch off the next person, and go to the end of the line.
   b. Same as A, except do a mule kick three times.
   c. Place a jump rope for each team on the turning line. Players run to the line, jump rope three times, run back and touch off the next player.
   d. Partner relay. Teams line up in partners holding inside hands. In two's, or partners,' players run to the turning line and run back to touch off the next pair. They must not release hands.
2. *Relays using beanbags.*
   a. Each team has three beanbags placed in one of two circles about 25′ ahead of the starting line. Draw circles with chalk. The first player runs to the beanbags, transfers them one at a time and with one hand, to the other circle; then he runs back to touch of the next person. The second person does the same thing, moving the beanbags back to the first circle. And so on. Vary this relay by stipulating that the left hand must be used, or the right hand or both hands.
   Same relay can be done using Indian Clubs instead of beanbags.
   b. Carry and Fetch Relay — The first person in each line has a beanbag. He runs to the turning mark, places the beanbag on the floor, runs back and touches off the next person. The second player runs and gets the beanbag, brings it back and hands it to the third player, and so on. One takes it up, and the next player brings it back.

One, two or three beanbags may be used, the player making a separate trip for each beanbag. Erasers, Indian clubs or other objects may be used.

3. *Relays using balls.*
   a. Arch Ball. Each team has one ball.

   The first person in the line stands holding the ball in front of him with both hands. At the starting signal, he passes the ball back over his head to the second person in the line. The ball is passed down the line in the same manner. Each person must handle the ball. The last person brings the ball to the head of the line, starts it again over his head, and stays at the front of the line. When the team is finished, all players will be back in their original positions.

   b. Over and Under Relay. Each team has one ball.

   The first person passes the ball though his legs to the player behind him. The second player passes the ball over his head to the third player who passes it between his legs, and so on. The last player carries the ball to the head of the line, starts it again by passing it through his legs and stays at the head of the line.

   c. Soccer relay — Each team has a soccer ball placed on the ground in front of the leader. Each player dribbles or kicks the ball around an object (chair, stick, Indian club) 25′ to 30′ away from the starting line, and back to the next person in line. He must get the ball to the next person at the starting line. No hands may be used on the ball.

   d. Dribble and Pass relay. Each team has a basketball.

   The player dribbles the ball about 25′ to the turning line, stops, turns and passes the ball back to the next person in line and goes to the end of the line.

   e. Teacher and Class formation. Each team has a softball or fleece ball. The leader throws the ball to each person in turn, in the line. Each throws it back to him. The throwing distance should be 15′ to 20′. After the leader has thrown to the last person in the line, he goes to the end of the line, and the next player becomes the leader. Continue until all have had a turn at being the leader.

   Vary with different kinds of throws such as underhand and overhand throws.

                    X1   (Leader)

   X7  X6  X5  X4  X3  X2

**3. Fifth Grade Relays** (Many relays from Fourth grade may be used)

    *1. Running or stunt relays.*

       a. Rescue Relay. Teams line up in single file with the leader standing on the turning line, facing the team, about 30′ away. At the starting signal, the leader runs to the starting line, joins hands with the first player in line and runs with him back to the turning line. The leader stays there, and the first player runs back and 'rescues' the second player. Each time, the last one brought over to the line returns to bring another person.

       b. Shuttle Relay. Half of each team is on the starting line and half on the turning line. Lines should be 40′ to 50′ apart.

| 5 | 3 | 1 | | | | 2 | 4 | 6 |
|---|---|---|---|---|---|---|---|---|
| X | X | X | | | | X | X | X |
| 1 | 1 | 1 | | | | 1 | 1 | 1 |
| O | O | O | | | | O | O | O |
| — | — | — | | | | — | — | — |

No. 1 runs across, touches off No. 2 and stays there.
No. 2 runs across, touches off No. 3 and stays there.
The race continues until each has run once. Players will end on the opposite side from where they started.

A shuttle race may be done in which each child runs twice (or a repeat of the entire race) in which case, each child will end in his original position.

       c. Base Running Relay. (Use in softball season)
Each team lines up behind a base. At a signal, the first player in each team runs counterclockwise around the bases, touching each base until he returns to the base from which he started. He touches off the next player and goes to the end of the line. When all the players on the team have run around the bases, the team is finished.

       d. Sack Race. Each team should have a gunny sack.
Place the gunny sack on the ground in front of the first player. At the starting signal, the pupil picks up the sack, steps into it, pulls it up to his waist and hops forward to the turning line. He may return to the starting line the same way.
One variation is to step out of the sack at the turning line and run back, handing the sack to the next player.

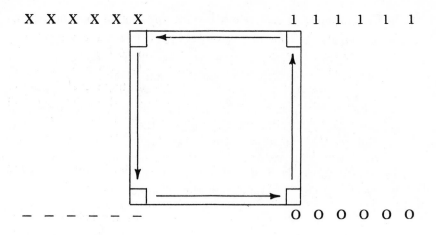

2. *Relays using balls.*

  a. Soccer Relay. Teams line up in partners with the partners being about five feet apart. Each team has a soccer ball placed on the ground in front of the leader. At the starting signal, the partners run to the turning line while passing the ball back and forth between them. At least three passes must be made each way. Return to the starting line the same way. No hands may be used on the ball.

  b. Run, Toss and Catch. Each team has a volleyball. A volleyball net or rope.

  The leader holds the ball in his hands. At the starting signal, he runs to the net, tosses the ball over the net and catches it on the other side, he runs back to the line and hands the ball to the next player.

  If the player fails to catch his own throw over the net, he must regain the ball and toss it again until a catch is made.

  Two players, holding a stick or a rope as high as they can reach, may substitute for the volleyball net or rope.

  c. Basketball Relays. Each team has a basketball.

   (1) Dribble the ball to the turning line, or around an object, dribble back to the starting line, hand the ball to the next person and go to the end of the line.

   (2) Same as (1) in shuttle formation.

   (3) Line up 25 to 30′ away from the basket. Dribble the ball, shoot a basket, recover the ball and pass it back to the next person in line. The player must shoot until he makes a basket.

   (4) The player dribbles the ball to the turning line, stops, pivots, and passes back to the next person in line and stays on the

turning line. When the team is finished, all players will be on the turning line. The distance between the starting and turning line should be no more than 20 feet.

(5) Each team forms a circle with the players 5 to 8 feet apart. The leader has a basketball. At the starting signal, he passes the ball around the circle three times. Each time the ball comes back to him, he counts out loud "One", "Two" or "Three." When the ball has gone around the circle three times, the team is finished.

Vary this by passing either direction, and by using different kinds of passes.

d. Kangaroo Relay. Each team has a ball.

The player puts the ball between his knees and holding it there with his knees, hops or jumps to the turning line and back to the starting line.

4. **Sixth Grade Relays** (Many of the relays from the Fourth and Fifth grades may be used)

1. *Stunt and running relays.*

a. Use line formation, shuttle formation, circle formation for running, skipping, hopping and stunt relays.

b. Base Running relay — see 5th grade.

c. Sack race in partners. Gunny sack for each team.

Teams line up in partners (or two squads may combine to form one team.) The gunny sack lies on the ground at the starting line. At the signal, the first two players pick up the sack and each puts one leg in the sack, pulling the sack up to waist level. In this fashion, they walk, run or hop to the turning line and return.

d. Using short jump ropes, each team has a rope. Jump rope to the turning line and return.

e. Crab walk relay. Do the crab walk, head first, to the turning line about 20' from the starting line. Crab walk, feet first, back to starting line.

f. Obstacle relay. Combine stunts such as

Jump rope to a certain mark, lay the rope down; bounce a ball three times, shoot a basket, recover the ball and lay it down; pick up the rope and jump rope back to the starting line.

2. *Ball Relays*

a. Each team has a football. The player runs, carrying the football, to the turning line and back, handing the ball to the next person.

b. Each team has a football. The first person on each team kicks the ball to a line. It must cross the line. Recover the ball and carry it back to the next person. If the ball does not cross the line on the kick, the player must go and pick up the ball, touch it to the line before bringing it back to the next person. The ball may be picked with a drop kick, or a place kick with the ball resting on the ground.

c. The leader stands on a line 20 to 25 feet in front of his team. Each leader has a ball. He passes it to each person in line each of whom pass the ball back to the leader and go to the end of the line. When the leader has passed to each person in his line, the team is finished.

This may be done as a contest, the object of which is to see which team can make the most number of consecutive passes without a dropped ball.

d. Basketball Relays. See 5th grade basketball relays. Vary these with different formations and distances.

(1) Zig Zag Relay. Set up three Indian clubs (may use blocks of wood, chairs, Indian clubs, etc.) about 5′ apart for each team. Each leader has a basketball. At the starting signal, the first player dribbles the ball, going in and out between the obstacles and returns to the line in the same way.

Part  III

# Other Considerations

# Special Problems

## WHAT CAN THE CLASSROOM TEACHER DO ABOUT POSTURE?

The word posture refers to the position of the body. Posture commonly refers to the standing position, but there is also sitting posture and walking posture. The posture, or position, of the human body is determined by the bone structure — the skeleton — and the muscles and ligaments which hold the skeleton in place. The bone structure, muscles and ligaments enable the body to perform innumerable physical movements and, at the same time, put limitations on that movement. The bone structure of the knee and the muscles and ligaments which surround it, for example, allow the knee to bend forward, but strictly limit the distance that the knee can bend backward. When one considers the number of bones in the body, the shape of those bones, the number and strength of muscles and ligaments, the range of variation in posture is seen to be limitless.

Good posture for the individual is that position which allows him most efficient movement. Because of differences in structure and in strength, good posture is not necessarily the same for all persons. Efficient movement is movement that is performed with the least expenditure of energy. Efficient movement is smooth, controlled and graceful. This is why the champion tennis player, skier or swimmer appears to move with ease and grace. The poor performer appears to be working hard — and he is — because his movements are inefficient.

Standing posture is a physical activity because to stand requires that muscles and ligaments must work to hold the bones and joints in an upright position against the pull of gravity. Good posture, for most people, means that:

1. Shoulders are even, or level.
2. Hips are even, or level.
3. Head is up with chin in, or down.
4. Chest is up, not caved in; upper back has a slight outward curve.
5. Abdomen is flat, or slightly rounded; lower back has a slight inward curve.
6. Feet point straight ahead.
7. Weight is evenly distributed on the heels and the balls of the feet.

Good posture is not a stiff position, not a "military" posture. The shoulders should be relaxed. The knees should be "easy."

A child's posture is determined largely by his bone structure and by his muscular strength. If one leg is longer than the other (and this is not uncommon) the hips will not be even with a resulting adjustment in the position of the pelvis and the spine. If his abdominal muscles are weak, the abdominal area will protrude and there will be an exaggerated curve of the lower (lumbar) spine.

Since posture is determined largely by muscular strength, it is also secondarily affected by the amount of energy available. If the child is low in energy or vitality, his muscles will not be able to function to the extent needed to maintain good posture. Inadequate nutrition, poor sleep habits, the presence of infection or disease thus may have an effect on the individual's posture, as these factors influence the amount of energy available to do physical or muscular work.

Hearing or vision defects may cause the child to hold his head in an abnormal position so that he can hear or see more effectively.

Another factor which may influence posture is the individual's mental or emotional health. The confident, happy, secure, poised pupil is more likely to have good posture than the child with problems, fears and frustrations. It has been said that we look as we feel — and conversely, we feel as we look. Both are true. Actors and actresses know that posture is very important in conveying the idea of a particular character to the audience.

Posture is also a *habit* of standing, sitting and walking. A person gets used to standing in a certain way and this, to him, is normal — it "feels right." This is one of the reasons why it is so difficult to change an individual's posture for it involves changing a habit that affects all of the body's muscles and habits of moving. Merely telling a child to "stand up straight" is not likely to have any lasting effect on his posture.

Does posture have any relationship to health? It is doubtful that slight variations from what is considered good posture have any effect on health. Extreme variations from the norm, however, can definitely affect body movement and function. A child's posture which is far from the normal — to the point where it might be called a deformity — must be corrected, as far as possible, for the sake of the child's health. Such cases do not fall within the responsibility of the school but are a medical problem.

In spite of the complexities of posture, the various factors that affect it and the difficulties of changing a child's postural habits, it is worthwhile to do whatever can be done in the school situation to help children achieve and maintain good posture. Good posture definitely improves one's appearance and this is reason enough for trying to achieve it. Good posture makes one feel better both mentally and physically. Good posture provides a necessary base for efficient and graceful movement whether it be walking or playing a vigorous game.

The causes of poor posture should be obvious from the foregoing discussion. To summarize, they include:

1. Abnormal bone structure, such as one leg longer than the other.
2. Muscle weakness, or lack of sufficient muscle strength to hold the skeleton in good alignment.
3. A depressed, frustrated, insecure or timid personality.
4. Poor nutrition. Insufficient sleep. Fatigue.
5. Vision or hearing defects.
6. Ill fitting shoes, or shoes that give no support to the feet.
7. Poor body mechanics, or poor habits of standing, walking and moving.

There are a number of simple posture checks, or tests, which the elementary school teacher can use to determine whether or not a pupil has good posture and good body alignment. They include:

1. Much can be seen by merely observing the child stand, sit and walk. The classroom teacher can see which children have good posture and which ones may have incorrect or poor posture.
2. Looking at the child from the rear, are the shoulders level? Are the hips level?
3. From a side view, is there a fairly straight line from the lobe of the ear, through the middle of the shoulder joint, the center of

the hip bone, just in front of the knees and through the midddle of the foot just in front of the ankle bone? This is commonly referred to as the 'plumb line test.' The teacher may use a heavy string with a weight on the lower end. Hold the string opposite the child's ear, and check to see if the line falls through the proper points. A blackboard pointer, or yardstick, may be used for this purpose. Or a weighted string may be tacked to the top of a door frame as illustrated in the sketch.

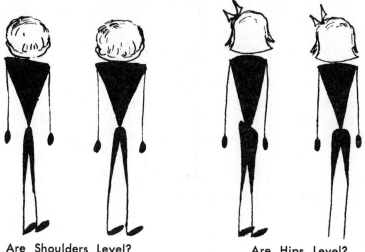

Are Shoulders Level?                    Are Hips Level?

4. Observing a child's walk, does he "toe straight ahead"? "Toeing out" is a harmful position as this means that the child's weight is falling on the inside of the foot, over the arch, instead of on the outside of the foot where there is bone structure to support it.

"Toeing in" is not a harmful position but does nothing to enhance the appearance of the individual. Severe toeing in, to the point where the child trips over his feet is, of course, a position that should be corrected.

Toeing out is usually accompanied by a condition called pronation, where the ankles are bent, or turned, toward the inside. This is a condition that leads to numerous foot troubles and should be corrected.

A simple way to check on how the child walks is to look at the heels of his shoes. If the heels are worn on the inside edge

'Plumb Line' Posture Check

of the shoe, it means that his weight is falling on the inside of the foot instead of the outside where it should normally be. If the child walks correctly, the heels will be worn on the back edge, or slightly to the outside of the heel.

The importance of good shoes for the proper growth and development of a child's feet cannot be overstressed. The foot troubles of many adults can be traced to improper shoes worn during the growing years. The shoe should provide protection from hazards on the ground, thus requiring a fairly thick sole, and should give the foot some support. This does not mean that the shoe should be inflexible with a steel arch support but some build-up in the arch is helpful to most children. A shoe that laces is more adjustable to the foot than one that buttons or snaps. The toe of the shoe should be broad, providing ample room for the toes, yet fit snugly around the heel.

Some parents spend considerable sums on cowboy boots for children. In most instances, these are too loose around the heel and ankle and the child soon runs them over, usually on the inner side of the ankle. A simple oxford type shoe is far better for the child's foot.

A good ankle high tennis or gymnasium shoe with a heavy sole is a satisfactory shoe for the child with a normal foot. The fact that "gym" shoes can be tossed into the washing machine eliminates the one-time objectionable odor.

## What the Teacher Can Do About Posture

1. Give a posture test. Refer any child who has gross deviations from the normal posture to the school nurse or to the parents.
2. Increase muscle strength, especially muscles of the trunk, by calisthenics and other physical education activities.
3. Inform the pupil or his parents if the child is wearing shoes which are harmful to his feet.
4. Look into the nutrition and sleep habits of the child who has poor posture.
5. See that children have desks and chairs which fit their height and structure. Lighting in the room should be conducive to good posture.
6. Try to make children posture conscious. Point out values of good posture. Use pictures, charts, illustrations.
7. Use cues such as:
   a. Stand tall. Push up *top* of head. Chin should be in, or down.
   b. Sit tall.
   c. Lift chest — not shoulders.
   d. Shoulders back (not up).
   e. Tuck buttocks under. Hips under. Tuck seat under.
   f. Flatten lower back. Pull tummy in. Pull abdomen in.
   g. Toe straight ahead. Feet parallel.
8. Be a good example of good posture.

A special word might be said about the unusually tall girl. There often are girls in the fifth and sixth grades who are taller than the boys. Because of this, they feel conspicuous and self-conscious and will adopt a slump posture to try to compensate for their height. Point out to them that the slump posture does not change their height, that they look much better and less conspicuous with good posture. Tall girls actually have an advantage in appearance as clothes look better on them than on the short girl. Most successful models are tall.

The classroom teacher is in a position to affect children's posture as she is with them for the whole school day. In being aware of the causes of poor posture and eliminating these as far as possible, and motivating children to want good posture, the classroom teacher can help them to achieve this goal.

## WHAT CAN BE DONE ABOUT THE CHILD WHO DOESN'T WANT TO PLAY?

The normal, healthy elementary age child loves to play. If he feels self confident, has status with his peers and is physically healthy, he will want to play and participate in all of the activities. If a child is reluctant to play, the teacher might ask herself the following questions in attempting to discover a reason:

1. Is the child healthy? A pupil returning to school after an illness may not have the physical energy to want to play. It may be advisable to have the child observe the physical education class for a few days or rest in the health room or the classroom until he has regained his normal vitality.
2. Does the child get enough sleep? Is he tired? In this day of the permissive home and the TV late show, there are large numbers of children who do not get an adequate amount of sleep. The elementary age child needs eight to ten hours of sleep every night for proper growth and development. Some need more than that. The teacher has little influence on this problem if the parents are unconcerned about it or are uncooperative. If a child shows other symptoms of lack of sleep — irritability, frequent colds, lack of energy, falling asleep at school — the teacher should so inform the parents and endeavor to convince them of the importance of sleep. With some youngsters, it may be for the good of the child to arrange for him to have opportunity to rest or sleep sometime during the school day.
3. Is the child inferior in physical education activities? No human being enjoys being in a situation in which he feels inferior. He will use all manner of subterfuge to avoid such a situation. The teacher needs to encourage the child, trying to get across the point that he must participate in order to learn and improve, or he will

be even farther behind the rest of the class. In extreme cases, the teacher may confide in the remainder of the class and enlist the aid of the child's peers to help him in gaining confidence in the activity and in himself. The child should be praised when he does something well. He may be given opportunity to perform extra duties or carry extra responsibilities that will enhance his status with the group. The wise classroom teacher, knowing the individual child and the class as a whole, will find ways of encouraging the timid or shy youngster and the poorer performer.

4. Is the child an attention seeker? Is he resisting play as a means of getting attention from the teacher or the class? Again, the classroom teacher is in a position to know her pupils — their weaknesses, strengths and idiosyncrasies. Some pupils seem to need much more attention from the teacher than others. Reasons for this are many, but the condition often indicates a lack of self-confidence, a lack of maturity and poise. Sometimes the child has what is to him a legitimate reason for not wanting to participate, such as lack of appropriate clothing. The teacher should try to bolster the confidence of such a youngster in any way possible but without sacrificing the needs of the rest of the class. If the teacher knows that the child is healthy and that no harm will be done by his participation, she should insist on his taking part in the class activities. The "attention seeker" problem must be attacked on all fronts — in the classroom and out — as this indicates a basic personality problem. There is nothing to be gained by allowing such a pupil to observe the class or to do something else. Once the activity has begun, the child usually will participate with joy and enthusiasm.

If the problem of a child's not wanting to play continues to exist and the teacher has not been able to solve it, it may be necessary to seek other help. If the school has a school nurse, the child might be referred to her for a physical check-up. If there is a guidance counselor on the staff, the counselor might be able to get some insight into the child's reasons for not wanting to play. If all fails, the child should be required to bring a written note from his parents or his doctor asking that he be excused from physical education, stating the reasons for such an excuse and the period of time for which the excuse is valid.

This problem does not arise very often but when it does it can be a very perplexing and time-consuming matter for the teacher. The classroom teacher's best weapon is her understanding of the individuals in her class and a knowledge of the motivating influences in their lives.

## WHAT IF ACCIDENTS OCCUR?

A program of safety and accident prevention should be part of the written policy of every school system and of every individual school. Twentieth century children have to grow up in an environment which presents many hazards; they must learn to live in it without being hurt and without endangering other people. The school should be a model of good safety practices so that the child will learn from the school environment as well as from living in that environment.

The following items are particularly important in connection with the physical education curriculum. Hazards on the school grounds — such as rocks, rubbish, holes, unsafe playground apparatus, electric installations, nearness to streets and traffic — should be eliminated or corrected where possible. When the hazards cannot be eliminated, some means of protecting children from them should be established. This might be done in a physical way, such as fencing the playground that is adjacent to a busy street, or by rules, policies or regulations that control where and how children may play. Such policies and regulations should be drawn up by the teaching staff and should be understood by all teachers as well as by the pupils.

A common hazard which need not exist is the slippery floor in the gymnasium and in other rooms and halls. This is usually caused by the type of wax used. Maintenance personnel should be instructed to use a wax or floor sealer that is not slippery, such as the kind used in hospitals and other public buildings. Sharp corners and protruding objects in the gymnasium should be removed or covered in some manner so that they will not cause injury if pupils run into them.

The responsibility of the school administration in preventing accidents is to provide an environment that is as safe as possible. It is also the responsibility of the school administration to lead and direct in establishing rules and regulations governing the moving and living of the pupils in the school buildings and on the school grounds. Because of its construction, arrangement of rooms and location each school presents its own hazards which must be recognized and controlled in the most effective manner.

The responsibility of the individual teacher concerning safety is to observe the safety policies of the school and to be safety conscious at all times.

Because of the nature of the activities, more accidents occur in physical education classes than in other areas of the school curriculum. Some accidents will occur in the best managed situations but these will be fewer and less serious if the teacher and pupils are aware of good safety practices. Many of the teaching suggestions listed for various activities are concerned with safety.

In recent years there has been an increasing number of liability cases in the courts against school administrators and school teachers concerning injury to pupils. Laws vary in different states, but the general rule that is applied in these cases is the rule of negligence. Was the teacher negligent and did this negligence cause, or contribute to, the accident? If the teacher observes safety procedures and conducts the class in "good faith," she is not likely to be accused of negligence. Children should have been taught safety rules and procedures and it is the teacher's responsibility to see that these rules and procedures are observed. Children should never be on the playground or in the gymnasium unless a teacher is there to observe and supervise.

The school should have an accident reporting system. Over a period of time, this provides the school administrator with a picture of where, and what kind of, accidents are occurring on the school campus, and points up the need to investigate these places or situations to see if the hazards can be eliminated. All accidents, whether or not considered serious, should be reported. It is a convenience to have a form on which the accident can be reported, giving details as to how it happened and the apparent injury. The form suggested by the National Safety Council is a good example. If the school carries accident insurance, the insurance company may provide reporting forms.

Every teacher should, ideally, have had a course in first aid. At the least, there should be one teacher on the staff who is trained in first aid procedure and who can be called upon in an emergency. There should be a first aid room, or a health room, where first aid supplies can be kept. Refer to the Red Cross First Aid Manual for suggested first aid supplies.

There are individuals who are "accident prone." Statistics show that, even among children, some have many accidents while others

# INSTRUCTIONS

A. Use Part **A** of the form to report any accident to a student at any place (home, school or elsewhere) any time of the day or night.

B. Use Part **B** of the form to report additional information about accidents to students while under school jurisdiction.

☐ Place an "X" in the box at the upper right-hand of the form for an accident sufficiently serious to require a doctor's care or to keep a child out of school one-half day or more. Only such accidents should be included in your annual summary to the National Safety Council.

**IMPORTANT:** In order that maximum use be made of accident reports, it is essential that the accident be described in sufficient detail to show the unsafe acts and unsafe conditions existing when the accident occurred. The description should answer such questions as: What was the student doing at the time of the accident? (Playing tag or football, operating lathe, cutting lawn, etc.) Was he using any apparatus, machine, vehicle, tool or equipment? How was he using it? Would it have been safer to do it some other way? Was another person involved in the accident in any way?

For further information see "What You Should Know About Standard Student Accident Reporting."

# STANDARD STUDENT ACCIDENT REPORT FORM

## Part A. Report ALL accidents to Students Occurring Anywhere, Day or Night

1. Name: _____ Home Address: _____

2. School: _____ Sex: M ☐; F ☐. Age: ____ Grade or classification: ____

3. Time accident occurred: Hour ____ A.M.; ____ P.M. Date: ____

4. Place of Accident: School Building ☐  School Grounds ☐  To or from School ☐  Home ☐  Elsewhere ☐

5. **NATURE OF INJURY**

| | | |
|---|---|---|
| Abrasion ____ | Fracture ____ | |
| Amputation ____ | Laceration ____ | |
| Asphyxiation ____ | Poisoning ____ | |
| Bite ____ | Puncture ____ | |
| Bruise ____ | Scalds ____ | |
| Burn ____ | Scratches ____ | |
| Concussion ____ | Shock (el.) ____ | |
| Cut ____ | Sprain ____ | |
| Dislocation ____ | | |
| Other (specify) ____ | | |

**PART OF BODY INJURED**

| | |
|---|---|
| Abdomen ____ | Foot ____ |
| Ankle ____ | Hand ____ |
| Arm ____ | Head ____ |
| Back ____ | Knee ____ |
| Chest ____ | Leg ____ |
| Ear ____ | Mouth ____ |
| Elbow ____ | Nose ____ |
| Eye ____ | Scalp ____ |
| Face ____ | Tooth ____ |
| Finger ____ | Wrist ____ |
| Other (specify) ____ | |

## DESCRIPTION OF THE ACCIDENT

How did accident happen? What was student doing? Where was student? List specifically unsafe acts and unsafe conditions existing. Specify any tool, machine or equipment involved.

_____
_____
_____
_____
_____
_____
_____
_____
_____
_____
_____
_____
_____

6. Degree of Injury: Death ☐  Permanent Impairment ☐  Temporary Disability ☐  Nondisabling ☐

7. Total number of days lost from school: ____ (To be filled in when student returns to school)

## Part B. Additional Information on School Jurisdiction Accidents

8. Teacher in charge when accident occurred (Enter name): ————

Present at scene of accident: No: ———— Yes: ————

**IMMEDIATE ACTION TAKEN**

9.

| | |
|---|---|
| First-aid treatment | By (Name): ———— |
| Sent to school nurse | By (Name): ———— |
| Sent home | By (Name): ———— |
| Sent to physician | By (Name): ———— |
| | Physician's Name: ———— |
| Sent to hospital | By (Name): ———— |
| | Name of hospital: ———— |

10. Was a parent or other individual notified? No: ——— Yes: ——— When: ——— How: ————

Name of individual notified: ————

By whom? (Enter name): ————

11. Witnesses: 1. Name: ———— Address: ————

2. Name: ———— Address: ————

**LOCATION**

12.

| | Specify Activity | | Specify Activity |
|---|---|---|---|
| Athletic field | ———— | Locker | ———— |
| Auditorium | ———— | Pool | ———— |
| Cafeteria | ———— | Sch. grounds | ———— |
| Classroom | ———— | shop | ———— |
| Corridor | ———— | Showers | ———— |
| Dressing room | ———— | Stairs | ———— |
| Gymnasium | ———— | Toilets and | ———— |
| Home Econ. | ———— | washrooms | ———— |
| Laboratories | ———— | Other (specify) | ———— |

**Remarks**

What recommendations do you have for preventing other accidents of this type?

————
————
————
————
————

Signed: Principal: ———— Teacher: ————

(National Safety Council—Form School 1)
REP. 100 M 106301

**Printed in U.S.A.**

Stock No. 429.21

have none or a few. Some experts believe that the accident prone may have an underlying psychological problem which shows itself in this manner. Boys as a rule have more accidents than girls probably because they are more aggressive, and also because of the male code of honor which encourages a boy to be more reckless and which seems to imply that being cautious is being a sissy. Without causing children to be overly cautious, the teacher must endeavor to make boys and girls safety conscious so that they will recognize dangerous situations and procedures and seek to avoid or remedy such practices.

## SHOULD RELAXATION BE TAUGHT IN SCHOOL?

An uninformed person would answer this question with an emphatic "No!" To many people, relaxation is in the same category as social adjustment which, since Sputnik, has become a naughty word. If the school is to meet the needs of boys and girls in this day and age, however, the idea of teaching relaxation is not as ridiculous as it may first sound. The greatest health problem in our country today — in terms of people involved and money spent for treatment and custody — is mental illness. Tension — actual physical tension and mental or emotional tension — often accompanies mental illness. Tension, inability to relax, is a contributory factor in many physical illnesses such as high blood pressure, stomach ulcers and allergies, to mention only a few. Being able to relax at will will not necessarily prevent these illnesses, of course, but being able to relax, to release the tension, may aid in preventing these disorders and in learning to live with them.

Even for the child, life builds up tensions, frustrations, mental and physical fatigue that can be partially relieved by short periods of relaxation. It has become an important asset in the maintenance of good physical and mental health.

As with other traits or characteristics, children vary greatly in their need for relaxation and in their ability to relax. The extremes are the high strung child and the phlegmatic individual. We must remember that even the apathetic youngster has tensions. Symptoms of the nervous, high strung, tense individual are irritability, habits such as blinking the eyes, biting nails, sitting in tense positions such as wrapping the legs around the chair, pulling hair or ears, thumb sucking, and unusual noisiness or extreme quiet. Inattention and restlessness are signs of tenseness and the need for relaxation and a break in the routine of the classroom. All elementary age children will benefit as children and as adults by knowing techniques of relaxation.

For some individuals the ability to relax seems to be a natural skill. For others it must be learned. Relaxing a muscle is a muscular skill in that it involves control of the muscle or group of muscles. There are many things the classroom teacher can do — in the classroom and in physical education classes — that will aid the pupils to learn to relax.

In planning the order of her school day, the teacher should try to create a situation in which tensions are at a minimum. The schedule should be flexible enough so that if there is an apparent need for a break, suitable activities can be inserted to vary the routine. Primary grade teachers usually do a better job of this than upper grade teachers. Fifth and sixth graders have tensions, too! There is not much logical reason for scheduling all of the so-called academic subjects — reading, arithmetic, writing, etc. — in one half of the school day and all of the more active subjects such as music, art and physical education in the other half of the day. The teacher must remember that children have a natural, instinctive desire to move and that forbidding the expression of this desire creates tensions. The quiet classroom with all children neatly in their places is not necessarily the most healthy classroom for boys and girls.

The room should be as comfortable as possible with attention given to ventilation, temperature and lighting, and appropriate furniture. Seats and desks should fit the child. It may look neater to have all desks and chairs of the same size and height, but the primary consideration should be whether or not they fit the children — and not whether the room looks neat and orderly. Boys and girls who are comfortable and at ease are much more receptive to learning than those who are too hot, breathing stale air or sitting in chairs that are not appropriate to their height or size.

The following are some activities which can be used for a short break in the classroom. If possible, windows should be open.

1. A five minute 'at ease' period in which children may get up, move around, talk to others, get a drink, etc. Some children need a snack such as a piece of fruit or a drink of milk.

2. A pupil may lead the class in a few calisthenic exercises which might include running in place, stretching, deep breathing.

3. A "Simon Says Do This" type of game.

4. A song, especially one accompanied by clapping or certain movement patterns.

As much as possible, the break should be child-directed so that this period serves as a break for the teacher as well as for the class. A short run to the playground or around the school building is an excellent way of relieving tensions and results in the children's being relaxed and ready to proceed with the next classroom subject.

To learn how to relax, the pupil must learn the difference in feeling between tension and relaxation. This is best done where children have room to sit or lie on the floor. Some suggestions:

1. Sitting on the floor —
   a. Stretch one arm out to the side, straight and stiff as a board. Muscles are tense. Let arm drop to side. Muscles are relaxed. Raise both arms in the same manner.
   b. Lean back on hands. Stretch legs out straight and stiff, feet together and toes extended. Muscles are tense. Relax, letting knees bend slightly and feet fall apart.
   c. Stretch arms and legs at the same time.
   d. Sit with crossed legs, hands resting on knees. Push up with top of head, lift chest and inhale. Hold for 3 seconds. Relax and exhale.

2. Lying on the floor —
   a. Stretch arms overhead and legs out straight. "Be as long as you can." Muscles are tense. Relax.
   b. Lie on stomach (prone position). Lift arms, heads and legs off the floor. Muscles are tense. Hold for three seconds. Relax.
   c. Kneel on hands and knees. Round back and pull stomach in to backbone. Muscles tense. Hold three seconds. Relax, letting stomach fall.

3. Standing —
   a. Stand on tiptoes, stretch arms overhead. "Reach to the sky." Hold three seconds. Relax, letting trunk and arms fall limp.
   b. Bend forward, letting arms and head hang. With swaying trunk movement, let arms swing from side to side.
   c. Push up top of head, lift chest and inhale. Muscles tense. Hold three seconds. Relax and exhale.
   d. Walk like a tin soldier. Walk like a rag doll.

In the foregoing where the tense position is held, begin by having pupils hold the position for about three seconds. Increase this to five or six seconds as the pupils gain in endurance and control.

Vocal cues are often helpful. e.g.,
1. Be a rag doll.
2. Pretend you are a dish of ice cream melting.
3. Feel soft like a piece of fur.
4. Feel limp.
5. Stand like a scarecrow.
6. Pretend you are a coat on a coat hanger.
7. Pretend you are floating on a cloud or on the water.

It is a good idea to include several of the foregoing relaxation techniques in each physical education class. Depending upon the activity of the lesson, relaxation might done at the beginning or the end of the class period. The teacher should emphasize "muscles tense" or "muscles relaxed" so that children learn to connect the words with the act and the feeling.

## WHAT SHOULD THE TEACHER TEACH IN PHYSICAL EDUCATION IF SHE HAS MORE THAN ONE GRADE?

Occasionally it is necessary, because of uneven enrollment and/or lack of space and teachers, for the school administrator to place children from two grades in the same classroom with one teacher. This creates problems for the teacher in curriculum selection in many subjects, physical education included. This problem should, of course, be solved in the manner that is best for the pupils and with the least disruption of their progress from grade to grade.

One solution is to arrange for the pupils to have physical education with another class of their own grade level and this may be the best answer to the problem. In a combined third and fourth grade room, for example, third graders might have physical education with another third grade class and fourth graders with another fourth grade class.

In smaller schools where there are, for example, ten third graders and ten fourth graders in one room — and no other third or fourth grade pupils in the school — the teacher has no alternative but to teach these children physical education in the same class. The teacher must select physical education activities from the third and fourth grade curriculum that will best suit the maturity, strength and skill of her class. It would be advisable to start with the third grade activities even though they may be repetitious to the fourth grade pupils. Fourth graders can serve as leaders or helpers — which they are usually happy to do. When the class can do the third grade activities satisfactorily, the teacher can proceed to fourth grade activities. In some areas of the curriculum such as calisthenics, ball skills, rope jumping, certain rhythm steps and formations and some games, the activities are similar for both grades and may be done together. The teacher should expect, of course, higher levels of knowledge, skill and sportsmanship from the fourth grade pupils.

Another method which could be used when teaching some activities is to divide the class according to grade level, with each grade participating simultaneously in activities for their own grade level. This requires careful planning on the part of the teacher and the assistance of dependable pupil leaders. For example —

1. Entire group together — warm-up run and calisthenics.
2. Third graders — rope jumping at one end of the gymnasium. Fourth graders, with teacher — tumbling at the other end of the gym.
3. Reverse, with fourth graders doing rope jumping and third graders tumbling.

The teacher with a combination room or combined grades should not consider this an entirely burdensome or unsatisfactory situation. Children can learn desirable social traits such as sportsmanship, tolerance for the poorer performer, willingness to help and to assume responsibilities by playing with children of a different grade level. This, after all, is the situation they will be exposed to in out-of-school hours. Much depends upon the tone set by the teacher and her leadership of the group. Some very wholesome and happy play situations are to be found in the small rural school where children of all ages play together.

## WHAT IS EVALUATION IN PHYSICAL EDUCATION?

### How Should the Teacher Grade the Pupils in Physical Education?

For the purposes of this discussion, evaluation is assumed to mean the process of ascertaining whether or not pupils are developing and growing toward the goals set up as the objectives of physical education. Evaluation should be considered as a teaching method or technique because pupils learn by evaluating their progress or lack of progress. Thus, pupils as well as teachers should evaluate progress and achievement. A grade is the mark which a teacher gives to a level or rate of growth or achievement. Grading is, therefore, one part of evaluation.

Since evaluation is a process and a teaching method, it should be more or less continuous throughout the grading period and not confined to the end of a six or nine week grading period.

The wise teacher will sense when evaluation by the class of their progress, or lack of it, will serve good ends and be useful as a teaching technique. Sometimes it is necessary to talk things over. Situations may arise in a game, for example, when the need for discussion and evaluation are obvious. Such questions as the following may be asked by the teacher to lead the discussion:

1. What is the rule about blocking the ball? (in line soccer)
2. What are the ways to block the ball? How many used more than one way to block the ball in our games today? How did you do it?
3. Did you see any example of good teamwork in our game?
4. Did you see any example of good strategy or smart playing?
5. How about our sportsmanship? Could it be improved? How? Did you see any example of good sportsmanship?
6. Can you think of any way to improve our game so that it will be more fun for everyone?

Sometimes evaluation is best done at the end of the class period when the events and situations are fresh in the children's mind. Sometimes it may be done at the beginning of the class period, in which case the teacher should remember mistakes or errors of the previous lesson and lead the class discussion to those topics.

Evaluation in physical education is often subjective rather than objective. On a spelling test, for example, the errors are obvious, the evaluation is simple and the grade is objective. Measuring — or evaluating — ball skills or sportsmanshp cannot however be done so easily or so objectively. Of course skill tests and personality diagnostic tests are available, but it is not likely that the classroom teacher will have access to these tests or the time and knowledge to use them.

To compound the difficulty of evaluating and grading in physical education is the fact that there usually is a greater range of ability in physical education activities within a class than in spelling or arithmetic or other classroom subjects. Also, the rate of improvement and learning is slower — for example, it takes less time to learn to spell a word than it does to learn to do a good underhand throw. The learning of physical skills is often a slow, gradual process requiring much time and practice.

There are, however, several ways of testing or evaluating progress in physical education that are objective and that can be used by most teachers. First, the fitness test can be used at all grade levels. Although fitness tests are not perfect, results give the teacher some information concerning a child's progress in strength, flexibility and coordination. All children who participate in a good physical education curriculum should make some progress in fitness between the beginning and the end of the school year.

Some skills can be measured objectively. A pupil either can or cannot do a two-step. Pupils should learn how to do the rhythm steps for their grade level. Stunts and tumbling activities and certain ball skills also can be judged objectively on a pass or fail basis.

Children should also improve in knowledge about physical education activities. The teacher can evaluate knowledge by observing whether or not pupils understand and observe rules of the game as they play. Do they use good strategy in playing the game? Do they observe safety procedures appropriate for the activity? From the fourth grade up, simple written tests on rules, strategy and safety can be used.

Pupils should improve during the school year in sportsmanship and grow toward desirable social traits — cooperation, leadership and followership, tolerance and consideration for others, etc. There should also be growth in self-control, self-discipline and dependability. These are difficult to measure, but the classroom teacher who is with the children for the whole school day can make good subjective evaluations of the growth of her class in these areas.

The system used for grading for report cards and for school records will depend upon the philosophy and policy of the school as a whole. There are two fairly common methods of grading in the elementary school:

1. The grade indicates the improvement of the pupil during the grading period.
2. The grade indicates the standing, or rank, of the pupil compared to other pupils of the same grade level.

It is possible in physical education, as well as in other subjects, for a child to earn a high mark by method #1 and be average, or below average, by method #2. In some school systems, two marks or grades are written on the report card using both method #1 and method #2.

The writer makes no judgment on which method of grading is better. It does seem, however, that the elementary age child who makes good progress, even though he is low compared to the rest of the class, should receive encouragement by being given a good mark. Progress toward all of the goals of physical education — skill, knowledge, social and individual traits — should be taken into consideration in arriving at a physical education grade.

Grading in physical education should be done as often and, as far as possible, on the same basis as grading for all other subjects in the curriculum. It often is helpful to the child to discuss his physical education grade with him so that he understands why he was given a certain grade and how he can improve it.

The philosophy of grading seems to be in flux, some school administrators and teachers believing that only Pass or Fail grades should be given. Others think that a child's improvement, compared to his previous achievement, should be the only consideration. Should a child grade himself? An idea, expressed by Bob Pangrazi in "Promising Practices in Elementary School Physical Education"[1] is receiving some approval. "Evaluation of student achievement must be accomplished on the basis of giving children the opportunity to try, to make mistakes, and to attempt new ideas, knowing that it is the effort and enthusiasm put forth toward physical education that is most important to both the teacher and the students. It should be noted that comparative grading has little if anything to do with meeting individual needs, respecting individual dignity, and leading each child to the maximum of his capacity to learn. It is to be hoped that comparative grading in the elementary schools will be abandoned." The individual teacher will have to blend her philosophy with that of her superiors to arrive at a satisfactory answer to this problem.

---

[1]Pamphlet published by American Association for Health, Physical Education and Recreation, 1201 Sixteenth Street, N.W., Washington D. C. 20036. "Promising Practices in Elementary School Physical Education." 1969. pp. 26 and 27.

# 10

# Activities Related
# to Physical Education

There are several school programs or activities in a number of elementary schools that are closely related to the physical education curriculum. Where there is a physical education specialist on the staff, this person is usually responsible for some or all of these programs. The classroom teacher has no direct responsibility for these programs — as she has for the teaching of the physical education curriculum to her class — unless she has been especially designated to be in charge of one or all of them. The classroom teacher needs to know about these activities, however, as they are the natural outgrowth of the physical education class curriculum. They include free play, recess, noon hour and after-school activities such as intramurals and interschool competition. These activities provide times when boys and girls can practice the skills learned in the physical education class and an opportunity for the pupils to start forming interests in and habits of profitable use of leisure time. It should be clearly understood that these activities supplement the physical education instructional period and in no case should be used in lieu of that period.

## FREE PLAY

The term "free play" is used to describe free activity on the playground or in the gymnasium. Pupils are free to participate in the activity of their choice and to organize their own individual or group play. A teacher should be present to supervise, but she takes no responsibility for organizing or directing activities. She is there in case of emergency or accident and to see that school safety rules for use of equipment and for playground behavior are observed. The free play period gives the pupils an opportunity to select, organize and direct their own play activities and thereby practice what they have learned in classes in a free situation that is not directed or controlled by a teacher. Free play, in fact, provides a laboratory in which the pupil can practice and in which the teacher can observe the pupils in a natural play situation and evaluate their learning, or lack of it.

## RECESS

The word recess is often used by the uninformed as synonymous with physical education. The physical education class is teacher planned and directed, and all children participate in the same activities as in any other subject in the curriculum. Teachers should use correct terminology so that pupils will learn the difference between recess and physical education. Recess may be a break period (see Relaxation) or it may be a free play period. Depending upon the length of the school day, many teachers plan their physical education class in one half of the day and a recess period in the other half. This is a good arrangement, especially in the primary grades where children become more restless and have a greater need for frequent activity than in the upper grades. Children should be encouraged to play some physical activity during recess and not use this period for talking or combing hair or catching up on classroom work. Sufficient physical education supplies, such as balls, should be available for any activity the pupil wishes to play.

## NOON HOUR

Most elementary school children spend the noon hour at school. After lunch there is usually time for play before the afternoon session of school begins. The activities available to children during this period will depend upon the size of the school, the number of children and the space and facilities which can be used. The noon hour may be a free play period, activities may be organized, or there may be a combination of both. There should be enough activities so that all who wish to play may have an opportunity to do so. In most schools it is not the responsibility of the classroom teacher to plan the noon hour activities for her children unless she wishes to do so. Teacher supervision however is a professional and legal necessity whenever and wherever children are playing.

Some activities for noon hour play are:

1. Table games such as word games, checkers, and dominoes which can be played in the classroom.
2. Rhythms. It is fun for all ages, including the faculty, to participate together in rhythmic activities.
3. Free play on the playground.
4. Team games or sports organized in tournament style or impromptu.
5. Other games such as hopscotch, croquet, tetherball.
6. Activities such as rope jumping and playing with balls.

Because children must leave the school on buses immediately after school, some schools conduct intramural sports tournaments during the noon hour. While it is very desirable to have intramural sports as part of the school program, they should, if possible, be carried on after school rather than at noon. If this program must be conducted at noon, the person in charge should see that the participants eat lunch. Some children would rather play than eat! If the activity is competitive and strenuous it may be advisable to have the participants eat lunch after playing instead of before. Good health practices must be observed in all aspects of the program.

## INTRAMURALS

The word intramural refers to activities that take place within the school. Intramurals, referring to physical education, means a program of competitive activities within the school. The existence and nature of such a program depend largely on the size of the school. Some activities which require only a few players — table tennis, horseshoes, croquet, basketball shooting, hopscotch, marbles, tetherball, track events, etc. — can be conducted in the small school as well as the larger one. In larger schools, tournaments in team games can be very interesting for the pupil and satisfy the need for competition and for more intensive play than is possible in the physical education class.

Competition and tournaments should be arranged so that children of nearly equal ability play with and against each other. In team games, the teacher in charge may divide the group into approximately equal teams, or if there are, for example, three fifth grade rooms, each room may enter one or more teams. In some activities, including volleyball, softball, dodgeball and others, co-ed teams (boys and girls together on the same team) work out very well.

Certain policies or principles apply to both the intramural and interschool sports programs. They include:

1. Every child who wishes to participate should be allowed to do so. Some activities will naturally be limited to certain grade levels. No child should be forced to participate, but each should be encouraged to do so, even if poorly skilled. Ideally, every child in the fourth, fifth and sixth grades should participate in some intramural or interschool activity as this provides an excellent opportunity to develop interest in things which can be used in leisure time in the high school and adult years. Programs should be provided for girls as well as boys.
2. Pupils who, for some reason, cannot participate physically, can be used as assistants — to officiate, keep score and help with equipment and supplies. Teachers should encourage these children to take part in the program as this experience is valuable training which may lead to a lifelong interest in sports as a manager, scorekeeper, newspaper reporter, etc.
3. Parents should be aware of the existence of the program. If activities are held after school, the school should have written statements from the parents permitting the child to stay after school. (See attached sample form.)
4. Children should have had a current physical examination and should be covered by some type of accident insurance. The nature of these depends upon the school health policies.
5. The program should be under adult supervision at all times, preferably a member of the teaching staff. Some school systems pay teachers extra compensation for assuming the responsibility of the intramural or interschool programs.
6. Newspaper publicity should be limited and should emphasize group rather than individual achievement.
7. In some instances, educators need to beware of over-eager parents or outsiders who may attempt to influence or control the program.

## INTERSCHOOL ACTIVITIES

The word interschool refers to competition between schools rather than within one school. Some educators are opposed to competition between schools at the elementary school level. As is the case with many topics, the question is not "competition or no competition" but "what kind of competition?"

Sample

Parent Permission Form

Dear parent:

The .............................................. (name of school) will conduct an after school sports program for fourth, fifth and sixth graders. Boys play on Tuesdays and Thursdays, girls on Mondays and Wednesdays from 3:30 to 4:30 p.m. Activities include flag football, basketball, softball, track, tumbling, table tennis, tetherball and other games. This program makes it possible for boys and girls to have extra instruction in these sports and extra playing experience.

These activities are conducted on the school campus and are under the supervision of a member of the teaching staff.

For the protection of your child, will you answer the following questions and return the lower half of this sheet to your child's teacher.

---

Principal's name

— — — — — — — — — — — — — — — — — — —

Child's name ...................................................................

1. Does he have his parents' permission to participate in the after school sports program?

   Yes ......................          No ......................

2. Has he had a physical examination by a doctor within the past year?

   Yes ......................          Date of examination ................

   No ......................

3. Does he have school accident insurance or some other type of accident insurance?

   Yes ......................          No ......................

   What kind? ................................................................................

---

Parent's name

---

Address

---

Telephone number

If competition is controlled, limited and adapted to the elementary age instead of being patterned after high school or college athletics, it can be a valuable experience for elementary age boys and girls. Again, every child who wishes to participate should be allowed to do so. Squads or just ten or twelve players, eliminating other children, should not be selected. There is no reason to limit the number on the squads. It can be a thrilling experience for a 10 or 11 year old to practice with the squad, sit on the bench and perhaps get into the game for a few minutes. In many cases, this will be the only time in his life when a boy — or a girl — will be on the team. Games should be of limited length, with frequent substitutions. School uniforms are not necessary. A cap or a T-shirt with a letter or the school name on the front meets the needs of the team and the child at this age level. Activities should be those included in the physical education class curriculum. Good officials should be provided. If adults are not available, high school boys and girls are often good officials, and this is valuable experience for them too.

Good health practices should be observed including adequate pre-game practice, warm-ups before the game, safe playing areas, individual towels if towels are used, and a shower or cooling off period after the game.

## PLAY DAYS

A play day is an occasion when pupils of one or more schools meet together for a day, or part of a day, to participate in games or other activities. The purpose of a play day is to have fun and to give all children an opportunity to play with others in their school or from another school. Note that the emphasis is on having fun and playing *with,* not against, other children or teams.

Play days can be organized with only one sport such as volleyball or softball or dodgeball, or may include a variety of activities such as relay races, games, individual contest and rhythms. Play days often include a picnic lunch.

A successful play day requires careful planning ahead of time or children (and teachers) will become confused and frustrated. It is helpful if the children know what they are going to do before the play day begins. A schedule of the day's events and where they are to occur should be posted in the classroom or in a hall where all can see it. Older children can help in the planning and can also assist in conducting the activities of the younger children. A loud speaker system is very helpful in giving instructions and directions at the play day.

A sample schedule for an afternoon play day:

12 noon — Picnic lunch on the school grounds or in the gymnasium or play room.

12:30 — Moving pictures in the play room, or a talent show of previously selected numbers. There might also be group singing.

1 p.m. — *Primary grades*

Novelty races — Kangaroo race

Sack race

Partner race

Backward race

Running race

(Children line up behind starting line. Ten can race at one time.)

*Upper grades*

Group divided into color teams, 12 to 15 on a team. Each team identified by a color. (May use crepe paper streamers.) Play Line Soccer, 10 minute games. Each team plays 2 or 3 games depending on time consumed.

1:45 — Color teams as upper grades. Play at least two games of Steal the Bacon.

Same teams — novelty races

2:30 — Rhythms — all children participating. Marching, Jolly is the Miller, Pop Goes the Weasel; Gustaf's Skoal with older children choosing partners from primary group.

3:00 — The end

## TOURNAMENTS

### 1. Ladder Tournament

Players draw numbers for their place to start the tournament. The object is to move up the ladder by challenging and defeating the person directly above — or the second place above. If the player wins, he moves up and the defeated person must move down. If the challenger does not win, positions remain the same. The tournament should have a time limit. Whoever is at the top of the ladder at the end of the time period is the winner, or the champion. Tournament forms may be secured from sports stores.

Or names can be written on slips of paper and the ends put through a slit in a piece of cardboard. Or, nails may be driven into a board and names put on round key tags.

Advantages of the ladder tournament:
1. It is good for a small number of players.
2. It almost runs itself. A child can challenge the person above him, and arrange when to play. The teacher is not required to schedule the game.
3. All participants are able to play a number of games whether they win or lose.

Disadvantages of the ladder tournament:
1. It can accommodate only about 10 players in a reasonable length of time, i.e. two to three weeks. Children lose interest after so long a time.

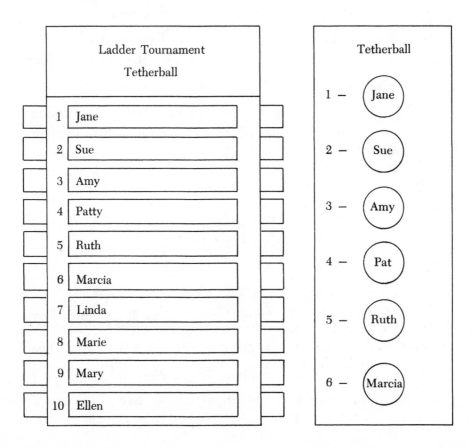

## 2. Round Robin Tournament

In this kind of a tournament, every team or every player plays every other team regardless of who wins or loses. The winner is the team which has the most number of wins when the tournament is finished. If there is an odd number of teams, one team has a "bye" or pass each playing day. A double round robin is the name given to a tournament when each team plays every other team twice. Advantages of the round robin tournament —

1. Every team plays every other team whether it wins or loses. No one is eliminated.
2. The round robin is a good tournament for small groups. It is best for four to eight teams. Too long a time is required to run off the tournament if there are more than eight teams.

Disadvantages of the round robin tournament —

1. It does not lend itself satisfactorily to large groups.
2. It requires a person in charge to schedule the games and keep track of wins and losses.

Following is a method of drawing up a round robin tournament for five teams. There will be one less round than there are number of teams.

1 vs. 2

1 vs. 3        2 vs. 3

1 vs. 4        2 vs. 4        3 vs. 4

1 vs. 5        2 vs. 5        3 vs. 5        4 vs. 5

| First Day | Second Day | Third Day | Fourth Day | Fifth Day |
|-----------|------------|-----------|------------|-----------|
| 1 plays 2 | 1 plays 3 | 1 plays 4 | 1 plays 5 | 1 — Bye |
| 3 plays 4 | 2 — Bye | 2 plays 5 | 2 plays 3 | 2 plays 4 |
| 5 — Bye | 4 plays 5 | 3 — Bye | 4 — Bye | 3 plays 5 |

Win and Lose Record

| | Won | Lost |
|---|---|---|
| Team 1 | | |
| Team 2 | | |
| Team 3 | | |
| Team 4 | | |
| Team 5 | | |

Another method of drawing up a round robin tournament is to write the team numbers in two columns in a counterclockwise manner as follows for six teams:

1 6
2 5
3 4

For subsequent rounds, leave team #1 in the same place and move each team up one place, i.e.:

| 1 – 5 | 1 – 4 | 1 – 3 | 1 – 2 |
|---|---|---|---|
| 6 – 4 | 5 – 3 | 4 – 2 | 3 – 6 |
| 2 – 3 | 6 – 2 | 5 – 6 | 4 – 5 |

## 3. Elimination Tournament

Any number of individuals or teams can be accommodated in an elimination tournament. The tournament bracket must start with 4, 8, 16, 32, or 64 lines. If there are 12 teams, for example, the tournament bracket would start with 16 lines, and four of the teams would receive byes or passes for the first round. Places on the tournament can be determined by a draw. More usually, the teams known to be stronger are placed in opposite halves of the tournament; this is called "seeding" and results in a better tournament. When a team loses, it is eliminated from further play. Advantages of the elimination tournament—

1. Any number of teams or individuals can be accommodated.
2. This tournament can be played off more quickly than a round robin or ladder tournament.

Disadvantages —

1. A team may play only one game if it loses in the first round.

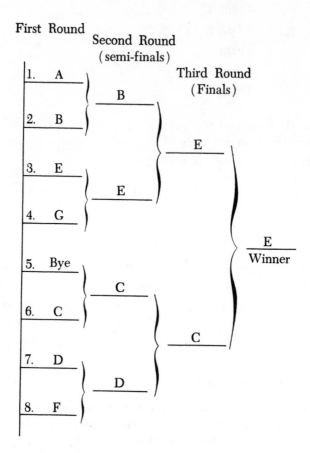

In the tournament shown, there are seven teams. C, who drew a bye, advances to the second round without playing. A plays B, E plays G, D plays F. Winners advance to the second round and losers are eliminated.

## 4. Consolation Tournament

A "consolation" round may be added to an elimination tournament. This gives every team an opportunity to play at least two games. If a team loses its first game, it goes into the consolation tournament. If it loses a second game, it is eliminated.

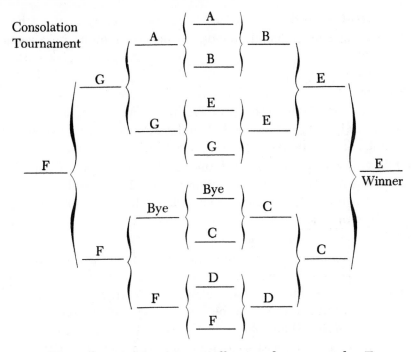

First place in tournament illustrated was won by E.
Second place was won by C.
Third place (winner of consolation) was won by F.

## PHYSICAL EDUCATION DEMONSTRATIONS

There are several goals that can be achieved by having public demonstrations of physical education activities. A public program is a motivation for both children and teachers. It gives children a reason for "polishing up" certain activities. It is a worthwhile experience for children to take part in at least a limited number of public programs as such experiences contribute to their poise and self assurance. Lastly, it should not be forgotten that it is fun to do things well before one's parents and friends.

The demonstration is also a means of showing parents, administrators and other teachers the content and progression of the physical education curriculum. If carefully planned, the demonstration can be an effective means of building understanding of, and support for, the physical education program.

In planning the physical education demonstration, the following points should be considered:

1. The date for the demonstration should be set early in the school year and teachers should be notified several months in advance as to date and general plans. For a demonstration that takes place in a gymnasium, the winter and early spring months will be the best time.

2. The program should preferably be an evening program so that more parents can attend and should be on a Friday evening if possible. It may be part of a PTA meeting or program.

3. Children from the fourth grade up can benefit from participating in such a demonstration. All children should be asked to participate. It is difficult to manage more than 150 children in this type of a program.

4. Children and teachers may help in selecting activities for the demonstration, but the program should be finally planned by one person who will be sure that there is a balance of activities, including games and sports, relays, self-testing activities and rhythms. All activities should be for the grade level which demonstrates them and should be from the accepted physical education curriculum. The demonstration is not an exhibition. It is preferable to have the demonstration last no longer than an hour and a quarter.

5. If possible, it is good procedure to have the audience sit around the edge of the floor, with the participating children sitting on the floor in front of the audience. This adds color, informality and enthusiasm to the program, let children see what is done in other grades and eliminates the baby sitting chore which teachers have if children have to wait in another room until it is their turn to participate.

6. In practicing for the demonstration, an effort should be made to avoid disrupting the school schedule as much as possible. Most of the rehearsing can be done in regular physical education classes, with perhaps one rehearsal of the whole program in sequence.

7. Special costumes are not necessary. Children can wear gymnasium clothes or play clothes for sports, relays and self-testing activities, and wear street clothes for rhythms.

8. Refer to suggestions for demonstrations in self-testing activities and rhythms sections.

Sample program for fourth, fifth and sixth grades:

1. Conditioning exercises
   Beater Goes Round — sixth grade boys
2. Stunts and Combatives — fifth grade boys and girls
3. Irish Reel
   Oklahoma Mixer — fourth grade
4. Boys' Basketball Drills — fifth and sixth grade boys
5. Conditioning Exercises
   Net Ball — sixth grade girls
6. Three Relays — fourth grade
7. Virginia Reel
   Oh Susanna — fifth grade
8. End Ball — fourth grade
9. La Raspa
   Oh Johnny
   Grand Square Quadrille — sixth grade

### BIBLIOGRAPHY FOR ELEMENTARY PHYSICAL EDUCATION

*Books*

1. *Becoming Physically Educated in the Elementary School.*
   Corbin, Charles B.
   Lea and Febiger, Philadelphia
   1969. 366 pages.
   A scientific approach to physical education with much research quoted. More detailed and philosophical than most books. Extensive bibliography. No pictures but numerous sketches and diagrams. Good sections on gymnastics and tumbling. Not classified by grade.
2. *Developmental Movement.*
   Mosston, Muska
   Charles E. Merrill Books, Inc., Columbus, Ohio
   1965. 317 pages.
   Progressive activities to develop agility, balance, flexibility and strength. Exclusively related to conditioning in four areas mentioned. Excellent sketches for every activity. Could be used by classroom teacher to progressively increase difficulty of activities.
3. *Dynamic Physical Education for Elementary School Children.* Third Edition.
   Dauer, Victor P.
   Burgess Publishing Company, Minneapolis, Minn. 55415
   1968. 384 pages.
   A complete, illustrated text including presentation of all types of activities for the elementary school physical education curriculum. Special emphasis on sports skills for the major sports of basketball, football, soccer, softball and volleyball.

4. *Fun and Fitness Through Elementary Physical Education.*
   Bryant, Rosalie and Oliver, Eloise
   Parker Publishing Co., Inc., West Nyack, New York
   1967. 313 pages.
   Separate chapter on 'warm-ups.' Practical and helpful teaching suggestions
   and hints. Written with a light tone and sense of humor. No pictures, but
   some stick drawings.

5. *Head Over Heels.* (Gymnastics for Children).
   Drehman, Vera L. Illustrated by Alene Holdahl
   Harper and Row, New York
   1967. 216 pages.
   Tumbling, marching, apparatus work, track events and a few games
   for children. Profusely illustrated. Emphasis on apparatus work. Many
   events presented are too difficult for beginning performers.

6. *Health and Physical Education for the Elementary School Classroom Teacher.*
   Clark, H. Harrison and Haar, Franklin
   Prentice-Hall, Inc., Englewood Cliffs, New Jersey
   1964. 375 pages.
   Interesting and informative chapter on child growth and development.
   Chapter on health services with emphasis on the teacher's responsibility.
   Outline of material for health instruction, lists of health resources including print and non-print materials. A few physical education activities described, classified by grade level. This book would probably be of most
   value to the supervisor or principal seeking an over-view of the health
   and physical education curriculum, rather than the classroom teacher.

7. *Illustrated Games and Rhythms for Children.* Primary Grades.
   Geri, Frank
   Prentice-Hall, Inc., New York
   1955. 196 pages.
   No theoretical discussion, all activities humorously illustrated. Music writ-
   ten. Useful source book for the classroom teacher.

8. *Introduction to Movement Education.*
   Kirchner, Glenn, Cunningham, Jean, and Warrell, Eileen
   Wm. C. Brown Co., Dubuque, Iowa
   1970.
   Definition and explanation of movement education. Profusely illustrated.
   Detailed lesson plans for primary and intermediate grades. Bibliography
   includes visual aides, 'human resources,' and printed materials. Chapter on
   apparatus, equipment and supplies. Includes instructions for improvised
   equipment and names of apparatus supply companies.

9. *Lead-Up Games to Team Sports.*
   Bale, O. William and Volp, Anne M.
   Prentice-Hall, Inc., Englewood Cliffs, New Jersey
   1964. 180 pages.
   Spiral bound, paper back. Lead-up games classified by sports, i.e., basketball, soccer and speedball, softball, touch football and volleyball. A handy
   and useful source book. Well diagrammed and illustrated.

10. *Movement Experiences for Children:* Curriculum and Methods for Ele-
    mentary School Physical Education.
    Schurr, Evelyn L.
    Appleton-Century-Crofts, New York
    1967. 569 pages.
    Kindergarten through eighth grade. Includes chapters on over-view, teach-
    ing process, foundations of movement, movement experiences. Good. Per-

haps more extensive than some other books. Most activities classified by grade level.

11. *Physical Education for Children.*

  Halsey, Elizabeth and Porter, Lorena
  Holt, Rinehart & Winston, New York, New York
  1958. 395 pages.

Good introductory chapters on child development. Discussion of growth patterns of children through preschool and elementary school years. Emphasis on movement exploration and creative dance. Pupils should be able to read and understand game descriptions as many of them are written by children.

12. *Physical Education for Elementary Schools.* Third Edition.

  Neilson, N. P., Van Hagen, Winifred and Comer, James L.
  Ronald Press Co., New York, New York 10016
  1966. 536 pages.

Contains a comprehensive physical education program, grades one through eight. Activities are grouped according to grade, and according to type of activity within a grade. A good general source book for teachers.

13. *Physical Education in the Elementary School.*

  Larson, Leonard and Hill, Lucille F.
  Henry Holt and Co., New York
  1957. 376 pages.

Some interesting discussions about activities, classifications, charts and evaluations. Activities arranged by grade level.

14. *Physical Education in the Elementary School Curriculum.* Third Edition.

  Miller, Arthur G. and Whitcomb, Virginia
  Prentice-Hall, Inc., Englewood Cliffs, New Jersey
  1969. 366 pages.

Grade level for activities is indicated. Chapters on integration with other subjects including social studies (games and dances of other countries) language arts, arithmetic (new math). Ideas for special days. This edition includes a chapter on movement exploration, definition, principles, teaching techniques and references. Sketches and diagrams. No pictures. A good 'solid' book, valuable to the teacher because of the extra things included which are not in most other books.

15. *Play with a Purpose.* Elementary School Physical Education.

  Anderson, Marian H., Elliot, Margaret E., and LaBerge, Jeanne
  Harper & Row, New York, New York
  1966. 549 pages.

Emphasizes the 'movement' approach. Section One, activities based on movement skills; Section Two, activities based on ball skills; Section Three, activities based on dance skills. Some grade level classification.

16. *Stunts and Tumbling for Girls.*

  Horne, Virgina Lee
  Ronald Press, New York, New York 10016
  1943. 219 pages.

An old, but one of the best, sources of information on the teaching of tumbling.

17. *Teaching Physical Education in the Elementary Schools.* Fourth Edition.

  Vannier, Maryhelen and Foster, Mildred
  W. B. Saunders Co., Philadelphia, Pa.
  1968. 460 pages.

Good over-all source book. Many diagrams and stick figures.

*Pamphlets*

1. *Drills and Ceremonies.* Manual FM 22-5. Department of the Army, Washington 25, D. C., 1953. Marching commands and drills. Must be adapted to elementary school level.
2. *Physical Conditioning.* Manual number 21-200. Department of the Army, Washington 25, D. C., 1957. Good sections on calisthenics and marching. Material on games and relays. Must be adapted to elementary school level.
3. *Physical Education,* Junior Division, Grades 4, 5 and 6. Ontario Department of Education. Canadian Association for Health, Physical Education and Recreation, 515 Jarvis Street, Toronto 5, Ontario, 1960. Good reference especially for self-testing activities, activities with small apparatus and track events. Strong section on creative dance. Good illustrations.
4. *Promising Practices in Elementary School Physical Education.* American Association for Health, Physical Education and Recreation, 1201 Sixteenth Street, Washington, D. C. 20036. 1969. 115 pages. A series of articles, by different authors, describing new ideas and trends in elementary physical education, with emphasis on movement exploration. Appendix contains annotated bibliography, list of AAHPER publications and audiovisual resources. Policies and principles.
5. *Youth Physical Fitness.* President's Council on Physical Fitness. Superintendent of Documents, U.S. Government Printing Office, Washington, D. C., 20402. 1967. 108 pages. Contains physical fitness screening test. Conditioning exercises. Illustrated with stick figures and line drawings. Teachers should have a copy of this pamphlet.

*Other Sources of Information*

1. American Association for Health. Physical Education and Recreation, 1201 Sixteenth Street, N. W., Washington, D. C. Publications on all phases of physical education, health and recreation. Also film bibliographies. Write for brochure listing publications.
2. The Athletic Institute, 805 Merchandise Mart, Chicago, Illinois. Slides, films and publications on physical education, health and fitness. Most of the material is designed for high school and college students but some for elementary school level. Write for brochure listing materials available.
3. State Departments of Education.
   State Departments of Education have material on physical education in the elementary schools. Many states have courses of study, or guides for the elementary teacher. Every teacher should have a physical education guide for the state in which she is teaching.

References for Fitness — at end of Chapter 2, Fitness, page 52.

Part  IV

# Physical Education
## for Junior
## High School Girls

# 11

# Physical Education for Junior High School Girls

## INTRODUCTION

The physical education curriculum for junior high school girls should be a continuation and progression of the elementary school physical education program and should consist of activities that meet the needs and interest of 12, 13, 14 and 15 year olds. Most girls of this age like and enjoy physical activity. The junior high girl can be delightful—or exasperating—depending upon her somewhat mercurial mood. She enjoys team or group activities as well as individual activities. Young people of this age are very conscious of peer approval, admire superior performers and are tolerant of poorer performers. The instructor as well as the selected (or un-selected) leaders of a class can do much toward furthering the acceptance of an activity and the enthusiasm with which students participate in it.

Junior high girls are aware of the need for physical activity in order to have healthy, attractive bodies. If properly motivated they will enter into physical education activities with 'vim and vigor.' Sportsman-like behavior is accepted. Being 'fair' is extremely important. Opportunities for leadership, for creativeness, for exploring one's physical limits, for group membership can, and should, be provided by means of a variety of activities throughout the year.

A daily period of physical education, with at least 30 minutes of actual activity, is desirable. Girls should 'dress down' for class and showering after class should be an accepted procedure if facilities are available, and if the activity warrants showering for hygienic reasons. Excuses from physical education for menstrual periods are not necessary except perhaps in the case of a few individuals who might have special problems. Our culture now expects girls to participate in all kinds of activities throughout the month, and not be inactive for those four or five days of menstruation.

The activities offered or included in the physical education curriculum are determined to a large extent by the facilities, indoor and outdoor, that are available. Often a gymnasium must be shared with the boys' classes. Lucky is the teacher who has a 'girls' gym in which to work.

The curriculum described herein can be presented using facilities that include the use of a gymnasium about half of the year and the availability of an activity room approximately one third the size of a gymnasium. Outdoor space includes several soccer field size areas (also used for flag football, speedball and softball), a grass track and a long jump and high jump area. An all-weather track and a paved outdoor area permit a greater variety of activities—under sometimes more pleasant conditions. Climate and weather of course affect the selection and practicality of certain activities.

The curriculum here presented is not claimed to be an ideal curriculum for this age group, but it is a satisfactory one, and one that provides the students with opportunities to

1. Improve their physical fitness.
2. Become acquainted with, and improve skill in, basic team games such as soccer, speedball, flag football, volleyball, basketball and softball.
3. Experience individual or dual sports, including badminton, table tennis, volley tennis and other recreational games.
4. Participate in individual activities such as rope jumping, tumbling and track.
5. Enjoy physical activity, release tensions and have fun in the more informal situation of a physical education class.

If the instructor is qualified to teach dance, certainly some dance activities should be included in the curriculum. However, rhythmic experiences can be included in rope jumping, tumbling and calisthenics to make up for the lack of actual dance instruction. Co-educational (boys and girls classes combined) are appropriate for junior high—non-contact sports as well as folk and square dances—if the teaching personnel, both men and women, are qualified and cooperative. Some fitness testing may be included if results are used to show the students their fitness status and if attempts are made to improve weaknesses that have been made apparent by test results. In no case, should fitness test results be considered in grading students.

All of the activities included in this curriculum provide for vigorous, stimulating and satisfying exercise. They provide opportunity for the use of team strategy and knowledge of the basic rules. They provide a foundation for further participation in high school and in out-of-school life. They provide a basis for understanding and appreciating spectator sports including football, basketball, baseball, gymnastics and track.

Young teen-agers also enjoy playing some of the games and relays from the elementary grades curriculum. Sometimes after several weeks of hard work on a certain activity, it is a welcome relief to play a different game 'just for fun.' An occasional 'free play' day also provides a break for the students—as well as the instructor.

Following is a possible unit schedule for junior high girls:

1. Orientation, locker assignment and introductory activities ....1 week
2. Fall sport—soccer, speedball or flag football, perhaps on a three-year rotating plan ......................................................4 weeks
   (If fitness testing is included, it should be done the third or fourth week of school.)
3. Volleyball ..................................................................................4 weeks
4. Basketball ..................................................................................4 weeks
5. Rope Jumping ...........................................................................2 weeks
6. Tumbling ..................................................................................6 weeks
7. Individual sports, Badminton, Table Tennis, etc. ...............4 weeks
8. Track ........................................................................................5 weeks
9. Softball .....................................................................................4 weeks
   (Final fitness testing would be done the second or third week before the end of school.)

Activities do not, of course, have to be presented in this order. Facilities will probably determine when each sport or activity is taught. Some teachers might prefer longer units. For example, volleyball and basketball may be taught in alternate years for eight or nine weeks each.

A five to eight minute warm-up period should start every class regardless of the activity which follows.

Progression may be provided for within the activity, except in some cases; for example, seventh graders may play volley tennis while eighth and ninth graders play badminton. Seventh graders may have soccer as an activity while eighth and ninth graders play speedball. Seventh and eighth graders should use elementary age rules and regulations for track while ninth graders participate in high school level events.

No attempt is made, in this book, to include all of the game rules, skills and strategies. There are many excellent references in which this information can be found. Included herewith are some calisthenics which appeal to junior high girls, teaching suggestions for games and sports, suggestions for a tumbling unit and an outline for a track unit.

## CALISTHENICS

(See Chapter 2, p. 13, Fitness; especially exercises pages 21-32.)

The use of calisthenics or exercises at the beginning of each physical education period provide a way to get the students warmed-up, to get the kinks out and to be assured that everyone has had some physical activity during the class period. There should be a regular organization or formation for exercises whether this be circles, lines, squads or whatever. To start each class period with the same formation saves time and eliminates confusion.

Exercises should be selected so that each major part of the body is used. They might be done in this order:

1. One or two general over-all exercises which involve the whole body.
2. One or two trunk flexibility exercises, such as forward bending or side bending.
3. An exercise for the arms, shoulders and upper back.
4. Two exercises for the abdominal area.
5. An all-round, or over-all exercise.

The whole exercise series should be done continuously, done correctly with good positions and good posture, and with snap. A series of six to eight exercises should take no more than five to eight minutes of the class period.

Exercises done to music are generally more enjoyable. There are a number of records available with the instructions for an exercise routine and with the accompanying music. Or the instructor (or class) can devise their own exercise routine and select their own music.

Some stunts such as the crab walk, mule kick, coffee grinder, four and three legged walk may be included in the exercise series.

Running—or jogging—in place or around the gym or field, is one of the best conditioners and should be used several times a week either at the beginning or the end of the class period.

For variety, exercises may be done in a 'circuit.' A circuit is composed of eight to twelve exercises, each done at a station in the gymnasium and done a certain number of times. At each station in the circuit (use entire room) a sign is posted on the wall telling the exercise to be done at that place and how many times it should be performed. Students may start at any station they wish and should complete the circuit in the time allowed. Known exercises are used, and jogging or skipping laps may be included.

Junior high girls do not object to calisthenics, in fact, they enjoy them if there is variety from day to day, and if the students know the purpose of the exercises. Exercises with rhythm, that include clapping, tapping the floor, or other 'sounds' are especially appealing. Variation can also occur by having different students lead exercises or by a 'Friday Special' in which the students select their own exercises.

Following are some calisthenics for junior high girls. For others see pages 21-32 and references on page 370-371.

*General, over-all exercises:*

1. Jumping Jack and variations.

   A. Two-count jumping jack — Starting positions: Standing, arms at side. Count 1 — Jump to stride, arms above head. Count 2 — Jump to starting position. Do 20 to 100 times.

   B. Three-count jumping jack — Starting position: Standing, arms at side. Same as (A) except add Count 3 — jump in place.

   C. Combine A and B — With arms, do two-count jumping jack. With legs, do three-count jumping jack.

   D. Eight-count jumping jack — Starting position: Standing, arms at side.

      Count 1 — Jump to stride, arms above head.

      Count 2 — Return to starting position.

      Count 3 — Hop on left, kick right leg up, clap hands under right leg.

      Count 4 — Lower leg, slap thighs.

      Count 5 — Hop on right, kick left leg up, clap hands under left leg.

      Count 6 — Lower leg, slap thighs.

Count 7 — Jump on both feet, clap hands behind back.

Count 8 — Jump on both feet, slap thighs.

Repeat 10 times.

E. Combine jumping jacks with turns (facing in different directions) straddle jumps and tuck jumps.

Eight Count Jumping Jack—Count 3

2. Running in place. Do quietly on balls of feet, arms bent at elbows in relaxed position.

A. Change directions on each 25 counts.

B. Combine running in place with jumping jacks, i.e., 25 counts running in place, 10 jumping jacks. Do 50 to 100 times, counting "1" each time right foot hits the floor.

3. "Butterfly." Starting position: Standing, arms at side.

Count "Half" — Jump to stride, arms extended out to side, shoulder level. Jump to return to starting position.

"Whole" — Jump to stride, arms above head. Jump to return to starting position.

"Butt" — Hop on right, kick left leg up, clap hands under left leg.

"er" — Lower leg, slap thighs.

"fly" — Hop on left, kick right leg up, clap hands under right leg. Lower leg, slap thighs.

4. Locomotor sequence. Starting position: Standing, arms at sides, relaxed.

A. Walk forward four steps.

Jump to stride, jump together, jump to stride, jump together.

Walk backward four steps.

Repeat jump sequence.

    B. Repeat above with run, skip and gallop instead of walk.
       Repeat all three or four times.

5. Hopping Sequence.
    A. Hop on right foot eight times; hop on left foot eight times.
    B. Hop on right six times; hop on left six times.
    C. Hop on right four times; hop on left four times.
    D. Hop on right two times; hop on left two times.
    E. Hop on right once, left once, right once, left once.
       Repeat all four times.
       May do in place, or moving about the floor.

*Forward bending and trunk flexibility exercises:*

1. Four count 'airplane.' Starting position: Feet in slight stride position, arms straight out at side, shoulder level.
       Count 1 — Bend forward, touch right hand to left foot.
       Count 2 — Return to starting position.
       Count 3 — Bend forward, touch left hand to right foot.
       Count 4 — Return to starting position.

Arms should be straight throughout exercises, knees should be approximately straight. May do in sitting position, with legs straight in "V" position.

2. Eight count 'airplane.' Starting position: Feet in slight stride, arms out to side, shoulder level.
       Count 1 — Bend forward, touch right hand to left foot.
       Count 2 — Return to starting position.
       Count 3 — Bend forward, touch left hand to right foot.
       Count 4 — Return to starting position.
       Count 5 — Clap hands in front of body, shoulder height.
       Count 6 — Swing arms together forcibly down and through legs.
       Count 7 — Standing position, arms extended in front of body.
       Count 8 — Return to starting position.
    Repeat 10 times.

3. Forward Bending. Starting position: Standing, arms at sides.
       Count 1, 2, 3 — Bounce forward, body and arms relaxed, knees
                   comfortable, touch floor if possible.
    Repeat 10 times.
    May do in sitting position, legs extended together.

4. "Fire Cracker." Starting position: Standing with feet slightly apart, arms at sides.
       Count 1 — Clap hands in front of body, shoulder level.
       Count 2 — Clap hands above head.

Count 1, 2, 3 — Bend forward, slap thighs, knees and feet.

(Rhythm is Count 1 slow, Count 2 slow, Count 1, 2, 3, fast.)
Repeat 10 times.

5. Trunk Twist. Starting position: Standing, feet slightly apart, arms extended up and out, 45 degree angle from shoulders.

> Count 1 — Keeping feet firmly on floor, turn to right as far as possible. Head should turn toward right.
> Count 2 — Return to front.
> Count 3 — Turn to left.
> Count 4 — Return to front.

Repeat all 10 times.

Trunk Twist—Starting Position

Trunk Twist—Count 1

6. Trunk Twist. Starting position: Standing, feet slightly apart, hands on hips.

        Count 1 — Keeping feet firmly on the floor turn to left.

        Count 2 — Return to front.

        Count 3 — Turn to right.

        Count 4 — Return to front.

Repeat 10 times.

May do in sitting position with legs straight, or folded (tailor sit) with arms in "do si do" position.

Trunk Twist, Sitting—Arms in "do si do" Position

7. Lateral or Side Bend. Starting position: Slight stride position, left arm at side, right arm in slight curve overhead.

        Count 1 — Keeping feet firmly on the floor, bend and bounce to left.

        Count 2, 3 and 4 — Repeat Count 1.

        Reverse, to right side.

Repeat five to eight times.

8. Hurdle Bounce. Starting position: Sit in hurdle position, left leg extended in front, right leg back with thigh at right angle to left leg.

        Count 1, 2, 3 — With right hand, try to touch left foot in three 'bounces.'

        Count 4 — Sit erect.

Repeat six to eight times.

Reverse.

**Hurdle Bounce Position**

*Exercises for arms, shoulders and upper back.*

1. Arm rotation. Starting position: Stand erect with good posture, arms extended, shoulder level out to side, palms up.

> Count 1 — Turn palms down.
> Count 2 — Turn palms up.

Repeat 20 to 30 times, turning palms as far as possible each turn.

2. Elbow pull. Starting position: Standing erect with good posture. Arms shoulder level, elbows bent, hands in front of chest.

> Count 1 — Pull elbows back.
> Count 2 — Repeat Count 1.
> Count 3 — Straighten elbows, fling arms back, shoulder level.
> Count 4 — Clap hands, arms extended in front of chest.

May be done in tailor sitting position (legs folded).

3. Shoulder shrug. Starting position: Stand erect with good posture, arms relaxed at sides.

> Count 1 — Lift shoulders as far as possible. Drop.

Repeat 10 times.

> Count 1 — Move shoulders front as far as possible.
> Count 2 — Pull shoulders back as far as possible.

Repeat 10 times.

May be done in tailor sitting position, with hands relaxed on feet.

4. Head push. Starting position: Stand erect, hands folded behind head and neck.

> Count 1 — Push head back against hands, hands resist. Hold 5 counts.
> Count 6 — Relax.

Repeat 10 times.

5. Hand touch. Starting position: Sit in tailor position, hands on floor beside hips.
  Count 1 — Clap hands over head.
  Count 2 — Return to starting position, tapping floor.
Repeat 20 times.
Vary number of floor touches and/or claps.

6. Push-ups. Starting position: Girls' push-up position with knees on floor. See page 25.
  Count 1 — Lower body, and touch nose, chin or chest to floor.
  Count 2 — Raise to starting position.
Repeat 10 to 20 times. Be sure only nose, chin or chest touches floor, not abdomen or thighs.
Girls should be encouraged to do push-ups in boys' position, page 25.

7. Arm fling on all-fours. Starting position: Kneel on all fours.
  Count 1 — Fling right arm up, look at hand.
  Count 2 — Let arm drop and swing under body.
Repeat 10 times and reverse.

8. Arm swing and drop. Starting position: Stand erect with good posture, arms at sides.
  Count 1 — Fling both arms up.
  Count 2 — Let arms drop, relaxed, and swing in front of body.
Repeat 20 times.

*Abdominal Exercises*

1. Head and shoulders curl. Starting position: Lie on back.
  Count 1, 2, 3, 4, 5 — Raise head and shoulders off floor and hold.
  Count 6 — Lower head and shoulders and relax.
Repeat 10 times.
Make exercise more difficult by folding arms on chest, or by folding hands behind neck.

**Head and Shoulders Curl**

2. Rocking sit-up. Starting position: Long lying (body out straight), arms on floor above head.

      Count 1 — Raise arms and upper body, raise legs (bending knees) and grasp knees with arms.

      Count 2 — Lower legs and body, to starting position.

Repeat 10 times.

Make exercise more difficult by holding legs 4 or 5 inches off the floor during entire exercise.

Count 1

Count 2

Rocking Sit-up

3. Leg cross over. Starting position: Long lying, arms out to side, palms down.

      Count 1 — Keeping shoulders on the floor, raise right leg, cross over and touch left hand with right foot.

      Count 2 — Return to starting position.

      Count 3 — Raise left leg, cross over and touch right hand with foot.

      Count 4 — Return to starting position.

Repeat 10 times.

4. Leg extension and bend. Starting position: Long sitting, legs extended, lean back on forearms.

      Count 1 — Slide feet along floor till heels touch seat.

      Count 2 — Return to starting position.

Repeat 10 times.

Make exercise more difficult by holding legs 4 or 5 inches above floor during entire exercise.

5. Knee swing. Starting position: Long lying position, arms extended out to side, palms down.

      Count 1 — Raise knees to chest.

      Count 2 — Swing knees to right to touch floor. Keep shoulders on floor.

      Count 3 — Bring knees back to center position.

      Count 4 — Return to starting position.

      Reverse.

Repeat 10 times.

6. Leg bend and extension. Starting position: Kneel on all fours.

      Count 1 — Bring right knee in to touch nose, rounding back.

      Count 2 — Extend right leg back and up.

Repeat 10 times.

      Repeat with left leg.

7. "V" sit. Starting position: Long lying position, arms extended out to side.

      Count 1 — Raise upper body and legs off floor to form a "V."

      Count 2, 3, 4, 5 — Hold.

      Count 6 — Relax, and return to starting position.

Repeat five times.

"V" Sit

Some Records for Exercises

1. *Keep Fit, Be Happy*
      Bonnie Prudden
      Warner Bros. Records, B-1358
   Vocal instructions by Ms. Prudden and counting for exercises. Piano and orchestra music. 30 exercises, described and illustrated on record folder. Appeals to teen-agers. Pleasing voice and suggestions. Good.
2. *Club 15 Exercise Routine*
      Muriel Grossfeld, Teen-age consultant for Campbell Soup Co., CSC 200, Box 1515, Maple Plain, Minnesota 55359
   Vocal instructions by Ms. Grossfeld and counting for exercises. Piano music with some percussion. 29 exercises described and illustrated on record folder. Exercises for two girls, working in partners, on one side of record along with instructions for a short gymnastic routine. Good.
3. *U.S.A. in Motion*—Vol. 1, #2010.
   *U.S.A. Physical Fitness*—Vol. 2, #2020 (mostly marches)
   *U.S.A. on the March*—Vol. 3, #2030 (marches)
      United Sound Arts, Inc., U.S.A. Inc.
      40 Hamburg Tpk., Riverdale, N. J.
4. *Herb Alpert Tijuana Brass*
      A & M Records, SP 4110
      A & M Records, SP 1219
      A & M Records, SP 103
5. *Fitness for Teens*
      Bonnie Prudden
   Send for catalog of their offerings to Institute for Physical Fitness, Inc., 112 Central Park South, New York, New York, 10019.
6. *Kimbo Records*
      Box 55, Deal, New Jersey 07723
   Send for catalog of records to use for calisthenics, rope jumping, ball gymnastics, etc.
7. *Pass Me By*
      Peggy Lee
      Capital Record, #5346
8. *Rhythms for Physical Fitness*, Junior and Senior High School, PE 3
      Educational Recordings of America, Inc.
      Bridgeport, Conn.
9. *Educational Record Sales*
      157 Chambers Street, New York, N. Y. 10007
   Send for catalog of their offerings for the junior high school level.

## References for Calisthenics and Fitness
(Also see pages 52-53, at end of chapter on Fitness)

1. *"Club 15," an approach to living*
      Edited by Muriel Grossfeld, U.S. Olympic gymnast.
      Published by Campbell Soup Co., Club 15, Box 1515, Maple Plain, Minnesota 55359.
      Pamphlet, 28 pages. 1965.
   Illustrated exercises. Diets and health care. Appeals to teen-agers. Good.

2. *Improve Your Body*
    Prudden, Bonnie
    Free from Equitable Life Assurance Society of the United States,
        393 Seventh Ave., New York, N. Y.
    Pamphlet, 28 pages.
Illustrated exercises, describes their purpose, comments about diet and
health. Good.
3. *Special Exercises for Physical Fitness*
    Nelson, Dale O.
    Mercury Publishing Co., Salt Lake City, Utah
    Pamphlet, 32 pages. 1964.
Illustrated exercises and their purpose, classified according to warm-up,
strength, flexibility, endurance and exercises to be avoided.
4. *Aerobics*
    Cooper, Kenneth H., M.D.
    Bantam Books, Inc., 271 Madison Ave., New York, 10016
    1968. Paperback, 180 pages.
A system of achieving and maintaining physical fitness, mainly aimed at
adults but useful for the physical education teacher. Contains interesting
and valuable information about fitness and health. Every secondary physical education teacher should be acquainted with this book.
5. *The New Aerobics*
    Cooper, Kenneth H., M.D.
    Bantam Books, Inc., 271 Madison Ave., New York, 10016
    1970. Paperback, 188 pages.
Updated and expanded version of *Aerobics*. Answers some questions about
exercise. Useful as a guide to the physical education teacher.
6. *Fitness for the Modern Teen-Ager*
    Wessel, Janet A.
    Ronald Press, New York
    1963. 213 pages.
An approach to fitness, written to the teen-ager. Photographs (some getting
a little old), many exercises, ways of self-evaluation.

## SUGGESTIONS FOR TEAM SPORTS

(See Chapter 6, Games and Sports, pages 159)
(Also basketball p. 204; softball p. 209; Volleyball p. 225;
soccer p. 217 and flag football p. 219)

1. *Simplified Rules*
    The official rules for sports can be simplified or adapted to meet
the needs of beginning players and to fit a certain teaching situation.
For example, the serve in volleyball may be made from a line three feet
to five feet inside the back boundary, instead of from behind the line.
In softball, baselines and the pitching distances may be made shorter
than in the official rules. However, the instructor should strictly enforce
rules that involve a learned skill, for example, 'travelling' or 'steps' in
basketball and the rules governing the pitch in softball. The students

should not learn an incorrect skill which later they will have to re-learn. Rules are constantly undergoing evaluation and revision, and the instructor should try to be aware of any changes and use the latest interpretations.

❖   ❖   ❖

2. *Selection of Squads*

The selection of squads for games and sports should be as objective as possible. There are many ways to do this.

A. The class lines up on a line alphabetically by last name. Count off according to the number of teams desired.
B. The class lines up according to height, then proceed as in A. In games such as volleyball and basketball where height is an advantage, this is a good method to use.
C. The class lines up at random. Proceed to count off.
D. Count off 1, 1, 2, 2, 3, 3, 4, 4, instead of 1, 2, 3, 4.
E. The instructor may divide the class into teams and post the lists.
F. The instructor may select captains, captains meet and divide the class into teams.
G. The class may elect captains who then meet and select teams. Games are more fun and interesting if the teams are as equal as possible in ability. The instructor should try to give each girl an opportunity to be captain or leader of a team sometime during the school year. It is sometimes surprising how a leadership role will give a girl confidence and self-assurance. Captains should be expected to assume some responsibility for the class and their team. They can assist with equipment, form team line-ups and take the lead in deciding team strategy.

❖   ❖   ❖

3. *Skill Drills*

Depending upon the facilities available, the sport involved, the size of the class and the length of the unit, different formations for practicing ball skills can be used. Variety helps to maintain interest and avoid boredom. Some frequently used formations are:

A. Circle.
B. Circle with a leader in the center.
C. Line.
D. 'Teacher and class' with the leader some distance in front of the team.

```
        x x x x x
                    or          x  | x x x x x
            x                      |
```

E.  Double line.          x x x

                                  x x x

F.  Shuttle formation, two lines facing each other.

                 →
              x x x |    | x x x
                         ←

G.  Fan formation.          x

                    x       x

              x           x

                   x

H. Scatter formation with students scattered about the floor in an informal manner.

I. Buddy formation, with two people to one ball.

Most of these formations can be used for relays using the skills practiced during the skill drill. Relays are a contest between two or more teams and thus the speed element is introduced and the situation becomes more nearly like that in an actual game. Do not add the speed factor until the skill has been fairly well mastered. Relays are particularly useful for ball handling practice.

                        ❋      ❋      ❋

### 4. *Skill Tests*

A skill test can be devised from almost any skill. How many volleyball serves can you get across the net and in bounds out of ten trials? How many times can you hit a target (taped on a wall) out of ten trials using a softball pitch? Or a skill test may be timed. How many bounce passes, with a basketball, can you make in 30 seconds? This may be done against a wall, or with a partner. How many baskets can you make in one minute? How fast can you run from home to first to second to third to home?

Skill tests may be used to motivate the students to practice a skill. They may be used to evaluate or score a student's ability. Most books on sports and many of the Sports Guides contain series of skill tests. Certain tests have been found to be quite reliable statistically, and show a true picture of a girl's ability. Skill tests must be objective and controlled so that all scores are fair. Skill tests take a considerable amount of class time as each girl must take the test and be scored, but in a four or five week, or longer unit, they are well worth the time spent on them.

                        ❋      ❋      ❋

### 5. *Large Classes*

Sometimes the teacher is confronted with large classes and it becomes a problem in a basketball unit, for example, to be sure that the 30 or more students get an opportunity to practice and play the game. "Sideline Basketball" is one answer to this problem. Divide the class into two teams and have them line up along the sidelines. The first five (or six) players from each team take their places on the playing floor, and play a regular game. After six or eight minutes, or a quarter, the players rotate off the floor and six more girls take their places. Those on the sidelines take out of bounds plays and may be passed to at any time by those playing the game. The 'sideline' players can watch the game and must be alert to catch a ball that might be passed to them. The same arrangement can be used in soccer and speedball.

As many as eight or nine players can be accommodated on a volleyball team. However, some opportunity to play with six on a team (the official number) should be provided. Other class members might do skill practice along the boundaries until they get into the game.

In softball as many as 12 can be used on a team. Others might play Work-Up or practice skills. With poorly skilled players, "Speed-Up Softball" is a good game to use. In Speed-Up the pitcher is a member of the batting team and merely tosses the ball to the batter, making it as easy as possible for the batter to hit. The batter gets three pitches during which she must hit, or be called out. Foul balls are counted as one of the three pitches. All other softball rules apply. This game gives the batter and all players on the field team much more action than in the regular game of softball.

✸     ✸     ✸

## 6. Written Tests

Written tests on rules and strategy may serve the same purpose as skill tests. They motivate students to learn rules and help the instructor to evaluate the students' knowledge of a game. They should not be used too often, perhaps only at the end of a unit, and a student's physical education grade should not depend wholly on the results of a written test.

✸     ✸     ✸

## 7. Class Tournaments

Tournaments within the class add interest and are fun. The last week and a half of a six weeks unit might be spent in tournament play. As stated previously, teams should be as even in ability as possible, so that preferably no team loses every game. The instructor should keep a record of wins, losses and scores and post this information so that all know the standings. A round robin tournament (see p. 338) with four teams is in most situations the best to use. If there are only two teams, a "little world series" of five or seven games can be played and a champion determined. Tournament play gives a team an opportunity to develop team play and strategy. As a finale in a unit, "All Star" teams may be selected.

This may be within a single class, or by grade level, i.e., a seventh grade all star team, an eighth and a ninth. All Star selections are honorary and in most situations do not actually play as a team.

\*   \*   \*

8. *References*

There are Official Sports Guides for the following sports:

Basketball

Soccer-Speedball

Softball

Volleyball

These may be secured from the American Association for Health, Physical Education and Recreation, 1201 Sixteenth Street, N. W., Washington, D. C. 20036. They are also usually available at college book stores. In addition to the rules, the Guides contain articles on techniques, skills, skill tests, written tests and other aspects of a game. The junior high school teacher will find these Guides extremely helpful in teaching as well as enabling her to keep up to date on the latest rules changes. Cost is around $1.50 each. Also, write to AAHPER for their "Catalog of Publications."

SELECTED REFERENCES

1. *Athletic Institute Catalog 70.*
    Athletic Institute, 805 Merchandise Mart, Chicago, Illinois 60654.
    A catalog of visual aids to use in the teaching of sports.
2. *Dynamic Physical Education for Elementary School Children.*
    Dauer, Victor P.
    Burgess Publishing Company, 426 South Sixth Street, Minneapolis, Minn., 55415
    1968. 384 pages.
    This book for elementary school children contains a great deal of information on the technique of sports skills, ways of practicing skills and some rules.
3. *Individual and Team Sports for Girls and Women.* Second Edition.
    Vannier, Maryhelen and Poindexter, Halley Beth
    -W. B. Saunders Co., Philadelphia
    1968. 622 pages.
    Written primarily for the high school and college student, but helpful to the junior high teacher of individual and team sports. Includes bibliography and audiovisual aids for each sport. Sports included are archery, badminton, bowling, golf, fencing, swimming, tennis, track and field, gymnastics, basketball, field hockey, lacrosse, soccer and speedball, softball and volleyball.
4. *Lead-Up Games to Team Sports.*
    Bale, O. William and Volp, Anne M.
    Prentice-Hall, Inc., Englewood Cliffs, N. J.
    1964. 180 pages.
    Lead-Up games classified by the sport, i.e., Basketball, Soccer and Speedball, Softball, Touch Football and Volleyball.

5. *Physical Education Activities Series.*
   Wm. C. Brown Co., Dubuque, Iowa.
   1966, and 1970 revisions
   Separate, paperback books on almost every sport. About $1.00 each. Write for list of books available.
6. *Saunders Physical Activities Series.*
   W. B. Saunders Co., Philadelphia. 1966.
   Separate, paperback books on a variety of activities. Written to the high school or college student. No teaching or coaching suggestions. About $2.00 each. Write for list of books available.
7. *Team Sports for Girls and Women.* Fourth Edition.
   Meyer, Margaret and Schwarz, Marguerite
   W. B. Saunders Co., Philadelphia
   1965. 376 pages.
   A thorough, detailed teaching aid for teachers of team sports. Well diagrammed. Coaching suggestions and methods of skill practice. Includes chapters on basketball, hockey, soccer, softball and volleyball.

## TUMBLING

Most junior high age girls enjoy tumbling activities. During a unit on tumbling a satisfying level of improvement can be made by even the poorer students, and there is no limit to what the well coordinated girl can accomplish, adding to and improving on the basic stunts or movements. Once a few basic skills have been learned, they can be combined into a routine. Even two consecutive forward rolls, with good approach and a good finishing position is fun to do and pleasing to observe. Tumbling contributes to the realization of all of the objectives of physical education — fitness, coordination, agility, body control, creativity and fun. It provides a good foundation for free exercises and gymnastics done at the high school level.

Based on experience, the author makes the following suggestions:
1. All tumbling stunts should be done on mats and not on the bare floor.
2. A good warm-up is a prerequisite to tumbling. Exercises that provide stretching, increase flexibility and improve strength in the abdominal area, arms and shoulders should be included.
3. The use of music adds a great deal to the pleasure of performing. It seems to 'smooth out' the stunts, and causes the students to perform with rhythm. Any records that have a good steady rhythm, that are satisfying to hear, not too fast, nor too slow (no marches) will work for this purpose.
4. Do not force a girl to do a stunt. Fear is usually the reason why a girl does not want to do a certain thing. Encourage her, urge her, and perhaps take her to a corner of the room and give her special help.

5. Do not lift a student (as on a forward or backward roll). She must learn the skill, or technique, and how to control her own body.

6. After a stunt has been described, presented and tried by the class, select those who do it well and let them demonstrate for the class. Students learn from each other.

7. Allow no 'horseplay' in class. Students should not touch or speak to a person who is doing a stunt. Accidents occur when one is distracted.

8. The instructor should try to position herself where she can see the entire class.

9. The class should be so organized that the best use is made of the available time and mats.

10. The large or heavy or obese girl may be a problem in the tumbling class. Encourage her to do only the stunts that she feels she can do. The instructor may find ways in which these girls can assist with the class in various ways.

11. A good beginning, with good posture, and a good ending add greatly to the appearance of a stunt. All stunts should be 'finished.'

12. Be free with praise for work well done, be aware of improvement—and say so.

*Basic Stunts*

1. Forward Roll. (see pp. 103, 122 and 129)
2. Backward Roll. (see pp. 113 and 122)
3. Cartwheel.
4. Shoulder Stand. (see p. 112)
5. Head Stand. (see p. 123)
6. Hand Stand. (see p. 130)
7. Round Off.

*Suggestions for teaching the forward roll:*

1. Start all in squat position, chin on chest. Emphasize shoulders, not head on mat.

2. After three or four practices, start from standing position.

3. Add "step, jump" before the roll. (Jump should be on both feet, i.e., a two-footed take-off.) Finish in good position with arms extended, shoulder level or above head. Stretch at end of roll.

4. Variations
   a. Legs in 'straddle' position.
   b. Forward roll with walk-out, one leg straight, ending with a one leg stand.

Forward Roll in "Straddle" Position

*Suggestions for backward roll:*

1. Start from squat position, chin on chest, palms up with thumbs near ears. Rock to get momentum for roll. Stay 'curled' and land on feet.
2. The hand position is most important. 'Push off with the hands.' The student actually lifts her body during this roll.
3. Do same from standing position. Back must curl as soon as seat hits mat.
4. Backward roll with extension; straighten arms and body into a hand stand position before bending at hips and landing on feet.

Extension on
Backward Roll

Starting down from
Backward Roll with extension

*Suggestions for the cartwheel:*
1. Draw a chalk line, or place a masking tape line down the center of the mat. Aim to have hands and feet touch the line.
2. Movement should be smooth and rhythmic, the slower (with control) the better.
3. Arms and legs should be equal distance apart. Head up.
4. May end in stride position with arms up in a "V."

Cartwheel

Shoulder Stand

*Suggestions for shoulder stand:*
1. Brace hips with hands, elbows on the mat.
2. Vary position of legs, i.e., straddle legs, or one foot on opposite knee.

*Suggestions for the head stand:*
1. Student must have triangle base with head and hands forming a triangle.
2. Get hips over head, then raise legs.
3. Arch back to get balance.
4. Variations
   a. Roll down—round back and roll down as in forward roll.
   b. "Drag up"—start from prone lying position, head and hands on mat in triangle, raise hips (keeping legs straight) over head, raise legs. Arch back to get balance.
   c. Legs in straddle position, or one foot on opposite knee.

Head Stand

"Drag up" to Head Stand

*Suggestions for the round off:*

1. May start as in cartwheel with one hand hitting the mat first and then the other, or both hands on the mat at the same time.
2. Kick legs up to as near a hand stand as possible, turn body and snap both legs down to the mat at the same time, ending facing opposite direction from start.
3. Keep arms straight, head up, arms extended over head at finish.

Finishing a Round Off

Starting a Round Off

**Hand Stand**

*Suggestions for the hand stand:*

1. Hands on mat, shoulder width apart.
2. Head up.
3. Kick up one leg at a time.
4. Arch back to get balance.

*Combinations of stunts:*

1. Forward roll, one-half jump turn, backward roll.
2. Cartwheel, round off, backward roll.
3. Head stand with roll down, forward roll, forward roll.
4. Forward roll, prone fall, head stand with drag up.
5. Forward roll with walk-out, double cartwheel, forward roll.
6. Round off, backward roll, backward roll with extension, backward roll.
7. Cartwheel, forward roll with walk-out, round off, backward roll with extension.
8. Cartwheel, round off, forward roll.
9. Forward roll, three small jumps, tuck jump, forward roll.
10. Partners doing same stunt side by side, or starting at opposite ends of the mat.

❊    ❊    ❊

As a culminating activity for the tumbling unit, students may create routines consisting of a continuous combination of stunts, stands and poses. The instructor may limit this, for example, to two or three trips across the mat, or a time limit of one, two or three minutes. Students may work alone or with a partner. Four or five practice sessions should be allowed before "show time." Music should be provided. Students will enjoy their routines for the class and will be happy to watch their classmates.

Poses and positions,
combined with tumbling
stunts, may make a
pleasing routine.

Students can learn
beginning balance
beam techniques on a
low beam.

SELECTED REFERENCES FOR TUMBLING

1. *An Illustrated Guide to Tumbling.*
   Baley, James A.
   Allyn & Bacon, Inc., Boston
   1968. 164 pages.
   A very helpful, well illustrated book. Valuable in teaching beginning tumbling, as well as for more advanced students.
2. *Gymnastics for Girls.*
   Hughes, Eric
   Ronald Press, New York
   1963. 264 pages.
   Good for the teaching of tumbling and free exercises. Some photographs, many sketches.
3. *How to Improve Your Gymnastics.*
   Athletic Institute, 209 S. State Street, Chicago, Illinois
   Pamphlet, 50 pages.
   Describes activities on the balance beam, even parallel bars, uneven parallel bars; also free exercises and vaulting. Well illustrated.
4. *Stunts and Tumbling for Girls.*
   Horne, Virginia Lee
   Ronald Press, New York
   1943. 216 pages.
   This is an old, but still very useful book especially for the inexperienced teacher of stunts and tumbling. Starts with very simple stunts. Many sketches and pictures. Emphasizes safety.
5. *Visual Aids for Physical Education,* a set of four charts illustrating stunts, tumbling and pyramids.
   Kripner, Joseph
   Joseph Kripner, 1709 W. 83rd Street, Chicago, Illinois
   Large charts suitable for bulletin board use. Helpful in showing students how activities should be done.
6. *Head Over Heels.* (Gymnastics for Children)
   Drehman, Vera L. Illustrated by Alene Holdahl.
   Harper & Row, New York
   1967. 216 pages.
   Tumbling, marching, apparatus work, track events and games for children. Profusely illustrated. Emphasis on apparatus work. Written for younger children, but very helpful as a reference for beginning tumbling and apparatus work.

# TRACK

Track is a very worthwhile activity to include in the physical education curriculum for junior high school girls. This more or less individual activity appeals to some girls who do not get enthusiastic about team sports. Track is very objective; it is a true measure of one's ability and over a period of time, indicates one's improvement.

Track contributes to the development of physical fitness. It improves agility, coordination, strength and endurance. Nearly all girls will find at least one or two events in which they can do quite well.

If a girl is not 'built for speed' perhaps she can excel in the shot put or softball throw.

If track is done in the early spring, weather conditions may require that track instruction be started indoors in the gymnasium. The techniques of racing starts, the softball throw, hurdling, standing long jump, high jump and the shot put can be effectively taught in the gym. Fleece balls, or soft softballs, should be used for practicing the softball throw against a wall; mats should be used for the long jump and to land on in the high jump, or a foam pad may be used for the high jump. A bamboo pole or rope should be used (instead of a metal pole) for the high jump. Cardboard boxes or cartons may be used in place of hurdles to teach proper pacing and hurdling form. Indoor shots are available for practicing the shot put inside. Three or four events may be conducted simultaneously with the students rotating from one event to the next.

Most girls need some motivation or goal or objective to really practice a track event, instead of just practicing for practice sake. A point system, where points are given for different levels of achievement, is one way to meet this need.

After a week and a half or two weeks of 'indoor' track, classes can usually be moved outdoors to continue practice on all events. Practice times are scheduled so that all girls have the opportunity to experience and practice all events.

Each student, after a suitable practice period, should be timed or measured in each event included in the point system. Second or third trials may be allowed, if time permits, and a girl's best time used as her score. Measuring and timing must be accurate to be worthwhile and fair, and therefore should be done by the instructor or a capable student who has received instruction in that particular event. After a student has completed all events, her total score is compiled. These scores may or may not be used as a track 'grade,' depending upon the philosophy of the instructor.

As a culminating activity, grade level or school track meets may be held, however, seventh and eighth graders should not, as a rule, compete against ninth graders, unless an age classification is used instead of grade level. Simple ribbons may be awarded for first, second and third places. School records in each event, and for each grade, should be kept from year to year.

Many high schools now have girls' track teams, and track is an increasingly popular spectator sport. The Olympics, the A.A.U. sponsored Junior Olympics, track meets on television all help to stimulate interest in this activity. It justifies its place in the physical education curriculum because of its contribution to fitness and because it stimulates interest in the whole area of track performance, while the girl is in school, and also outside of school.

## A Point System for Track

| 50 Yard Dash | | Running Long Jump | |
|---|---|---|---|
| *Time* | *Points* | *Distance* | *Points* |
| 7.1 sec. & under ........10 | | 13' & more ...............10 | |
| 7.2-7.4 ................... 9 | | 12' to 12' 11" ........... 9 | |
| 7.5-7.7 ................... 8 | | 11' to 11' 11" ........ 8 | |
| 7.8 ........................... 7 | | 10' 6" to 10' 11" .... 7 | |
| 7.9-8.1 ........................ 6 | | 10' to 10' 5" ........... 6 | |
| 8.2-8.4 ................... 5 | | 9' 6" to 9' 11" ........ 5 | |
| 8.5-8.7 ................... 4 | | 9' to 9' 5" ............... 4 | |
| 8.8-8.9 ................... 3 | | 8' 6" to 8' 11" ......... 3 | |
| 9.0-9.1 ................... 2 | | 8' 6" ot 8' 5" ........... 2 | |
| 9.2-and more ........... 1 | | Below 8' ................... 1 | |

| Softball Throw | | Shot Put | |
|---|---|---|---|
| *Distance* | *Points* | *Distance* | *Points* |
| 135' & more ...........10 | | 28' & more ...............10 | |
| 120' to 134' ........... 9 | | 26' & 27' ................... 9 | |
| 110' to 119' ........... 8 | | 24' & 25' ................... 8 | |
| 100' to 109' ........... 7 | | 22' & 23' ................... 7 | |
| 90' to 99' .............. 6 | | 20' & 21' ................... 6 | |
| 80' to 89' .............. 5 | | 18' & 19' ................... 5 | |
| 70' to 79' .............. 4 | | 16' & 17' ................... 4 | |
| 60' to 69' .............. 3 | | 14' & 15' ................... 3 | |
| 50' to 59' .............. 2 | | 12' & 13' ................... 2 | |
| Below 50' .............. 1 | | Below 12' ................ 1 | |

| High Jump | | 50 Yard Hurdles | | 220 Yard Run | |
|---|---|---|---|---|---|
| *Height* | *Points* | *Time* | *Points* | | *Points* |
| 3' 10" or more ........10 | | 8.0-8.3 sec. or less ....10 | | 32.9 sce. or less ......10 | |
| 3' 8" & 3' 9" ........... 9 | | 8.4-8.5 ................... 9 | | 33.0-33.9 ............... 9 | |
| 3' 5", 3' 6", 3' 7" .... 8 | | 8.6-8.8 ................... 8 | | 34.0-34.9 ............... 8 | |
| 3' 2", 3' 3", 3' 4" .... 7 | | 8.9-9.1 ................... 7 | | 35.0-35.9 ............... 7 | |
| 3' 0", 3' 1" .............. 6 | | 9.2-9.5 ................... 6 | | 36.0-36.9 ............... 6 | |
| 2' 9", 2' 10", 2' 11" .. 5 | | 9.6-9.8 ................... 5 | | 37.0-37.9 ............... 5 | |
| 2' 6", 2' 7", 2' 8" .... 4 | | 9.9-10.1 ............... 4 | | 38.0-38.9 ............... 4 | |
| 2' 3", 2' 4", 2' 5" .... 3 | | 10.2-10.5 ............... 3 | | 39.0-41.0 ............... 3 | |
| 2' 0, 2' 1", 2' 2" ...... 2 | | 10.6-10.8 ............... 2 | | 42.0-44.0 ............... 2 | |
| Below 2' ................... 1 | | 10.9 and more ........ 1 | | 45 and more ........... 1 | |

| Name | | Points |
|---|---|---|
| 50 yd. dash | | |
| 50 yd. hurdles | | |
| Running Long Jump | | |
| High Jump | | |
| Softball Throw | | |
| Shot Put | | |
| 220 yd. run | | |
| Total _____ | | |

At the end of the track season, each student may be given a three by five card on which the instructor has recorded her scores and points.

Good Running Form

## Track Events
### (See pages 133-143)

Some official rules may need to be simplified for the junior high age group. Following are brief rules for the various events, and some teaching suggestions.

*RULES for running events:*
1. At the start, every part of the body touching the ground must be behind the starting line.
2. Two false starts will disqualify a runner.
3. Runners must stay in own lane.
4. Runners may not jostle or interfere with another runner.
5. No competitor leaving the track will be permitted to rejoin the race.

*Suggestions for running:*
1. A standing or crouching start may be used. Starting signal is "Runners take your mark," "Get set," "Go."
2. Lean slightly forward.
3. Arms should swing easily forward and backward from the shoulders. There should be no sideward movement.
4. Relax. Good running looks effortless.
5. Feet should point straight ahead.

*       *       *

*RULES for hurdle races:*
1. All rules that apply to running events also apply to hurdle races.
2. There are four hurdles in a 50 yard race.
3. A runner is not disqualified for touching or knocking over a hurdle.
4. A runner must go completely over the hurdle and not around the side of it.
5. Seventh and eighth graders use 18" hurdles. Ninth graders use 30" hurdles.

*Suggestions for hurdling:*
1. Run or float or step over the hurdles. Do not jump.
2. Take off from same foot at each hurdle. Land on same foot after each hurdle.
3. Take the same number of steps from starting line to first hurdle each time. Take the same number of steps between hurdles each time. COUNT.
4. Practice steps or paces from starting line running along side of hurdles.
5. Assume hurdle position on the ground to get the feel of the position.
6. Stretch forward (or lead) leg. Lift back leg and bring it forward as quickly as possible.

*RULES for running long jump:*
1. The jumper may use as long an approach run as she wishes.
2. The jump is disqualified if the jumper goes over the take-off line or board.
3. Each jumper is allowed three jumps, or trials.
4. Measurement is made from the mark in the jump pit nearest to the take-off line or board.

*Suggestions for running long jump:*
1. Speed in the approach run is important. The jumper should hit the take-off board at top speed. Discourage too long a run.
2. Reach up and forward with the arms while bringing knees forward and nearly up to the chest.
3. Reach forward, lean forward on landing.

❋   ❋   ❋

*RULES for the high jump:*
1. The length of the approach run is unlimited. Approach may be made from either the right or left side.
2. The competitor must take off from one foot. Two-footed take-offs are not allowed. (No diving.)
3. A jumper is allowed three trials to clear a certain height.
4. In case of a tie, the jumper with the fewest number of misses is the winner.

*Suggestions for the high jump:*
1. Start with the pole (or rope) 18″ to 20″ high until all have established their approach, and have determined the take-off foot. A long run is not necessary.
2. Scissors jump
   a. With approach from left of bar, take-off from right foot.
   b. Lift left leg over the pole, and then right leg. (Kick up *inside* leg.)
   c. Bring head back, lift seat, land on left foot.
   d. Use arms to aid lift.
3. The instructor should not allow a 'flop' jump or any kind of a back or shoulder landing unless a foam landing pad is available.
4. With the exception of Suggestion #3, allow girls to experiment with jump techniques until they discover what is best for them.

❋   ❋   ❋

*RULES for the softball throw:*
1. The throw is made with an official softball (inseam).
2. The throw is made from behind a line.

3. The contestant may not step over the line until the throw had been marked by the official.
4. Throws are measured from the throwing line, perpendicularly, to the point where the ball hits the ground.
5. Contestants may stand at the line and throw, or may run up to the line and throw.
6. Each competitor is allowed three throws, her best throw being her score.

*Suggestions for softball throw:*
1. A certain amount of height on the throw is helpful.
2. Throw with the entire body and follow through in the direction of the throw.

⁕    ⁕    ⁕

*RULES for the shot put:*
1. Seventh and eighth graders use a six pound shot. Ninth graders use an eight pound shot.
2. The shot shall be put from the shoulder with one hand only. During the attempt, the shot shall not pass behind or below the shoulder.
3. The competitor may not cross the line until the put has been marked by the officials.
4. Each competitor may have three puts, or trials, the best put being her score.
5. Measurement is made from the spot where the shot first hit the ground, perpendicularly, to the throwing line.

*Suggestions for the shot put:*
1. Practice the movement without the shot in hand.
2. Right hand behind neck, palm toward the front, elbow away from the body.
3. Bend over right knee, shoulders level and facing away from direction of throw.
4. Rotate body and lift as shot is pushed forward.
5. Right arm follows through in the direction of the target.

⁕    ⁕    ⁕

SELECTED TRACK AND FIELD REFERENCES

1. *Track and Field Techniques for Girls and Women.*
      Foreman, Ken and Husted, Virginia
      Wm. C. Brown Co., Dubuque, Iowa
      1965. 184 pages, paper bound.
   Discusses all track events, techniques, conditioning exercises. References. Very helpful to the instructor.

2. *Track and Field for Girls and Women.*
> Scott, Phebe M. and Crafts, Virginia
> Appleton-Century-Crofts, New York
> 1964. 217 pages.

Describes techniques of track events. Photographs. How to conduct a track meet. Good.

3. *Track and Field Guide,* 1968-1970.
> Compiled by the Division for Girls and Women's Sports.
> American Association for Health, Physical Education and Recreation,
> 1201 Sixteenth Street, N. W., Washington, D. C. 20036

Contains official track and field rules and standards, as well as number of helpful articles on skills, ways of practicing, etc. Every track instructor should have a copy of this Guide.

# Index